EVIDENCE CONSIDERED
A RESPONSE TO EVIDENCE FOR GOD

Evidence Considered

A Response To Evidence for God

Glenton R. Jelbert

ISBN: 978-1-947858-01-5

To all my friends and family

To my amazing wife and children, Chris, Sophie, Miriam, and
Timothy for their love and support

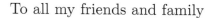

"The truth will set you free." — John 8:32

Contents

Introduction

I was a Christian for more than three decades. I had the usual questions and experiences but held fast through them all. The feeling of struggling to understand the Bible or of feeling like your prayers go nowhere is somewhat familiar to Christians, I think. But I held on because I believed that there was convincing evidence for the claims of the Bible. I believed that people had witnessed Jesus alive again and then gone on to be tortured to death, rather than admit that they had not seen him. I read, I studied, I led Bible study groups, I went to church, and I prayed despite the long, dark nighttime of the soul. I prayed that I would be the "good and faithful servant."

One day in the middle of 2015, a question popped into my head: What do atheists make of the evidence for the resurrection? I had read many popular books by atheists but felt that none of them adequately addressed that question specifically. Of course, such books exist, and with the internet, it was easy enough to find them.

I was unafraid of the truth. I was sure that I would find the gaping holes in their arguments, and the cognitive dissonance that atheists must have to hold their worldview together. I was convinced that my faith would only get stronger as a result of this study. It rocked my world to discover that within a couple of months I was ready to become an atheist. It shocked me, even more, to find out that I had a greater sense of contentment than I had ever had before. The journey from one to the other was disquieting at first, and so I started to write. After all, Christianity had been a large part of my identity. Many atheists dismiss religion on general grounds, saying for instance that the atheist and the Christian are both atheists when it comes to the vast majority of religions (Ra, Jupiter, Odin, etc.), but the Christian suddenly loses their skepticism when it comes to this one set of claims. Whatever the merits of this approach are, I have not followed it here. The issue is that it causes the two sides not to engage with each other. Christianity is the dominant religion of the culture in which I live, and so I wanted to tackle Christian arguments directly, robustly, and with integrity.

I expect that most Christians will agree with most of what I have said, that some Christians will agree with all of it, and that nearly all Christians will agree with some of it. Christians should welcome a close and critical examination of apologetic arguments as part of their search for the truth. As Peter exhorted (1 Peter 3:15), if you are a Christian you should "always be ready to give an answer ... concerning the hope that is in you."

One of the benefits of writing is the opportunity to read and learn. A book that grapples with these issues is the collection of essays edited by William Dembski and Michael Licona entitled *Evidence for God: 50 Arguments for Faith from the Bible, History, Philosophy, and Science.* I am open to evidence, and so I read this book closely and with fascination. I admire the quest for truth and the broad scope of apologetics that it covers: it took me on a journey deep into areas that I had not considered before. However, as I worked through it, reading and learning as I went, I realized that I wanted to bring my own thinking to bear on these questions. I do not seek to belittle or attack the writers, nor to critique *Evidence for God*, but rather to test their arguments and findings.

Of course, to be a Christian, you need only to find one of the arguments convincing. But you do need at least that. So my hope is that this book will help you to refine your thinking and take you into areas that you have not necessarily considered either. *Evidence for God* contains four sections:

1. The question of philosophy;

2. The question of science;

3. The question of Jesus; and

4. The question of the Bible.

Each section contains essays by various apologists. I have mirrored that structure in this book. In each chapter I summarize the argument made in *Evidence for God*, quoting frequently (with the kind permission of the publisher) to try to ensure that I am not responding to a straw man of the argument. I have included sufficient detail so that it is not necessary to have read *Evidence for God*. I have not shied away from any of their arguments but wrestle with each in turn. Even if a particular chapter's topic does not interest you, you may find my response reveals a new facet for you. If it does not, feel free to skim or skip, as each chapter is self-contained, and I reference other chapters where necessary.

Even with 50 arguments, several major reasons for belief remain uncovered. For example, a personal experience of God, or the existence of the church. I discuss these and an overview of the argument from nature in the fifth section. A personal experience, in particular, is the reason most Christians I have spoken with choose to believe, even in the face of other evidence, which is why I wanted to be sure to cover this topic. This book attempts to show why I am unconvinced by any of these arguments.

For many people, their religion is tied up with their lives, families, friends, and identity. Even to think of abandoning their faith is uncomfortable. In my own life, I realized that I was censoring my thinking at least partly because of this, so I can hardly criticize anyone else for it. But I hope that you can read this book with an open (though critical) mind and that it helps you in your quest for the truth.

I want to make a brief comment on the term atheist and the concept of certainty. Atheists are often vilified as a group or counted among the religious. The word "godless" is synonymous with debauched and evil. But atheists are simply people who are not theists. There is nothing more to it, and therefore, though people can, of course, choose to define their own labels, everyone is either a theist or an atheist. If your answer to the question "is there a god?" is yes, then you are a theist; if it is anything else, you are an atheist. Atheists do not universally adopt this definition, but it will suffice for my purposes. Whatever definition you use, no atheist of whom I am aware accepts a definition in which God is rejected on principle or as a matter of faith. The usual consensus of atheists is that there is insufficient evidence to accept god; for many (perhaps most) this goes beyond god to include the supernatural more broadly.

Many people choose the term agnostic. But, by my definition, an agnostic is either a theistic agnostic or an atheistic agnostic. The former believes there is a god, but that his/her/its nature cannot be known (many Christians believe this on some level when you dig a little); the latter believes the question of the existence of god is undecidable in principle. In this sense, the agnostic makes an assertion about the unknowability of god that goes beyond the theist-atheist dichotomy. Many atheists are skeptical of the agnostic's ability to know what is knowable.

Most people who use the term agnostic today mean that they personally do not know about god, not that god is unknowable in principle. This definition is equivalent to the defining position of an atheist, which is "I am not persuaded that there is a god." However, the connotations are that agnosticism is less threatening than atheism, with the former having a subtext of "I do not want to talk about it," while the latter is seen as more antagonistic to the religious. However, there is no belief associated with atheism; rather a lack of one. Note "atheism," not "atheist" in the preceding sentence—people may have all manner of beliefs. My point is that those beliefs are not strictly part of their atheism. Some atheists actively believe that there is no god, but this is a stronger position. Most atheists will agree that such a statement cannot be proven. But the burden of proof is on the theist, so if the theist's evidence does not convince you, you should be an atheist, at least if you wish to be rational.

It is clear that *Evidence for God* is Christian apologetics in the second half of the book (on Jesus and the Bible), but the first half is often an argument for a form of deism rather than theism. Even saying the Christian God is inadequate, as different Christians have such diverse views. As we get into these arguments, I will try to make clear why I believe these distinctions are important.

Quotations from *Evidence for God: 50 Arguments for Faith from the Bible, History, Philosophy, and Science* edited by William Dembski and Michael Licona (©2010) were used by permission of the publisher, Baker Books, a division of Baker Publishing Group.

I include Bible verses in my text if it is necessary for the point I am making. Otherwise, in this paperback version, I put the reference in a footnote. I encourage you look up the references, read the context and maintain a healthy skepticism of all claims, including mine. Unless otherwise noted, I have used the World English Bible (WEB) because this is the only version that is both in the public domain and written in modern English. The WEB is based on the American Standard Version which in turn is a revision of the Authorized Version/King James Bible. The WEB therefore combines the familiar feel and authority of the King James with a contemporary readability. In each verse I quoted I compared the WEB with other established translations to ensure that the meaning was unchanged.

A book of this scope is a daunting task and would not be possible without support. I owe an enormous debt to the many brave and wise souls who have written and talked on this subject to the point where it is now a relatively safe topic with which to engage; it was not always so. I would like to thank Sarah Peeler, without whom Chapter 5 would not have been possible—any wisdom or insight you find in that chapter probably comes from her; Professor John Sutherland for taking the time to read Chapter 10 and share some of his vast knowledge and expertise with me; Professor Antoine Panaioti for helpful comments in the section on philosophy; Ulrich Paquet for his help on evolutionary computing; various people who have read early drafts of the essays and the book and provided comments and insights: Adam Clulow, Rachael Wolfgang, William Jelbert, Charmaine Jelbert, Sarah Peeler, Ryan Peeler, Vaughan Wittorff, Nic Ross,

Evan Nurcombe-Thorne, Bruce Martin, Tom Willcock, Jason Elder, and Jess Lewis. Bill Hohn provided comments on the finished product that have now been included. Numerous other people have engaged me in discussions, and I am sorry I cannot mention them all here.

Ivan Lopez, Adam Verreault, and Joseph Stevick all helped with the stencil for the cover of this book, which was designed by the brilliant Josh Wright.

Most of all, my wife, Christine Jelbert, who talked, read, supported, argued, helped, encouraged, and listened. She is the best of all possible wives.

If you find anything inaccurate in this book or have any comments or questions, please reach out to me at `glentonjelbert.com`.

Glenton Jelbert
California, 2017

———— *Ratione Veritas* ————

Part I

The Question of Philosophy

CHAPTER 1

The Cosmological Argument

I first consider an essay by David Beck[1] on the "cosmological argument." Beck draws the conclusion that "God is real based on observations that things we see around us cannot exist unless something or someone else makes them exist." He notes that almost every culture and religion has made an argument like this, and quotes Thomas Aquinas for the argument best known within the Western Tradition:

> We see things in the world that can exist and can also not exist. Now everything that can exist has a cause. But one cannot go on *ad infinitum* in causes ... Therefore one must posit something the existing of which is necessary.

According to Beck, the argument requires three basic steps:

1. What we observe and experience in our universe is contingent. In other words, everything we experience depends upon something else. Everything we know is contingent.

2. A network of causally dependent contingent things cannot be infinite. Beck gives the analogy of a moving train. Each car you see is being pulled by the one in front of it, which in turn is being pulled by the one in front of that. Eventually, you need an engine.

---

[1] David Beck is a Professor of Philosophy at Liberty University.

3

3. Therefore, a network of causally dependent contingent things must be finite.

This argument allows him to draw the conclusion that there must be a first cause in the network of contingent causes.

He then raises and dismisses four possible objections:

1. It is not God. The conclusion is only a vague and undefined first cause, perhaps the Big Bang, not an infinite creator God who is personal and relational.

2. Infinite series are possible.

3. We do not know about the whole universe, and so have no way of knowing that everything is contingent. Beck diverts a little here to talk about the possibility of multiple gods.

4. What caused God?

Beck deals with the first of these objections (that it is not God) by saying that it is already enough to defeat atheistic naturalism because there is at least one non-contingent component. He also agrees that it tells us only a little about God ("Those who use this objection often seem to suppose that unless we know everything about God then we do not know anything"), but that this should suffice.

For the second point on the possibility of infinite series, he asserts that his cosmological argument relies on a concurrent relationship rather than a chronological one. In other words, each cause exists because of another concurrently existing cause. This, he asserts, cannot be done in an infinite network.

The third (that we do not know about the whole universe) he agrees is true but says that what "the argument shows is that if there is something that is contingent, then there must be something that is not." He admits that the cosmological argument by itself does not eliminate the possibility of multiple gods but states that only one infinite being can exist because "infinity minus or plus anything is still infinity." While this statement is alluring, it is inaccurate, at least mathematically: infinity minus infinity can be anything from negative infinity to positive infinity including zero.

The fourth (what caused God?) he says, misses the whole point of the argument. The cosmological argument shows that a series of contingents must be finite and must eventually lead to a non-contingent.

He concludes that "we cannot make sense of the universe, the reality in which we live, apart from there being a real God." It would, I think, have been more honest to say "apart from there being a cause."

Response

I find this line of argumentation rather fascinating. There are several important points to be made in response. The first is this: even if we grant everything that Beck has argued, it still gets us no closer to any form of theism. Simply put, Beck's argument is that logically there must be something that started all this off, some reason why there is something and not nothing: let us call that 'god'[2]. The atheist (if granting the argument) would say: let us just admit that we do not know what that is, but we can call it X if you need to name it. This is not telling us a little about god—it is telling us absolutely and precisely nothing since we are explicitly equating god with the unknown X. The fact that all religions are equally able to use this argument shows this.

Beck claims that this already defeats naturalistic atheism, but I would disagree. The game show Jeopardy recently gave a definition of atheism as "the active, principled denial of the existence of god." You would need both this (absurd) definition of atheism and an extremely vague and meaningless definition of god for this to constitute any kind of defeat. A definition of atheist as someone who does not believe there is a god, is the equivalent of saying that since the case has not been made, the burden of proof lies with the theist/deist. Note the subtle distinction between this definition and one that states that an atheist believes there is no god: the former is simply unpersuaded, while the latter is actively believing a non-existence.

In other words, the argument as given proves nothing, and certainly nothing about Jesus, or resurrections, or virgin births, or any other religion

---

[2]I will take **God** (with an upper-case "G") to mean the theistic God, a supernatural being about whom specific, personal claims are made, such as a virgin birth or a miraculous resurrection. Most often I have the Christian God in mind during my discussions, but if not specified, it is likely to be applicable to the Gods of other major religions also. Apart from supernatural powers, 'God' is intimately involved in human affairs.

When I refer to **god** (with a lower-case "g"), I mean the deist's supernatural being. This is a god who was involved in creation in some way. But it is not a god who cares about human affairs or who has a personal relationship with people. It is also not a god who is supported by or supportive of any of the major theistic religions. It is a supernatural being, however. Talk of us all being god or of nature being god reduces the concept of god to something so broad as to make this conversation meaningless.

Theism and deism do not cover the full spectrum. Generally, the deist's god is not active any more. But what of a god who continues to sustain the universe, perhaps by sustaining the laws of physics, but who is not interested in morality or relationships with humans? Though this may be a theistic God because of its on-going participation in the universe, it is not easily associated with the Gods of the major religions. In fact, it is far more similar to deism than theism. So apologists who see a sustaining God in nature and claim that they have found a theistic God have merely stretched the definition and still have all their work ahead of them to get to their chosen religion. In general, when we see the word God, we will need to be careful about the definition.

or creed. But even the cosmological argument itself is disputable philosophically, which is all that is needed to deny the underlying premise. In
other words, not only does it prove nothing if it were sound, it is not clear
that it is sound. The objections Beck dismisses are not trivial.

Firstly, if the original cause is not god but rather some physical phenomena, then the cosmological argument falls apart. Beck refers to "a
vague and undefined first cause," but I think the phrase "an unknown first
cause" would be more accurate. Beck says "Those who use this objection
often seem to suppose that unless we know everything about God then we
do not know anything." That, however, is not the point. The cosmological argument is telling us nothing because it is looking for evidence in the
unknown.

This will be a theme of many arguments in this book: lack of knowledge
is not evidence for God; it is evidence of ignorance.

Secondly, it is not clear that an infinite causal chain could not exist:
perhaps it is an infinite series of big bangs. There is no particular reason
why this is conceptually impossible[3]. It is hard to imagine validating such
a claim empirically, but it is equally hard to imagine repudiating it empirically. The fact that an infinite series of big bangs fits the cosmological
argument at least as well as a first cause shows that it is on rocky ground
philosophically. Others have added the argument that if time started at
the big bang, then the concept of causality could break down at that point,
making the question of first causes meaningless.

His assertion that he is referring to "concurrent dependency relations"
is difficult to fathom. The atoms in your body trace their existence to a
time before the formation of the earth. What possible concurrent cause
could they have for their existence?

Thirdly, while Beck agrees that we have limited knowledge, he believes
that the argument shows that there must be at least one non-contingent
thing. He says "there can only be a single uncaused or infinite being."
Note that he has subtly switched from "cause" to "being." This shift is
important for his argument since god is a being (at least by any reasonable
definition), but Beck asserts knowledge that he does not have. That is, he
asserts either that cause and being are interchangeable, or that the first

---

[3]Certain quantum theories predict that the universe has no beginning. These
are not widely accepted, but it is known that quantum mechanics (the theory of
the very small) and general relativity (the theory of the very big) are not compatible, which is why a unifying theory is needed. In general this is not a problem,
but there are cases where both apply, such as black holes and the early universe.
Just the possibility that this theory is correct undermines the cosmological argument. For a popular article on this quantum theory, see Lisa Zyga, 2015, phys.org,
No Big Bang? Quantum equation predicts universe has no beginning. Available at
phys.org/news/2015-02-big-quantum-equation-universe.html

cause is required to be a being. He fails to make either case.

Fourth, he refers to the possible objection "What caused God?" But this is granting that which needs to be proved, and cunningly putting it into the mouth of the skeptic. We do not grant that God has been established, so any talk of what caused him/her/it is worthless. Perhaps such statements are used rhetorically, like the absurd notion that "God is dead." As I mentioned above, an unknown first cause is not the same thing as a god unless god is defined so loosely as to be meaningless, and no assertions will overcome our ignorance on this.

The fundamental point is that we do not know. The biggest, single breakthrough of the scientific revolution was the ability to admit this simple fact[4]. Note, science does not say that it cannot be known. Quite the contrary: the admission of ignorance is an invitation to explore. But it avoids the error of drawing a conclusion prematurely. Beck says that "we cannot make sense of the universe, the reality in which we live, apart from there being a real God." This is an admission that the feeling of not knowing is disquieting, which Beck soothes with the notion of God. Religious beliefs have filled this gap for millennia through numerous gods, theistic and deistic, not because the god is real but because the psychological discomfort is real. The cosmological argument peers into the distant and murky past and claims to see something that just cannot be made out. As such, it is not evidence for God.

---

[4]For more on the key scientific breakthrough of the ability to admit ignorance, see the wonderful book *Sapiens: A Brief History of Humankind* by Yuval Noah Harari.

CHAPTER 2

The Moral Argument

For my next chapter, I consider Paul Copan's[1] essay entitled "The Moral Argument for God's Existence." His argument is "if objective moral values exist, then God exists; objective moral values do exist; therefore, God exists." He goes on to say that to "resolve our ethics crisis, we must recognize the character of a good God (in whose image valuable humans have been made) as the necessary foundation of ethics, human rights, and human dignity." He does not elaborate on what this "ethics crisis" is. He then presents three sections each supporting a claim (which do not quite equate to the above argument, but I suppose mean to):

1. Objective moral values exist: they are properly basic;

2. God and objective morality are closely connected;

3. Non-theistic ethical theories are incomplete and inadequate.

Firstly, he claims that moral values exist whether or not a person or culture believes them. He says that humans "do not have to find out what is moral by reading the Bible. Such knowledge is available to all people" and quotes scripture to back this up. "So people (including atheists) ...will have the same sorts of moral instincts as Christians." He says that

---

[1] Paul Copan is an author, speaker, and Professor of Philosophy and Ethics at Palm Beach Atlantic University.

9

moral principles are "discovered, not invented." And that "[m]oral reforms
...make no sense unless objective moral values exist." Finally, he quotes
Kai Nielsen (an atheist philosopher) as saying:

> It is more reasonable to believe such elemental things [wife beat-
> ing, child abuse] to be evil than to believe any skeptical theory
> that tells us we cannot know or reasonably believe any of these
> things to be evil.

Secondly, he says that atheists often say that they can be good without
God. He argues that what they mean is that they can be good without
believing in God, but that they cannot be good without God because they
would not exist. Humans are made in God's image so they can know what
is good even if they do not believe in God.

> Intrinsically valuable, thinking persons do not come from imper-
> sonal, non-conscious, unguided, valueless processes over time. A
> personal, self-aware, purposeful, good God provides the natu-
> ral and necessary context for the existence of valuable, rights-
> bearing, morally responsible human persons.

He does not elaborate on or support either of these claims.

Thirdly, he says that while ethical systems that make no reference to
God (e.g., Aristotle, Kant[2]) can make "very positive contributions to ethical discussion, ...their systems are still incomplete. They still do not tell
us why human beings have intrinsic value, rights, and moral obligations."
Naturalistic evolutionary ethics cannot be correct because then morality
would not be objective. It "could easily undermine moral motivation."
He argues that the problem with skepticism is that it assumes a trustworthy reasoning process to arrive at the conclusion that reasoning cannot be
trusted.

Response

His first point is that objective moral values exist. He asserts that everyone has a conscience, even without the Bible. Sadly, this is not true.
Psychopaths do not experience remorse and conscience in the same way
as others do[3]. Theologically this is hard (or repugnant) to explain, especially the part about them being made in God's image, while evolutionarily

---

[2]Philosophy Professor, Antoine Panaioti points out that Kant does speak of God in
his writings on ethics. In fact, Kant made a moral argument for God.

[3]Psychopaths are discussed by Robert D Hare in his excellent book *Without Conscience: The Disturbing World of the Psychopaths Among Us.*

it makes complete sense. Evolution tells us that if certain (good) social behaviors are advantageous to the group, they will spread through the population. But some small percentage of the group could remorselessly take advantage of these norms and also be very successful, as long as that percentage does not get too high (which would impact the group's success). That is what you would expect, and it is what you get. There is no need to appeal to an objective morality. You see similar behaviors in animals, whose instincts are shaped in a similar way and for whom the notion of morality may not be well-defined.

Another point on this is that he is admitting that there is no moral behavior that a Christian could do that an atheist could not do. On the other hand, religious people have committed plenty of repugnant and immoral acts on account of a warped religious justification from one of their books or leaders. To take one of many possible examples, consider that when Moses expounds upon the fourth commandment, he says that "whoever does any work in [the sabbath] shall be put to death" (Exodus 35:2). This punishment is clearly repugnant and immoral. Even the staunchest believers have quietly dropped this. If God wrote the ten commandments and inspired the rest of the Bible, he did a poor job of demonstrating that morality is objective. Even if we have not yet established the exact nature of morality, we can agree that death penalty for working on the Sabbath is bizarrely cruel.

A second example, is that if Christians do not persecute me for my current beliefs, it is because their religion no longer overwhelms their basic humanity. We would only have to go back a few hundred years to obtain a very different situation, where their basic humanity was suppressed by their religious convictions. In fact, it is still the case now in some parts of the world and for some individuals. I will discuss other aspects of Christian morality in Chapter 5 and Chapter 38.

We now understand where the fundamental moral urges come from (evolution) while also having the agency to think about situations and decide what we want to be. We can codify the logic of these urges in such things as the golden rule ('do as you would be done by'), or understand a desire to maintain our reputation or to love our families, which are all comprehensible by evolution. But we can also decide not to be racist or homophobic, regardless of whether or not those urges arise from evolution. We have the agency to reason and reject a primeval urge to aggression and to decide that such aggression is immoral. To get to this point, we needed to relinquish the belief that such behaviors had divine warrant. We might like morality to be objective, and it may be possible to get there through science or peer-review as I will discuss below, but the case is far from made that morality

is *necessarily* objective. Just this level of doubt causes Copan's argument
to collapse.

His second point is that if there is no God, there is no objective morality. He asserts this as though it were self-evident, but it is not. What is
evident, is that humans are masters at believing in things that do not exist,
and using them for effective collaboration. Companies, countries, money,
human rights, and Gods are all things that work because people collectively
believe in them[4]. Even if you believe in God, you would probably accept
that the vast majority of humanity's Gods are imaginary beings that shape
or shaped collective human behaviors because of our belief in them (a more
repulsive option is to believe that other Gods are actually demons or something of that nature, a type of belief that has caused endless moral problems
and sectarian violence throughout human history[5]). It might be difficult
to see how valuable, thinking humans come from valueless, unguided processes, but that does not mean it is impossible.

His third point is that without God, ethical discussions are incomplete
because they do not tell us why morality exists. He argues that the naturalistic evolutionary origins of morality cannot be correct because then
morality would not be objective. It would be equally valid to turn this
around and assert that morality cannot be objective because it arises from
naturalistic evolution. I will discuss the objectivity issue below.

He states that subjective morality could undermine moral motivation,
but this is itself undermined by his point that everyone has a conscience,
and in any event has nothing to do with the underlying truth of the issue.
A naturalistic explanation is superior for explaining the existence of such
things as psychopathy, moral gray areas, bigotry, and an evolving sense of
morality. In fact, over time, religions have been on the wrong side of so
many moral arguments that it is hard to give them any credit. It is an
extraordinary hubris that supposedly humble Christians claim a monopoly
on morality while ignoring the atrocities committed by the religious and
justified by their books and leaders. The best we can offer is that there
may be a consistent way to view religion and morality, but that is also
easily done with atheism and morality. Note that the existence of good
Christians or evil atheists does not change this argument.

Sam Harris wrote a book[6] arguing that there is, in fact, objective moral-

---

[4]This point is discussed in detail by Yuval Harari in *Sapiens: A Brief History of
Humankind.*

[5]There are other options, of course. For example, some Hindu philosophers believe
in a supreme Cosmic Principle that manifests itself into different deities or avatars to
steer humanity from time to time. Thus Moses, Jesus, Mohammed, and others are just
avatars.

[6]Sam Harris, *The Moral Landscape: How Science Can Determine Human Values.*

ity, which can be studied scientifically. He debates the issue with William Lane Craig[7]. I will not get into their discussion here apart from the following. Craig's central point is that if there is a God, then you have a basis for objective morality; and if there is no God, then there is no basis for objective morality. Only in the questions and answers at the end of the debate, does he admit that his actual second point is that "he couldn't see how" objective morality could arise without God, which is a dramatically weaker argument!

The other issue is that objectivity versus subjectivity may not be such a neat dichotomy. I think most people would agree that science is objective. But is it? For example, gravity is a real, physical phenomenon, but Newtonian gravity is a description of it that works under certain circumstances. One could envisage a society that skipped straight to Einstein's theory of gravity, perhaps learning about manifolds, geodesics, and tensors from a young age, and never worrying about Newtonian gravity. But Einstein's theory of gravity itself breaks down under certain (quantum mechanical) conditions. The essence of science is models that describe empirical reality to a greater or lesser extent, and are agreed on by a peer-review process. A scientific understanding of morality could achieve a similar level of "objectivity" or "subjectivity." In other words, it is conceivable that an understanding of morality could have the same degree of rigor as science, regardless of whether you label this objective or subjective.

Ultimately, the discussion on morality is both important and fascinating. But it should be evident that (i) it is not clear whether morality is objective, (ii) it is not clear whether objective morality can only come from God, and (iii) even if i and ii were given, no-one has convincingly linked it to any specific God. In other words, this argument does nothing to establish any particular theistic claim, and religious apologists have all their work ahead of them.

---

[7]The debate can be seen on YouTube youtu.be/vg7p1BjP2dA: *Debate: Atheist vs Christian (Sam Harris vs William Lane Craig)*.

CHAPTER 3

Near-Death Experiences

Your attention is now drawn to the third essay: "Near-Death Experiences: Evidence for an Afterlife?" by Gary Habermas[1]. Habermas discusses accounts of near-death experiences, stating that they have been reported throughout history. He mentions reports with

> claims of floating above one's dying body, traveling down a dark tunnel, encountering or even being welcomed by a loving being of light, perhaps meeting deceased loved ones, hearing beautiful sounds and seeing wonderful colors, and then afterward losing the fear of death.

He says that critics sometimes claim that "even similar sightings such as these may indicate nothing more than the presence of common brain chemistry among humans."

However, Habermas continues, some near-death experience reports include verifiable data.

> For example, in dozens of [near-death experience] accounts, the dying person claims that, precisely during their emergency, they actually observed events that were subsequently confirmed. These observations may have occurred in the emergency room

---

[1]Gary R. Habermas is a Distinguished Professor and Chair of the Department of Philosophy and Theology at Liberty University.

when the individual was in no condition to be observing what was going on around them. Sometimes the data are reported from a distance away from the scene and actually may not have been observable from the individual's location even if they had been healthy, with the normal use of their senses.

He goes on to say that some of these reports occurred when the dying person had no heartbeat for an extended period and even no brain activity. Blind people have given accurate descriptions of their surroundings, without ever having seen anything before or since.

The example that he gives is one "well-documented case" of a little girl who nearly drowned and did not register a pulse for nineteen minutes. Here is the story as related and quoted by Habermas:

> Her emergency room physician, pediatrician Melvin Morse, states that he "stood over Katie's lifeless body in the intensive care unit." An emergency CAT scan indicated that Katie had massive brain swelling, no gag reflex, and was "profoundly comatose." Morse notes that, "When I first saw her, her pupils were fixed and dilated, meaning that irreversible brain damage had most likely occurred." Her breathing was done by an artificial lung machine. She was given very little chance of surviving.

> But then, just three days later, Katie unexpectedly made a full recovery. In fact, when she revived, she reproduced an amazing wealth of information regarding the emergency room, specific details of her resuscitation, along with physical descriptions of the two physicians who worked on her. All this occurred while she was completely comatose and most likely without any brain function whatsoever. As Morse recounts, "A child with Katie's symptoms should have the absence of any brain function and therefore should comprehend nothing."

> It took her almost an hour to recall all the recent details. However, part of the story made no sense in usual medical terms. Katie related that during her comatose state, she was visited by an angel named Elizabeth, who allowed her to look in on her family at home. Katie correctly reported very specific details concerning what her siblings were doing, even identifying a popular rock song that her sister listened to, watched her father, and then observed as her mom cooked a meal that she correctly identified: roast chicken and rice. She described the clothing and positions of her family members. Later, she shocked her

parents by telling them these details that had occurred only a
few days before.

Habermas states that the naturalistic explanations such as oxygen de-
privation cannot account for these kinds of detailed stories.

Habermas goes on to say that several descriptions in the Bible seem
like near-death experiences. Luke 16:19–31 is the parable of Lazarus the
beggar that "sounds somewhat similar to contemporary reports [of near-
death experiences]." Acts 7:54–60 is the stoning of Stephen in which he
says "I see the heavens opened, and the Son of Man standing at the right
hand of God!" And 2 Corinthians 12:1–10 describes Paul's vision of being
caught up to the third heaven. He admits that "tough questions" exist (a
phrase he uses three times), and states that more research is needed, but
that

> these occurrences still argue for a supernatural reality beyond
> this present reality, thereby presenting serious challenges to nat-
> uralism. This may be the chief worldview contribution of [near-
> death experience] research.

Response

Habermas is presenting us with a transcendental or non-physical interpretation of a near-death experience, that is the view that consciousness can
become separated from the brain under certain conditions and give us a
glimpse into a different realm. This view is at odds with the dominant neu-
roscientific view, which says that consciousness is a brain function. There
is a great deal of research available on near-death experiences, much of
it written long before 2010 (when *Evidence for God* was published), which
makes its absence from Habermas's essay surprising. The full Melvin Morse
story had not yet come to light by then, however, so we may excuse this
part (which I will discuss shortly), though it does show the danger inherent
in dealing with this kind of subject, where evidence is paramount because
of the ramifications of the claims.

To begin with near-death experiences in general, Kenneth Ring wrote a
book[2] in which he classified them on a five-stage continuum as:

1. feelings of peace and contentment;

2. a sense of detachment from the body;

---

[2]Kenneth Ring, *Life at Death: A scientific investigation of the near-death experience.*

3. entering a transitional world of darkness (rapid movements through tunnels: 'the tunnel experience');

4. emerging into bright light; and

5. 'entering the light.'

Karl Jansen published a paper in 1996[3] which concluded that

> ketamine administered by intravenous injection, in appropriate dosage, is capable of reproducing all of the features of the [near-death experience] which have been commonly described in the most cited works in this field.

He says that

> [a]s might be predicted in a mental state with a neurobiological origin, mundane accounts with less symbolic meaning also occur, e.g. children who may 'see' their schoolfellows rather than God and angels.

He states that

> Ketamine is a short-acting, hallucinogenic, 'dissociative' anesthetic. The anesthesia is the result of the patient being so 'dissociated' and 'removed from their body' that it is possible to carry out surgical procedures. This is wholly different from the 'unconsciousness' produced by conventional anesthetics ... anesthetists prevent patients from having NDE's ('emergence phenomena') by the co-administration of sedatives which produce 'true' unconsciousness rather than dissociation.

He also describes that this is not a coincidence, as the biochemical effects of ketamine are somewhat similar to the effect of cell death from lack of oxygen, a lack of blood, and from epileptic fits, and not at all like the effects of psychedelic drugs. This has also been known in recreational drug circles since the 1970s.

This would appear at a glance to wrap up the vast majority of the cases. But a challenge remains, in the form of cases where the person close to death has obtained some special knowledge, such as the story quoted above. In general, an attitude of skepticism will serve well, not accepting such claims

---

[3]Karl Jansen, *Using Ketamine to Induce the Near-Death Experience.* Available at ¡a www.lycaeum.org/leda/Documents/Using_Ketamine_to_Induce_the_Near-Death_Experience.9260.shtml.

until provided with extraordinary evidence. The case Habermas chooses to present is certainly not that. At first glance, it may seem impressive, as we have a doctor attesting to aspects of this story. It turns out that Morse is the only one attesting to these stories, and that he is a doctor with a particular interest in near-death experiences, who has written many books on the subject. Immediately, his interest in it should pique our suspicion that we need more evidence than Morse alone. Even in this story as given, it is unclear how Morse verified the various facts. But anyone can imagine how two stories could seem to correlate to an interested party.

"She said you had chicken. Did you have chicken?"

"Yes, that sounds right. Which night did you mean? It was a few days ago now, but I think so."

"Wow, so she saw you eating chicken!"

The point is that how you collect the evidence is important, and Habermas's story does not indicate that this was done with due care.

The story of Melvin Morse gets more interesting. In 2014 he was convicted of waterboarding his wife's eleven-year-old daughter and sentenced to three years in prison[4]. This would appear to be turning an interest into an obsession. However, the issue is the lack of evidence. Morse presents himself as a doctor and therefore a reliable witness, but his character would seem to be in question, and his evidence collection leaves a lot to be desired, and so his lone testimony is not convincing.

A comment on this: people bandy about stories like this, and one might be tempted to see the sheer number of them as evidence. But when given a single example to chase down, it tends to evaporate into nothing. This parallels my experience of trying to pin down evidence for faith in general.

We could stop here, as Habermas has presented no compelling evidence of a supernatural reality. But I would like to continue a little further—the truth is not so fragile that it does not bear closer examination.

In 2001, a project known as the AWARE study (AWAreness during REsuscitation) was begun, coordinated by Sam Parnia from Southampton University. This involved placing figures on suspended boards facing the ceiling in resuscitation units at many different hospitals. The boards are not visible from the floor. Parnia wrote, "anybody who claimed to have left their body and be near the ceiling during resuscitation attempts would be expected to identify those targets." So far, no-one has seen the boards. A second, larger trial is underway with results due on May 31, 2017. If someone did "see" the image, I would be more inclined to look for playful interns or reflective surfaces, but I do not think a healthy skepticism should

---

[4]See CBS News article dated February 13, 2014: `www.cbsnews.com/news/delaware-pediatrician-convicted-of-waterboarding-girlfriends-daughter`.

prevent us searching. This research is on-going, but so far there have not been any results that would require a separation of mind and brain.

Lastly, let us look at the theology of this, in which there are indeed some "tough questions." Habermas adduces three Bible verses.

Luke 16:19–31 which is a parable, and includes the idea of Hades as a place of torment. I think most modern Christians are dialing back on this idea of hell, a place of such obvious injustice that it throws the whole system into disrepute. But to stay focused, this is just a parable, and cannot be counted as a near-death experience.

Acts 7:54–60 relates the stoning of Stephen. However, Stephen says that he sees heaven open before they rush him outside and stone him. There is no indication that he was not the picture of good health at the time he claimed to have a vision so this too cannot be a near-death experience.

Finally, 2 Corinthians 12:1–10 is Paul's vision of the third heaven. We know that Paul was prone to visions, and it is at best speculation that this was a near-death experience: he does not even mention an illness or injury.

So these are all rather weak. Even Answers in Genesis (hardly a skeptical source) has an article dismissing visits to heaven on theological grounds[5]:

> Far too much of the present interest in heaven, angels, and the afterlife stems from carnal curiosity. It is not a trend biblical Christians should encourage or celebrate.

On the other hand, these experiences happen to people regardless of religion so even if it did reveal some realm beyond the natural (which it does not so far) it would not provide any evidence for god, gods, or any specific religion.

---

[5] John MacArthur, 2014, Answers In Genesis, *Are Visits to Heaven for Real?* Available at answersingenesis.org/reviews/books/are-visits-to-heaven-for-real.

CHAPTER 4

Naturalism: A Worldview

On to "Naturalism: A Worldview," written by L. Russ Bush III[1]. He begins by defining Naturalism as

> the belief that in the final analysis, nature is all that there is, and that 'nature' is essentially unmodified by anything other than itself ...either there is no God or God has no effect or influence on nature ...spiritual realities, according to naturalism, are either illusions or they are merely complex or unusual natural realities.

He argues that a materialistic worldview has been gaining ground since the eighteenth century. Before that most people believed in a divine creation, but naturalistic thinking "challenged that view and sought to replace it."

Bush is skeptical of naturalism, which, he says

> built itself on the idea that the universe (and everything in it, including life itself) came into being because of a natural quantum fluctuation (or by some other strictly natural means) ...life arose from non-life.

---

[1]L. Russ Bush was a distinguished Professor of philosophy of religion at Southeastern Baptist Theological Seminary. He died in 2008.

He states that

> a natural process of change is essentially random and/or undi-
> rected, but natural processes actually seem to 'select' some pro-
> cesses and activities in the sense that 'better' or stronger ones
> survive while others perish. Naturalists believe that this un-
> conscious, nondirected 'selection' process along with random
> genetic fluctuations (i.e., mutations) are the keys that explain
> the origin of the world of living things as we know it today.

He then discusses the implications of this belief system. He notes that
"personality arose (evolved) from the nonpersonal, from that which was
matter and energy only." And it had to do this "without direction or
guidance from any personal source." This, he states,

> would appear to violate the natural law of cause and effect. En-
> ergy dissipates. Complexity changes by simplifying. No system
> spontaneously becomes more complex unless additional energy
> and order are added from outside the system. A 'cause' must
> either contain the 'effect' or at least be sufficiently complex to
> be capable of producing the less complex 'effect.' Personality,
> however, is far more complex than the natural chemical and
> physical order of things observed in nature. How could this
> be? The naturalist usually assigns such questions to the intel-
> lectual dustbin. Personal beings are here (they and you and I
> exist), and thus naturalists accept that fact regardless of the
> significant improbability of highly complex and intelligent and
> self-aware personality naturally arising from the nonpersonal
> reality of nonintelligent and nonaware matter.

He points out that the same argument can be applied to life and to
rational thinking.

> Reason itself, in the naturalistic worldview, is nothing more
> than the natural and random result of a particular randomly
> changing original bit of matter. Reason is not really an inde-
> pendent evaluative process that can critique itself ... why should
> reason be trusted? How could naturalism be known to be true?
> The answer is: it can't.

Without allowing for divine revelation, we lose reason, truth, knowledge,
and meaning. "Naturalism dies of its own success."

Response

To consider Bush's essay, I need first to differentiate between methodological naturalism and metaphysical naturalism. The former is practiced by scientists the world over, including religious scientists, and expresses a philosophy of how to do science (it is epistemological, that is, related to how knowledge is acquired). The latter is ontological, that is, a more definitive statement about underlying reality. I am not going to defend the latter here, which may have arisen for many people out of the success of the former. The former is a pragmatic view, based on what has always been successful in practice. There are simply no cases in science of knowledge being advanced by hypothesizing anything more than naturalism.

At this point it is as well to mention something important, that will feature more as we go on with this book. The single, greatest scientific breakthrough was the ability of its practitioners to say 'I do not know.' Not in a defeatist way, but in a way that invites further exploration. It is something strikingly absent from the stereotypical images of gurus, sermons, and holy writings. These seem never to be short of an answer. Yuval Noah Harari in his book *Sapiens* makes the point brilliantly when he describes a map of the world drawn c1490 (just before the scientific revolution) beautiful and complete in every detail. But also completely wrong in many places because guesses were seen as an adequate substitute for knowledge. Another world map c1550 (shortly after the scientific revolution) is blank in regions where the cartographer does not know what is there. It is wonderfully inviting, almost begging the viewer to explore.

This is the very antithesis of the god of the gaps argument[2] which rushes

---

[2] "God of the gaps" is a term coined by Christian theologians to label a fallacious set of arguments. Sadly, it has not stopped many theologians from using such arguments. Though the ideas date back to the 19th-century, or perhaps earlier, an example of the criticism of the God of the gaps argument is from noted German theologian Dietrich Bonhoeffer, who wrote in 1944:

> How wrong it is to use God as a stop-gap for the incompleteness of our knowledge. If in fact the frontiers of knowledge are being pushed further and further back (and that is bound to be the case), then God is being pushed back with them, and is therefore continually in retreat. We are to find God in what we know, not in what we don't know.

We will come across this fallacy many times in the course of this book. It is related to the "argument from incredulity," where the arguer sees no explanation and deduces (incorrectly) that one could never be found. The more correct position in this common circumstance is to admit ignorance. In general, people do not feel comfortable with not knowing, a drive with both positive and negative ramifications. It is positive in that it encourages curiosity and exploration, which has led to some of the remarkable successes that humanity has had. It is negative in that God of the gaps arguments continue to be used long after they were recognized to be false, or, more generally, that there is a to fill every gap in our knowledge with god. Embracing the incompleteness of our knowledge has led to the fastest advances in human history, by far.

When Newton discovered gravity, he could correlate the speed of the planets and the shape of their orbits. However, gravity did not explain why they all revolved in the same direction, in the same plane, and in very nearly circular orbits. This must require divine intervention ("blind Fate could never make all the Planets move one and the same way in Orbs concentrick"[3]).

Laplace a century later used the same argument, except that he corrected the error and postulated that the reason for this was unknown. Now, of course, it is understood: our telescopes allow us to see other solar systems at different stages of evolution, and our computers allow us to model the gravitational dynamics, and the whole thing is unraveled. This discovery was discouraged by Newton's original statement and encouraged by Laplace's update. This, and millions of discoveries like it, forms the basis for our empirical belief in methodological naturalism: it simply works.

With this backdrop, let me engage with what Bush has argued. He says that naturalism "sought to replace" divine creation, but I disagree. Ironically, Bush is claiming there is intent behind naturalism, but natural causes will suffice. Naturalism gradually replaced theism because it worked better; it has more explanatory power for what we observe. There is no denying our roots: theism was humanity's first attempt to explain what we saw. Science is just better at it. Every technological advance and improved understanding of our universe has come out of science. Wisdom is a different and more subtle issue. I would argue that thoughtful, analytical, and observant people are the progenitors of wisdom, which is still a naturalistic explanation.

Bush then discusses the origins of personality. He has an explanation (God), and a reason why it cannot have evolved (the second law of thermodynamics: the entropy of a system always increases). He uses the intuitive idea of "order" (entropy is sometimes loosely said to be a measure of chaos), but a better definition of entropy is related to the ability of a system to do work. Most of our energy comes from the sun (the rest comes from the leftovers of an older, bigger, long extinct star in the form of geothermal and nuclear energy), and this energy is available to do work. This it does, by moving water and air around and through photosynthesis. The totality of life including personality constitutes a decrease in entropy which is offset by an extravagantly larger increase in entropy in the sun. Since we have the sun providing energy capable of doing work, there is no violation of the

---

tendency to rush prematurely to an explanation for a given phenomenon.

[3]Newton, 1717, *Opticks*.

second law of thermodynamics.

Bush then argues that the evolution of personality is highly improbable. What, exactly, is improbable? If we do not understand the process, we cannot figure out the probability. Any attempt to calculate the probability must make unjustified assumptions. At best they show that the assumptions are not correct. How did personality and life form? We do not know (at least in detail). But we are going to keep looking because Bush does not know either. It is certainly not a question for the dustbin: it is an area of active and fascinating research (see Chapter 10).

Finally, Bush talks about reason and how we can know that evolution will give us a trustworthy rationality. The answer is that we cannot. In fact, we know that we have evolved irrational behaviors like superstition and various biases (some would argue that religious tendencies fall into this category too, of course, but we will leave this aside for now). One can easily imagine pattern recognition evolving. That is to say, it could easily help individuals endowed with it to copulate more than individuals without it (by keeping them alive, for example). But there might not be adverse consequences for false positives (running away from a shadow or not eating a non-poison berry is less dangerous than not running from a predator or eating something poisonous). So an overdeveloped sense of pattern recognition could evolve, which we now see as superstition and confirmation bias. For example, if someone observed: "I swear something bad happens every time I see a black cat walking in front of me!" it is easy to imagine them confirming this to themselves.

On the other hand, one can also see the potential advantages of correct reasoning skills, and we have now evolved to the point where we can observe the success of our reasoning through empiricism and consensus building, both things that seem to post-date our rise to intelligence at least at the scale they are on now. The scientific revolution evolved out of rationality so immediately here is a counter-example of something evolving out of a less sophisticated antecedent, contrary to Bush's assertions.

At the end of the day, metaphysical questions like "Why should reason be trusted?" are academic curiosities, not something on which to hang your faith. Reason is trusted because it has provided useful, concrete, repeatable results and because there is no alternative. Perhaps we have an evil demon feeding us stimuli to simulate the world we see. But if so, what other option have we than to play along?

And, once again, Bush is arguing not just against Naturalism, but for the God of the Bible, and once again the chapter offers no gain for his cause. He is claiming to know much more than he does. Whether ontological naturalism is philosophically justifiable, I will leave to the philosophers.

Methodological naturalism is alive and well, buoyed by its empirical success, and seems to support metaphysical naturalism, but I can accept that this may not be enough. However, Bush's essay leaves me unpersuaded about any supernatural, deistic or theistic claim.

CHAPTER 5

Suffering for what?

Up for consideration next is Bruce A. Little's[1] essay entitled "Suffering for What?" Little presents a chapter addressing the question of suffering. Specifically, he seeks to classify the different kinds of suffering that a Christian may experience. "The reason for doing this is to see if some of the promises in the Bible regarding suffering apply only to certain categories of suffering." Little assumes the Christian God and the Bible and attempts to explain some of the contradictions that appear to arise from this assumption. So you could say that this is evidence for the consistency of God, rather than evidence for God in the first place.

Little argues that there are three categories of Christian suffering:

1. Christians may suffer when they live righteously for God;

2. Christians suffer simply because they are part of the human race living in a fallen world; and

3. Christians might suffer when they behave as evildoers.

Firstly, Little argues that in the oft-quoted verse Romans 8:28 ("We know that all things work together for good for those who love God, to

---

[1]Bruce A. Little is a Senior Professor of Philosophy at Southeastern Baptist Theological Seminary. He has been the Director of the L. Russ Bush Center for Faith and Culture at Southeastern.

those who are called according to his purpose."), the "all things" refers to
suffering for righteousness, and is therefore limited to this first category of
suffering.

Secondly, Little affirms that sometimes we just suffer for no particular
reason. It may be because of nature, chance or wicked people. And when
it does, "we should not apply the promises that pertain to suffering for
righteousness' sake."

Thirdly, Little goes on, if we are involved in wrongdoing, we will be dis-
ciplined by God. Or even by the state if we get caught: "[C]ivil authorities
are God's ministers to bring judgment on those who practice evil."

Response

It is commonly known and understood that correlation does not imply
causality. It is perhaps thought about less, though easily appreciated, that
a lack of correlation *does* imply a lack of causality. If I take my umbrella
with me everywhere I go, and sometimes it rains, and sometimes it does
not, then we can say that my carrying an umbrella is not correlated with it
raining. It is therefore not the case that my carrying of the umbrella causes
it to rain. But suppose I claimed that it did. You might point to this lack
of correlation as proof against it. "Ah," I counter, "but on the days it does
not rain, I am carrying with me something that is not a *real* umbrella. It
looks identical. In fact, it is indistinguishable, except that it does not cause
it to rain."

Something similar to this situation is quite common in religious apologetics. There are many uncorrelated variables out there which are, therefore, not causally linked. However, instead of accepting this, we are told
that there are hidden variables which are not accessible to us, and so do not
admit of evidence. 'Religion' and 'good behavior' is perhaps the most obvious example, where, for instance, if a Christian is caught behaving badly,
we are told: "she's not a *real* Christian!" This is known as the no true
Scotsman fallacy[2]. 'Prayer' versus 'answers to prayer,' where there is an
evident lack of correlation (sometimes it works and sometimes not): "that
was an answer. God was just saying no."

---

[2] "No true Scotsman" is an informal fallacy in which a generalized rule is protected
from a counter-example by the introduction of additional information. A simplified
example is as follows: Person A: "No Scotsman puts sugar on his porridge." Person B:
"But my uncle Angus likes sugar with his porridge." Person A: "Ah yes, but no *true*
Scotsman puts sugar on his porridge."

The term is attributed to British philosopher Antony Flew (who we will meet again
in Chapter 11 on page 75).

In the case under discussion, suffering is meant to serve God's good purpose. But what about the many instances when no good purpose appears to be served. One way out of this is to say that God is mysterious. How could we possibly understand his plan? However, Little argues that "all things" when understood contextually means some things. So if it does not work out, then you were in a different category. Little may be right about the contextual understanding of the chapter, but it means it is impossible to tease this out of the evidence. Or, put another way, Occam's razor would suggest that you drop the unnecessary assumptions and accept that all things do not work together for good.

The idea that evildoers are punished seems to me to be too hopeful. A big part of the reason for wanting to believe in a good God who brings justice in the end, is the obvious fact that evildoers often seem to fare so well. Some might call that wishful thinking, or too good to be true. But if you do happen to suffer for things you have done wrong, then you should not expect to be blessed for that or to think that any good that comes out of it exonerates you for the original evil. I would argue that this is common sense and does not constitute evidence for God.

Little sees God's hand in the punishments meted out by civil authorities in his third category. The sad fact, though, is that the church as a structure and Christians as part of that structure, with reasonable interpretations of teachings from the Bible, are often the cause of evil. Abuse is rife in the church, not despite the teachings, but because of them[3]. The rest of this essay will discuss this.

Most evangelicals would believe that God is sovereign (in control of all things). They also believe that this sovereign God inspired the words of the Bible as a guide for how we as humans should live our lives. But of course, the Bible is an ancient document written in ancient languages about ancient cultures, and as such, needs to be interpreted for application to our modern cultural experience, and churches do the bulk of that interpreting. Most people are quick to point out when someone else has a "wrong" interpretation of Scripture but are often completely unwilling to admit that they have used any interpretation at all to arrive at their viewpoint (we will see an example in Chapter 40). Most churches have a power structure in place which they draw from an interpretation of Scripture. And while there are many different forms of government in evangelical churches, every church believes that their particular interpretation is the correct, "biblical" one. Therefore all churches believe that their power structure was established

---

[3]I am grateful to Sarah Peeler, a good friend who has discussed the idea of abuse within the church with me, and opened my eyes to a great deal that I did not see before. Much of the rest of this chapter was paraphrased from emails she wrote to me on the subject, with her permission.

directly by God.

Because God is sovereign, He is actively involved in orchestrating which individuals end up with the positions of power (See Romans 13:1–7[4]). Thus, when someone in power sets a rule, those below must view it as a commandment coming directly from God. Because God is good, rules established by God are also assumed to be for our good, even when they are uncomfortable. If someone in power is setting rules that appear to be harmful, there are two possible causes:

1. The person in power is negligent, and God will eventually make it clear to the others with power that the toxic person must go; or

2. The rules are not harmful (though they might be painful) and you just need to submit.

Notable by its absence is representation for the injured party. Meanwhile, the church preaches the values of obedience, submission, humility, suffering with joy, and loving your enemy among others. Church attendees are reminded that God is in control, we owe everything to Him and should strive in all ways to submit ourselves to His will for our lives. Even the messages about God's goodness, love, and justice are often just reminders that because of these qualities we can trust that submitting to God will bring about good in our lives. About the only thing we can do is pray, and because this involves communicating directly with our sovereign God who hears and orchestrates all things for our good, it is considered to be incredibly powerful (more on this below).

So we have created a situation in which a group of people believes that they have been ordained by a sovereign God to dictate the beliefs and

---

[4]Romans 13:1–7 represents unsophisticated and reprehensible moral teaching, with its victim blaming and might is right mentality:

> Let every soul be in subjection to the higher authorities, for there is no authority except from God, and those who exist are ordained by God. Therefore he who resists the authority, withstands the ordinance of God; and those who withstand will receive to themselves judgment. For rulers are not a terror to the good work, but to the evil. Do you desire to have no fear of the authority? Do that which is good, and you will have praise from the same, for he is a servant of God to you for good. But if you do that which is evil, be afraid, for he doesn't bear the sword in vain; for he is a servant of God, an avenger for wrath to him who does evil. Therefore you need to be in subjection, not only because of the wrath, but also for conscience' sake. For this reason you also pay taxes, for they are servants of God's service, attending continually on this very thing. Therefore give everyone what you owe: if you owe taxes, pay taxes; if customs, then customs; if respect, then respect; if honor, then honor.

behaviors of their subordinates. They tell their subordinates that their highest calling in life is to submit and suffer in joy. Both those in power and those submitting believe that a good and loving God has orchestrated the situation. Therefore, whatever the authorities decide is both good and of God, and anyone who disagrees with the authorities should be considered to be in direct rebellion against God himself. It is easy to imagine that this is a recipe for disaster, and indeed the result is often one of coercion and abuse. A hallmark of this is the tendency to support the institution over the individual, the powerful over the powerless.

Of course, a structure like this is susceptible to conmen and charlatans, but often it is challenging to distinguish these from people who genuinely believe. Bill Gothard[5], who is alleged to have molested several women and girls, has been hugely successful in his ministry. His teachings include[6]:

- The **authority** principle: inward peace results when people respect and honor the authorities (parents, government, etc.) that God has put into their lives. It is based on the idea that God gives direction, protection, and provision through human authorities.

- The **suffering** principle: people should allow the hurts from offenders to reveal "blind spots" in their own lives. Genuine joy is a result of fully forgiving offenders.

It is easy to see the dangers inherent in these teachings, and that these teachings are easily inferred from the Bible, such as Romans 13:1–7.

I could say much about Mark Driscoll[7], another successful minister and personality cult leader. But of relevance to this discussion is a bylaw change that he proposed in September 2007 that would grant an indefinite term of office to the executive elders, effectively consolidating power with Driscoll and his trusted lieutenants. Two other pastors (Paul Petry and Bent Meyer) dissented to the changes and were summarily fired for "displaying an unhealthy distrust in the senior leadership." Driscoll announced at a conference that:

> They were off mission so now they're unemployed. This will be
> the defining issue as to whether or not you succeed or fail. I've

---

[5]Bill Gothard is an American Christian minister, speaker, writer, and founder of the Institute in Basic Life Principles. He stepped down from leadership in the Institute in Basic Life Principles after multiple allegations of sexual harassment and molestation in 2014.

[6]These teachings from the Institute in Basic Life Principles can be found here: `iblp.org/seminars-conferences/basic-seminar/basic-life-principles`.

[7]Mark Driscoll is an American evangelical pastor and author. He founded Mars Hill Church in Seattle, Washington, and resigned in 2014 amid public criticism and formal complaints from Mars Hill staff members and congregants.

read enough of the New Testament to know that occasionally
Paul puts somebody in the wood chipper.

One can see from these examples the central role Biblically supported,
Christian power structures play in church abuse. Of course, you can dispute
the interpretations of the Bible that are used here, but the theme remains.
Most tragic is that these issues exist in the vast majority of church structures and are supported (tacitly at least) by the vast majority of Christians.

Once a person gets in the position where they disagree with their authorities, they struggle to get out of it. Their fellow subordinates will
shame and blame them ("she should have been more submissive/obedient/
joyful," "he must not have prayed/studied/forgiven enough," "she's too
bitter/angry/divisive," "he wasn't a strong enough leader"), and they will
trust that the authorities must have been correct, regardless of any evidence to the contrary. Because the system is believed to be protective, if
someone is claiming harm then they must not have adhered closely enough
to the protective values. So the powerful get more power, and the weak
and vulnerable are blamed, abused, and pushed out.

It is often well-meaning people since they take all the theology so seriously. When you believe all is of God and God is good, then it is easy to
see something horrible and say "but it must somehow be good in a way I
do not understand." And then you end up calling evil good.

A pastor at a church I used to go to was loved by his congregation and
effective in his preaching, teaching, and ministry. The presbytery (a group
of mostly anonymous men) believed that his theology was not sound: he
believed that women could be pastors and elders. He did not preach on
this issue from the pulpit, or even talk about it widely, but had listed it as
a theological difference in his ordination exam.

They refused to ordain him and humiliated him in various ways. For
example, they said that he could no longer give communion after him having
done so for more than a year, so he would have to sit like a castigated
school boy while an ordained member of the presbytery (unknown to the
congregation) led the sacrament.

No-one in the church dissented. In fact, people blamed him for not
studying hard enough for the ordination exam. An elder would stand up
in church and defend the presbytery, spinning it with spiritual language as
though they had done it out of care and concern for the spiritual welfare of
the congregation. Eventually, the pastor left to go to another church where
he was ordained immediately and welcomed with open arms. In a company,
this kind of abuse would be grounds for a lawsuit, but in the church, it is
dressed up in religious language, and the victim is blamed.

A typical vehicle for blaming the victim is the "we are all sinners" narrative. Abusers repent and are welcomed back with open arms, while victims are shunned as resentful, bitter, and unwilling to forgive. The church above would say in effect that "yes, perhaps the presbytery was not kind—they are fallible humans after all. But let's not forget that the pastor answered that question 'wrong' (that is, truthfully). And in the end, the pastor proved himself to be the problem because he gave up after only three attempts at ordination. If he truly believed in God, he would not have been so faithless as to withdraw from godly correction. How else does God lovingly draw us to himself if not through the chastening of his anointed? If the presbytery treated the pastor unfairly, then surely God would have revealed that? What he needed to do was recognize his sin in the situation, repent, and submit. Let God take care of the alleged injustice."

A common reason for apathy and inaction in the face of abuse is the notion that prayer is a type of action. In the above example, when an elder announced that the pastor would no longer be able to give the sacraments, a member of the congregation said that it sounded like we needed to pray. There was much nodding and agreement, and everyone felt that they had achieved something. People were bothered by the way the presbytery had behaved and had it occurred in their work or family they would have voiced questions about it. But in this case, systemic injustice was perpetuated by good people doing nothing. And they were content to do nothing because they thought prayer was leaving it in God's hands. So the pastor was abused, the church tacitly allowed it to happen, and all of this was completely inevitable when you look at the way the church is structured. Given this pastor is a white man, imagine the abuse suffered by women, homosexuals, and minorities inside congregations around the world.

So, to Little's list of three types of suffering, we need to add a fourth: Christians often abuse and are abused by sincerely trying to adhere to the teachings of the church regarding submission to authority, forgiveness of their oppressors, love of their enemies, and the efficacy of prayer.

The existence of suffering is a big issue for many believers. Little introduces categories of suffering in an attempt to split the problem up and exonerate God. This does not constitute evidence for God, but might be useful for reconciling the problem if we somehow knew that God existed already. However, Little does not acknowledge the category of suffering that comes directly from sincere attempts to follow Biblical teachings. The existence of this type of suffering undermines his argument and hints at the all too human origins of the teachings. I am not trying to show that God does not exist, but merely to show that the evidence for God's existence is insufficient to accept it. In this arena, Little's chapter does nothing to undermine that view.

CHAPTER 6

Responding to the Argument from Evil

Another article on the problem of pain is David Wood's[1] essay entitled "Responding to the Argument from Evil: Three Approaches for the Theist." Wood presents three possible responses to the problem of evil, that is the question of how to reconcile the existence of evil with an "all-knowing, all-powerful and completely good" God. The three approaches Wood suggests are:

1. To point out problems with the problem of evil argument. Specifically:

   (a) Inconsistencies;

   (b) Ambiguous terms; and

   (c) Unproven assumptions.

2. To explain suffering:

   (a) Theologically; and

   (b) Philosophically.

3. To offer additional arguments for theism that outweigh evidence against theism.

---

[1]David Wood is an American evangelical missionary and Christian apologist. He is currently head of the Acts 17 Apologetics Ministry.

Here are the problems that Wood sees with the problem of evil argument.

1a Inconsistencies: Wood argues that since the argument from evil is attempting to establish the non-existence of God, the burden of proof is on the atheist to make the case. He presents the argument from evil as follows:

1. If God exists, there would not be any pointless suffering.

2. Since we cannot think of reasons for allowing certain instances of suffering, some suffering is probably pointless (e.g., an injured deer experiencing pointless pain as it slowly dies in the woods).

3. Therefore, God probably does not exist.

Wood then draws attention to the "probably," asserting that the atheist is claiming that "we shouldn't believe in something that seems improbable." But what about the design argument? Here the position is reversed: now the theist is saying that it is extremely improbable that life formed on its own, or that the universe just happened to be finely tuned for life, and the atheist responds that it may be improbable, but she is going to believe it anyway. This, Wood argues, is a clear inconsistency which levels the scales between atheist and theist. Any further argument in favor of theism will tip the scales that way.

1b Ambiguous terms: Wood then focuses on ambiguous terms. In this argument, the term Wood refers to is 'good.' "If we examine atheistic arguments carefully, we find that a 'good' being is one who *maximizes pleasure* and *minimizes pain*" (emphasis in the original). Wood then sets up a different version of the argument from evil that says that "If God existed, he would maximize our pleasure and minimize our pain." That is not the case, so God does not exist.

But what if 'good' means something else to a theist? What if God sees a greater good in "developing virtues, learning that we're not the center of the universe, [and] seeking God with all our hearts"? Pleasure is not at the top of Christian priorities, and so the whole argument from evil falls apart.

1c Unproven Assumptions: Wood considers the awareness assumption: "If God has reasons for allowing evil, we will be aware of these reasons." Wood states that "without this assumption, most versions of [the argument from evil] cannot get off the ground."

Wood next sets out to explain suffering, some of which he says can be accounted for both theologically and philosophically, by appealing to "what philosophers call 'theodicies.'"

2a Christian Doctrine: Wood notes that theologically "humanity is in a state of rebellion against God." The argument from evil "relies, to a large extent, on how awful humanity is and can become." The evil of the Holocaust or the Rape of Nanking[2] "fit quite well with the idea that humanity has turned away from God." He says that "the more examples of moral evil an atheist presents in support of his argument, the more evidence he's [giving] that human beings are extremely sinful." Wood argues that it makes little sense to have humans "at war with God," while God is expected to "give us a world of total pleasure."

2b Theodicies: Wood explains that a theodicy is an attempt to answer the question: "What morally sufficient reason could there be for God to allow evil?" He argues that there is the "free will" theodicy, which claims that a "world containing free beings is better than a world without free beings since only free beings can choose the good or genuinely love or be moral in any meaningful sense." Wood notes that this free-will is open to misuse, which is the cause of moral evil.

Secondly, there is the "soul-building" theodicy, which posits that "if becoming mature human beings ... is important, then a world with pain is better than a world without pain" since pain is correlated with times of personal growth.

Wood acknowledges that "such theodicies [do not] account for all of the evil in our world," but that nevertheless "[t]he fact that we can come up with *some* plausible explanations for suffering (despite our limited knowledge) is itself a serious blow to [the argument from evil]."

3 Outweighing the Argument from Evil: Finally Wood switches tack and says that even if the argument from evil provides some evidence against theism, it can potentially be outweighed by other evidence for theism. He states that there are "dozens of arguments for the existence of God," and mentions and briefly explains three of them:

---

[2]The Rape of Nanking, or Nanking Massacre was an episode of mass murder and mass rape committed by Japanese troops in 1937–8 against the residents of Nanjing, which was then the capital of the Republic of China, during the Second Sino-Japanese War. The number of people killed is disputed by scholars, but ranges from 40,000 to 300,000.

1. Design arguments: He cites the argument from fine-tuning, and the argument from biological complexity as the main two versions.

2. Cosmological arguments. And

3. The argument from morality.

Finally Wood notes that these responses should only be used at an appropriate time, as they offer little solace to the suffering. Nonetheless,

> the fact that theists can explain a fair amount of suffering (which is all that can be reasonably expected of limited beings) and that we have strong evidence that supports belief in God, it's clear that the only significant [atheist] argument fails on multiple levels.

Response

Wood here is doing a preemptive strike on an argument against the existence of God. I do not believe it is possible to disprove the existence of God in general, but I do believe that the evidence for the existence of God is insufficient. The purpose of *Evidence for God* is to present such evidence so it would appear to be circular for Wood in this chapter to claim that it exists. To claim that the argument from evil is the only significant atheist argument is equally false. In fact, I could grant Wood his whole thesis and admit that the argument from evil is utterly without merit and not find myself any closer to theism, let alone Christianity.

However, since we are here, I will address a few issues in Wood's arguments. I do not think he is correct in his dismissal of this discussion. Even if it does not prove that God does not exist, it surely makes us wonder about his nature. Wood's argument relies on a straw man fallacy[3], redefining the argument from evil in each section that he writes. I count at least four definitions, including a switch from evil to moral evil at some point in the procedure.

In his discussion on the inadequacy of the argument from evil, Wood talks about **inconsistencies, ambiguous terms**, and **unproven assumptions**.

In the first of these discussions (on **inconsistencies**), he argues that since we cannot think of a reason for allowing pointless suffering there

---

[3] A straw man argument is an informal fallacy it which someone appears to be refuting an opponent's argument, while actually refuting a different, weaker argument that was not advanced by that opponent.

probably isn't one. He then points out that it is extremely *improbable* that life formed on its own or that the universe is fine-tuned. Since these are both improbable, the theist and atheist are at a stalemate.

Note that Wood here is himself using an ambiguous term, in this case, *probability*. In the first instance, we are talking about the existence of a moral justification, while in the second instance, we are talking about the existence of a scientific mechanism. Saying that you cannot think of a moral justification for the holocaust is the same as saying that you believe the holocaust was wrong. To phrase it in terms of probability is to play word games. On the other hand, it is clear that life formed and the universe is finely tuned. It *seems* improbable, based on our current understanding, but it is plausible that at some point *Nature* will publish a paper that explains that such a thing was, in fact, inevitable or very likely because of a newly discovered mechanism. In other words, the probability has no meaning in the second case because we do not know enough to assess it.

The fundamental point is that we cannot think of a moral justification for pointless suffering, and we should not quash our morality based on the belief that it is beyond our comprehension. If we believe something is wrong, we should say so plainly and discuss it rationally. We should not change the subject, as Wood did.

In the second discussion (on **ambiguous terms**), Wood argues that "good" is ambiguously defined and that atheists seem to define it as maximizing pleasure while minimizing pain. But what if we define good as something else: developing virtues and seeking God? So let me accept Wood's definition and restate his argument from evil:

1. If God existed, he would help people to develop virtues and seek God.

2. People do not develop virtues and seek God.

3. Therefore, God does not exist.

So even with Wood's definition of good, the argument seems to hold.

I also take umbrage with the idea that atheists define good as hedonism, and that atheists cannot appreciate the potential glory in a tough situation. However, there are plenty of situations, both real and hypothetical, where evil destroys people, rather than builds their character. It is unpalatable that he dismisses the argument so glibly in the face of real evil and suffering. Note, also, that Wood defines good as seeking God, which downplays the many atrocities that have been committed in the name of God (see the previous chapter for a discussion of how sincere belief in the Bible contributes to abuse within the church).

In the third discussion (on **unproven assumptions**), Wood says that atheists are assuming that they would be aware of God's reasons for allowing evil. This is probably his strongest argument at least in the abstract. The religious (my former self included) hold it all together with a trust that God is in control in some way that is beyond understanding. This argument is a call to distrust your senses, your moral judgment, and your logic in favor of a nebulous notion that God has it all worked out. Perhaps Wood establishes that atheists cannot disprove God's existence with the argument from evil. If there were good evidence for the existence of God, then you would be forced to assume that He has secret reasons for the evil that we all see. But without good evidence for His existence, you can resolve this cognitive dissonance by simply abandoning belief in God.

Note that there is a contradiction between this argument and the moral argument discussed in Chapter 2. In the moral argument, we are meant to see our own morality as evidence of God. Here we are meant to suppress our own morality with the assumption that God has a bigger plan to which we are not privy. This tendency to take the evidence, split it in two, and deal with each part separately is a theme we will come across many times as we consider the arguments of *Evidence for God*.

Next Wood tries to explain the existence of evil. He notes that he cannot explain away all evil, but says that if he can explain some evil, we can imagine that a supernatural being could explain it all. He also notes that this truth is not of any comfort to people who are suffering. All of this seems rather inadequate to me.

He says that theologically humans are at war with God, so that explains their poor morality and the evil it produces. But most people display poor morality out of selfishness, which is easily understood naturalistically. For example, though we do not necessarily judge animals on a moral standard, their behavior is also often selfish (or at least tribal). Therefore, the "war with God" explanation for evil is unnecessary, and we can drop it.

The same applies to the theodicies. We have free will because God thought it was a good idea or we have free will because there is no God. Or God did not intervene because He wanted to make you a better person. In all these cases God is assumed to have a motivation that has the effect of making His inaction indistinguishable from what would occur if He did not exist.

Finally, Wood summarizes a few more arguments for the existence of God, to "outweigh" the argument from evil. This feels to me like he is changing the subject. However, the cosmological argument and moral argument we met and responded to in Chapter 1 and Chapter 2 respectively. The argument from design I have touched on briefly above and much of the discussion regarding the cosmological argument applies here too. We will get into this in much more detail in Section II.

In summary, the problem of evil, while not ironclad, is a serious blow to the idea of God, as any free-thinking person will acknowledge. It is possible to hold it all together, but it requires suppressing your own morality in favor of some mysterious Godly greater good. That these supposed truths offer no comfort to those in pain is a hint to their inadequacy. Ultimately, a person needs to decide whether there is sufficient evidence to believe in God. If there is, then the problem of evil will always be an uncomfortable reality and a question mark on the character or omnipotence of God. I argue that there is not sufficient evidence for God (I have not been convinced by anything in this book so far) and that this provides the obvious way to resolve the problem of suffering.

CHAPTER 7

God, Suffering, and Santa Claus

Remaining with the problem of pain, we now consider a second essay by David Wood: "God, Suffering, and Santa Claus: An Examination of the Explanatory Power of Theism and Atheism." Wood states that the previous chapter responded to the claim that theism does not explain the presence of suffering. To further expound why this is flawed, Wood wants to "compare the explanatory power of theism with that of atheism."

As a point of comparison, he discusses how a child believes that "Santa is the explanation for the presents under the Christmas tree." The child accepts this because it explains the observation. Later they realize that a simpler explanation exists (that parents put gifts under the tree), and so they reject the Santa hypothesis. Wood argues that the situation is qualitatively different for the "God hypothesis" because there are observations which are better explained by God than by an atheistic viewpoint.

Wood then argues that theism has explanatory power. He says:

> Suppose we have a set of facts—symbolized as a, b, c, d, e, f, and g—and we're seeking an explanation that accounts for these facts. Let us further suppose that hypothesis x accounts for facts a, b, c, d, e, and f, but that it's unclear how hypothesis x can account for g. Here it would be quite easy for a critic of hypothesis x to say, 'This hypothesis makes no sense in light of g; we should therefore reject hypothesis x.' But is it reasonable

43

to dismiss a hypothesis when it accounts for nearly every fact we're trying to explain?

Wood lists the facts for which theism accounts. Theism explains

1. why we have a world at all;

2. why our world is finely tuned for life;

3. the origin of life, including its diversity and complexity;

4. the rise of consciousness;

5. objective moral values; and

6. miracles.

On this last point, he gives the example of the resurrection:

> [A]ccording to all of the historical evidence available to us, Jesus died by crucifixion. We also know, historically, that Jesus's tomb was empty three days later, and that both friends and foes were soon claiming that he had appeared to them, risen from the dead. The only explanation that accounts for these facts without strain (and without appealing to absurd phenomena such as mass hallucinations) is that Jesus rose from the dead.

So if theism fails to account for suffering, it has to be seen in the context of all the other things that theism does explain.

But what does Atheism explain? Wood argues that atheism "explains, quite literally, nothing." It does not explain

> the existence of our universe or the fact that our universe is finely tuned. It doesn't explain the origin and diversity of life. It fails to explain the rise of consciousness or objective moral values or the evidence for miracles; indeed, atheism doesn't even account for the evil that serves as the foundation of the argument from evil.

The best atheism can do is say that if we "somehow end up with a finely tuned universe and diverse life, suffering won't be surprising."

But what if an atheist says that "atheism isn't meant to be taken as an explanation for anything." Wood says that to reject the theism hypothesis leaves you with no reasonable explanation of anything. He explains with a continuation of the analogy with Santa:

As we've seen, people who believe in Santa as their explanation for the presents under the tree eventually reject the Santa hypothesis when they realize that there's a far more reasonable explanation of the data. But suppose another person comes along and declares, "Santa didn't put those presents there, and neither did your parents. The presents are just there. Their existence is a brute fact."

The problem with this response is that, by taking away the explanations (Santa and one's parents) that actually account for the data, and by offering no substitute hypothesis to explain the data, we're left with data but no explanation. Indeed, if we had to choose between "Santa put them there" and "No one put them there," I think most of us would find the former explanation superior since it at least accounts for the presents.

Wood states that atheists "must offer a hypothesis at least as powerful as theism" calling this a "double standard." He concludes that "[i]f we're going to reject hypotheses because they fail to explain the data, we must reject atheism long before we reject theism."

Wood closes the chapter with an epilogue on gratitude, saying that until atheists have a reasonable explanation they will always have "much to be thankful for, and no one to be thankful to," accusing atheists of destroying a person's gratitude with the argument from evil.

Response

The ancient Egyptians saw the brute fact of the sun rising each day. They explained that this occurred because Khepri, the scarab god would push the sun across the sky ahead of him like a beetle pushing a ball of dung. It is unclear whether the ancient Egyptians ever took this "explanation" seriously, but the point is clear: a divine explanation is no explanation at all.

The point is that theists have been claiming for thousands of years that they had all the explanation that was needed, often resisting scientific advances. The god of the gaps argument arises precisely because of this. It was only with the scientific revolution that people realized that it is better to admit ignorance than to pretend to have an explanation. Humans do this all the time, and not just with God—just try to ask a four-year-old something; it is almost impossible to get a response of "I don't know."

Without scientists admitting their ignorance and beginning their quest of discovery, we would not even know about fine-tuning. So this pillar that seems so central to the theist argument now would just disappear. In fact, at any given point in time, there are things we understand and things that we do not. The god of the gaps fallacy postulates that god explains the things that we do not understand. Obviously, this is a shifting goal. As time goes by, we understand naturalistically things that we used to explain with god (such as the sun rising, rainbows shining or the fact that the planets revolve around the sun in the same direction and in the same plane), and so theists move on to whatever the current scientific difficulty is. In the old days, God scattered the stars across the heaven and molded us from clay. Now he tunes the universal constants. And if (when?) the origin of the universal constants is understood, theists will have to shift their arguments once again.

So theism cannot be said to "explain" anything. If you have to assume the existence of a supernatural being to make it work, then you might as well admit you do not know.

A second objection is the logic of how scientific knowledge works. Wood says: "But is it reasonable to dismiss a hypothesis when it accounts for nearly every fact we're trying to explain?" Wood asks this rhetorically, implying that the answer is "no", but in fact, the answer is a categorical "yes!" We reject hypotheses when they make a prediction that fails. This is the very essence of science. Likewise, the very essence of pseudoscience is adding a lot of extra clauses and exceptions to the base hypothesis so that the hypothesis can remain unchanged in the face of additional evidence.

And what of Wood's idea that atheism explains nothing? If we include all scientific discovery in this (which is reasonable because science is a naturalistic endeavor), it is hard to imagine a more wildly inaccurate statement. Science has impacted almost every aspect of our lives. I should clarify that there is an ambiguous term here, in this case, what constitutes an explanation. Science mostly occupies itself with a description of what is, rather than a value judgment. If we asked "why did the child die?" your archetypal scientist might answer in terms of the momentum of the bus and the mass of the child. It is certainly an answer, but perhaps not the metaphysical one for which the questioner was looking.

Nonetheless, most of the questions Wood presented were of the sort that looked for a scientific explanation, rather than a metaphysical one. The exception is the issue of the existence of suffering, which theism has trouble answering anyway, as Wood tacitly acknowledged both in this and the previous chapter.

But let us look at some of the questions and contrast the alternative answers that atheism and theism provide.

Why do we have a world at all? It is a good question, but let us make sure that we understand what we mean by it. If we mean to ask by what mechanism did the universe come to be here, then atheist and theist alike must admit that we do not know. "God made it" is no explanation at all, and the myriad creation stories are evidence of nothing more than a fertile imagination among the various human founders of these religions: they have certainly not proved to be factually or scientifically accurate.

If we mean by what mechanism did the *earth* come to be here, then we must admit that science has found far more compelling and correct answers than those invented by the various religions. The scientific description of the evolution of the solar system is magnificent and fascinating.

If we mean what is the purpose of the world, then we must consider the world in its totality, with its glory and wonder as well as the unnecessary suffering and decay. In other words, the argument from evil, which Wood admits is more easily explained without a good and omnipotent God, is inseparable from this question so the theist cannot legitimately claim to have a better answer than does the atheist.

If we mean individual purpose, then atheists are in the position of having to create their own. Whether or not this is better is a question of taste, but speaking personally I prefer it to my experiences as a Christian. So by most measures, atheists have a better explanation for this question, and otherwise, they are at least equivalent.

Why is our world finely tuned for life? Scientifically, the answer would appear to be that there is an extreme selection bias. If we are here to observe it, then the universe must be able to evolve and support life so it must be fine-tuned. If there were many universes, or if we were in an infinite sequence of universes then obviously we could only observe universes finely tuned for life. This is also known as the weak anthropic principle. Now, if the universe were not fine-tuned, that would be impressive evidence that we were somehow put here. But that is not the case.

The origin of life, including its diversity and complexity, is explained scientifically by evolution. This provides at a stroke, and with incredible efficiency, the mechanism for increasing complexity. If there were no diversity, then evolution could not occur, so the variation we see accords with evolution. The fossil record demonstrates increasing complexity with time, as has been appreciated since the ancient Greeks. We could reject evolution with just one fossil found out of place. On the other hand, Wood does not show how theists "explain" the diversity and complexity of life: what aspect of theism requires diversity and complexity?

If evolution explains the diversity and complexity, the abiogenesis event is not as well understood. That is not to say that we know nothing about it: the origins may be lost in the mists of time for now, but the basic concepts are somewhat understood and remain an area of research. And again, if scientists discovered the abiogenesis event (or sequence of events), where would that leave the theist? Once again, they would be forced to shift their focus elsewhere because the specifics do not matter when you already know the 'right' conclusion. We will return in more detail to abiogenesis in Chapter 10.

The rise of consciousness again poses no particular problem conceptually. Atheists have in evolution a mechanism whereby complexity can increase, and consciousness emerges from lower forms of consciousness. This does not decrease our wonder and sense of awe, but nor does it make us throw up our hands in despair.

Objective moral values. I dealt with the question of objective moral values in Chapter 2. Suffice it to say that it is not clear that there is such a thing, and if there were, it is not clear that we cannot find a scientific explanation for it. Nor is it clear that theism accounts for this, given the argument from evil.

Miracles. Last, we have the explanation of miracles in general and the resurrection of Jesus in particular. It cannot be shown that miracles, in general, are impossible, though an approach of skepticism commends itself. "Extraordinary claims require extraordinary evidence." However, I would like to delve into these two points in more detail.

Miracles in general.

Theism does not, in fact, explain miracles at all well because they feature in different, conflicting religions. Monotheistic religions claim a monopoly on miracles and have two approaches to claims made from outside the fold: either they are fake, or they are diabolical in origin. Neither of these approaches will do. In the former case, the theist admits that there are rational explanations for miracle stories and agrees completely with the atheist. This is probably true for the vast majority of miracle stories, which the theist and atheist both treat with suspicion. In this case, the theist has no better "explanation" than the atheist and must answer why he has applied a double standard to some of the miracles that happen to support the theist's particular perspective.

The latter is the uglier explanation, more popular once than it is now. It is obviously both caused by and a cause of prejudice, and it is noteworthy indeed how often people seem to be born into the 'good' religion, while all others are born into the false ones. We need also ascribe to the devil a very devious mind as he performs quite wondrous healings and other general good deeds to dupe people into following him. It is hard to imagine a Martian arriving on Earth and being able to pick the good religion from the bad by the miracles alone.

But this misses the major point, which is that these miracles invariably evaporate upon closer examination. We have always found more prosaic and human explanations, and so this is a reasonable place to start. Most Christians have noticed a marked decrease in the frequency of miracles, and in the modern age of ubiquitous cameras and phones, evidence for miracles is notable by its absence. Most reasonable Christians conclude that miracles are more of a first-century phenomenon. At first pass, this seems consistent, as this was the century of Christ himself and so surely an exception can be made to the usual rules? Unfortunately, this is circular reasoning. The only way into the circle is to accept the evidence, which means examining the evidence critically and without the presupposition. When we do this, the evidence for these miracles is unexceptional compared with the evidence for other miracles that we would ordinarily reject.

For example, Sathya Sai Baba is a man who died as recently as 2011, and about whom you may not have heard. Yet there are hundreds of thousands of people who believe that he was divine based on witnesses reporting miraculous healings, resurrections, clairvoyance, and bilocation. His mother even claimed that she conceived him miraculously. Despite all this, we tend to believe that, far from being an incarnation of Sai Baba of Shirdi as he claims, he was just a conman (or perhaps deluded). The witnesses are dismissed by us because they are ardent followers of his, ready to believe in him rather than critically examine alleged incidents. Why do we not apply the same standard to objectively worse evidence obtained in similar circumstances contained in the Bible? The gospel writers were not even witnesses of the miracles but reported other people's traditions uncritically.

Consider Balaam's Donkey (Numbers 22:21–41), which Wells relates, drawing on the work of David Strauss[1]. The well-known story is that Balaam's donkey sees an angel and stops moving. Balaam, unable at first to

---

[1] G. A. Wells, *Cutting Jesus Down to Size: What Higher Criticism Has Achieved and Where It Leaves Christianity*

see the angel, beats the donkey, and eventually, the donkey says "What have I done to you, that you have struck me these three times?" Balaam responds to the donkey, not commenting on the oddness of the situation. Even if Balaam himself related this to you, and even if Balaam were known to you to be a person of good character, you would "find it more probable, beyond all comparison, that [it is] an untrue account, rather than a miraculous fact."

An examination of the evidence reveals an entirely human origin for the miracles of Jesus, which is that they are passed down as a tradition rather than as eyewitness accounts. This atheist position is a better "explanation" of the miraculous accounts. Let me give you some examples (Wells discusses these examples in more detail). There are several instances where there are two accounts of a miracle in the same book of the Bible. For example, Mark has two accounts of miraculous feedings: one of the five thousand[2] and one of the four thousand[3]. The incidents are so similar that it beggars belief to suppose that there were two separate events involved. In the second feeding, the disciples ask "From where could one satisfy these people with bread here in a deserted place?" revealing themselves to be preternaturally stupid since they have just witnessed the first feeding, or that perhaps the traditional story evolved into two and Mark copied them both down. This argues against the gospels being written by eyewitnesses.

Furthermore, Strauss notes (also in Wells) that many of the New Testament stories result from a kind of oneupmanship over previous holy men. This is actually a common theme in religion. For instance, the story of Noah's ark mostly replicates the earlier Gilgamesh story[4].

The New Testament has Jesus supplying food miraculously and raising

---

[2]Mark 6:30–44

[3]Mark 8:1–21

[4]Gilgamesh is an ancient king whose supposed reign was in approximately 2700 BCE (creation.com suggests a date of about 2300 BCE for the Biblical flood (creation.com/the-date-of-noahs-flood)). The *Epic of Gilgamesh* is regarded as the earliest surviving great work of literature, and features a character called Utnapishtim. Utnapishtim is told by the Sumerian God Enki to abandon his worldly possessions and create a giant boat for him, his family, the craftsmen of his village, the animals, and grains. A violent storm then breaks out for six days and nights, causing the gods to go into hiding, and killing everything else that is not on the boat. After twelve days on the water, Utnapishtim opens the hatch of his ship to look around and sees the slopes of Mount Nisir, where he rests his ship for seven days. On the seventh day, he sends a dove out to see if the water has receded, but the dove finds nothing and returns. Then he sends out a swallow, and just as before, it returns. Finally, Utnapishtim sends out a raven, and the raven sees that the waters have receded, so it circles around, but does not return. Utnapishtim then sets all the animals free, and makes a sacrifice to the gods. The gods return, and Enlil gives Utnapishtim and his wife the gift of immortality.

Scholars believe that this story substantially pre-dates that of Noah's ark and regard both as mythical.

the dead, which were both done by Elisha[5]. In fact, Luke[6] has a story of
Jesus meeting a funeral procession of the only son of a widow and raising
him to life, just like Elisha's story. This story does not feature anywhere
else even though Luke says (7:17): "This report went out concerning him
in the whole of Judea, and in all the surrounding region." Luke is at pains
to point out that the bystanders glorified God, saying "A great prophet has
arisen among us!" so that the reader could be clear that Jesus was at least
up to Elisha's level.

Wells goes further:

> Some gospel incidents were, says Strauss, invented in order to
> show that Jesus was a greater prophet than Moses. The forty
> days' temptation in the wilderness parallels Moses's time on
> Sinai; and since Moses had been transfigured upon the moun-
> tain top, Christ must also have a transfiguration to show that he
> was in no way inferior. All this, although it may still shock the
> laity, is barely disputed any more even by relatively conservative
> theologians. A. E. Harvey, in so *bien-pensant* a work as his 1970
> *New English Bible Companion to the New Testament*, specifies
> a number of details peculiar to Matthew in the gospel transfig-
> uration stories and says that "they perhaps show Matthew at
> work, deliberately presenting Jesus as the new Moses, the defini-
> tive lawgiver" (p.70). That early Christians constructed their
> picture of Jesus from the Old Testament is obvious from the
> statement of Paul—the earliest extant Christian writer—that it
> consists of prophetic writings, written down for our instruction
> in order to elucidate facts about Jesus (Rom. 15:3–4;16:25–26).
> In other words, if study of scripture showed that the Messiah
> was to behave in a certain way, then, for early Christians, Je-
> sus must have behaved in that way, whatever eyewitnesses or
> historical records said or failed to say.

Furthermore, the earliest Christian documents are letters ascribed to
Paul, which have no suggestion of any miracles worked by Jesus even though
the early Christians regarded miracles as of great importance.

He goes on to point out that Paul himself comes close to denying that
Jesus worked miracles when he says "For Jews ask for signs ... but we
preach Christ crucified" (1 Corinthians 1:22–23). Mark[7] has even Jesus
saying "Why does this generation seek a sign? Most certainly I tell you,

---

[5] 2 Kings 4:42–44 and 2 Kings 4:32–35
[6] Luke 7:11–17
[7] Mark 8:12

no sign will be given to this generation." This is a strange thing to say after just feeding four-thousand people and perhaps comes from an earlier tradition that pre-dates the miracle traditions.

Wood asks us to choose between "Santa put them there" and "No one put them there" and suspects that we would rather choose the former as it at least explains the presence of the presents. No! Given those two options, I would have to question the accuracy of the latter statement. Even if someone of extraordinary reputation made the statement, I would delve deeper into the evidence: "How do you know?", "Who witnessed the tree?", "Were they in the room the whole time?", "Did they perhaps fall asleep?", "Could David Copperfield have introduced the presents without being noticed?" The comforting rush for an "explanation," and the corresponding aversion to the unknown, apparently leads to a willingness to believe nonsense.

The Resurrection in Particular

Wood gives the example of the resurrection: "We also know, historically, that Jesus's tomb was empty three days later, and that both friends and foes were soon claiming that he had appeared to them, risen from the dead." I will discuss the empty tomb in Chapter 34 and the resurrection claims in Chapter 35. There is no evidence outside of the Bible for the resurrection. The only real evidence is in the Gospels and Acts. Paul's claim to be a witness when he saw only a vision, cheapens his assessment of other witnesses. You may never have seen a summary of the evidence from the gospels so allow me to present one now. This will make it clear how many direct contradictions of this key gospel event exist.

To start with the women visiting the tomb: Some number (1, 2, 3 or a group at least 5) of women go to the tomb. There are either guards there (Matthew) or not (other Gospels). The tomb is open already, or it is opened by an angel when they arrive. They go in and find a man sitting there, or it is empty, and two men appear after a while. The man/angel/men (if present) either say that Jesus will see them in Galilee, or remind them of what Jesus said to them in Galilee or just ask why she is weeping. The women return and are either visited by Jesus or not *en route*. Then they are quiet about what they see (Mark), or they tell the apostles, or they just tell Simon Peter, or Simon Peter and the other disciple. Peter either does or does not run to the tomb to see for himself, with or without the other apostle. Mary goes back to the tomb and sees two angels and Jesus or not (depending on whether the verses John 20:2–10 are (as they appear[8]) a

---

[8]Here is John 20:1–11, with John 20:2–10 italicized. Note how naturally it flows

clumsy addition to demonstrate how the author of John was quick to have faith).

Then to continue to the actual appearances: The earliest manuscripts of Mark have no appearances. Mark has a later addition with Jesus appearing to two unspecified people, and then at a table, presumably in Galilee and then ascending. Matthew has the eleven on a mountain in Galilee, with no ascension. Luke has him appearing to the two near Jerusalem and then appearing through a locked door to the eleven in Jerusalem. Jesus gives strict instructions not to leave Jerusalem and ascends apparently on the day of his resurrection. Acts (by the same author) has the ascension 40 days later, but also in Jerusalem. John has them in Jerusalem twice (8 days apart) and then in a boat in Galilee, using the story of the miraculous draught of fishes which Luke has at the beginning of Jesus's ministry. These are all supposed to be from eyewitness accounts, from the same group of witnesses who experienced the same thing at the same time. Note also that Jesus appears to the eleven, not Paul's twelve. Every single one of these stories has the supposed witnesses either not recognizing Jesus, or doubting that he is really alive[9].

The above is a summary of all the Gospel evidence for the resurrection. I know of no theological exposition that harmonizes these disparate accounts. As I mentioned, I will discuss this in more detail in Chapter 35.

To end this chapter, I want to point out that the universe owes you no

---

when John 20:2–10 is removed, and how there appears to be a continuity error when it is included:

> Now on the first day of the week, Mary Magdalene went early, while it was still dark, to the tomb, and saw the stone taken away from the tomb. *Therefore she ran and came to Simon Peter, and to the other disciple whom Jesus loved, and said to them, "They have taken away the Lord out of the tomb, and we don't know where they have laid him!"*
>
> *Therefore Peter and the other disciple went out, and they went toward the tomb. They both ran together. The other disciple outran Peter, and came to the tomb first. Stooping and looking in, he saw the linen cloths lying, yet he didn't enter in. Then Simon Peter came, following him, and entered into the tomb. He saw the linen cloths lying, and the cloth that had been on his head, not lying with the linen cloths, but rolled up in a place by itself. So then the other disciple who came first to the tomb also entered in, and he saw and believed. For as yet they didn't know the Scripture, that he must rise from the dead. So the disciples went away again to their own homes.*
>
> But Mary was standing outside at the tomb weeping. So, as she wept, she stooped and looked into the tomb, . . .

[9]Bart Ehrman, *How Jesus Became God: The Exaltation of a Jewish Preacher from Galilee.*

explanation. Theism does not explain anything in any meaningful sense anyway; it merely gives you an amorphous structure at which you may vaguely wave your hand instead of tackling the question and facing your ignorance. Atheists do not claim to have all the answers, while theists seem to believe they have a magic wand that explains everything. This despite the fact that many different theists all believe this of themselves to the exclusion of all others. Even Christians I know, secretly (or not so secretly) look down on other Christians as being not quite up to scratch. I am ashamed to admit that I probably did the same thing myself.

On the question of gratitude, Wood's epilogue got me thinking. I believe it is important to be grateful, even if there is no God at which to aim this. Atheists can be grateful for our existence, our families, our friends, the people who cooperated to give us food and technology and medicine, for nature, for beauty, for love. Having a sense of gratitude for all this and much more is good. All of these things have their roots in the physical and tangible world around us. To try to aim that gratitude towards God is perhaps to miss the more important contributions of the people around us, and is not, as Wood implies, a better sense of gratitude. But regardless, gratitude towards something intangible does not constitute evidence that the intangible is somehow real.

Part II

The Question of Science

CHAPTER 8

Creator and Sustainer

Examination of the question of science begins with a look at Robert Kaita's[1] article entitled "Creator and Sustainer: God's Essential Role in the Universe." Kaita mentions that

> Einstein posed a question that scientists, as scientists, still cannot answer. He asked why the universe is comprehensible. We do not know, for example, why there are only a few laws of physics. The same law of gravity can be used to describe how we are held to the earth, but also how immense galaxies are attracted to each other to form clusters.

Kaita states that we "do not know why [the universe] had a moment of origin, which is now commonly called the 'big bang.'" And that "we do not know why enough [carbon] was created [inside the stars], relative to heavier elements, to make life possible on Earth."

He notes that some scientists appeal to the anthropic principle (that we cannot observe a universe in which we cannot survive[2]) to explain all this,

---

[1] Robert Kaita is a Principal Research Physicist at the Princeton Plasma Physics Laboratory, where he is head of boundary physics operations for the National Spherical Torus Experiment-Upgrade and deputy head of research operations.

[2] The anthropic principle is the philosophical idea that observations of the universe must be compatible with the conscious and sapient life that observes it. Usually, the weak anthropic principle is meant, which observes that there is a selection bias going

but that other scientists, including himself, "are perfectly comfortable in saying that our universe is all the work of a creator." He adds: "It takes just as much faith to claim that there is no creator behind what I just described as it does to believe that there is one."

He then gives the example of his own work as an experimental physicist, noting that equipment needs constant interventions to keep going. He says that we "can imagine hardware wearing out with time, but there is no fundamental reason why the software that runs on them should be as 'immutable.' "

Kaita is making two appeals. His primary appeal is that the laws of physics are so unchanging, and mathematics works so well to describe them, which seems so unlikely. His secondary appeal, which he does not spell out as distinctly, is that our collective experience is that things degrade with time and need maintenance to keep going. What could explain all this? For Kaita the answer is found in Genesis 8:22: "While the earth remains, seed time and harvest, and cold and heat, and summer and winter, and day and night will not cease."

This is God's promise to humanity, and Kaita asserts that "it is God who ensures this regularity." Those who rely on the anthropic principle to explain the persistent patterns have "a focus primarily on [themselves] in the here and now." He hints at the "egocentrism" and lack of gratitude in humanity, pointing to an event in Luke 17 where Jesus heals ten men from leprosy and sees only one return to thank and praise him.

Kaita then states that the real miracle of modern science is that "we can do, and can continue to do, science at all. In that sense, all scientists tacitly believe in the 'miracle' to perform their work."

He sums up by drawing attention to our response to this reality.

> We can focus 'anthropically' on ourselves, and run off with blithe disregard of what a blessing our very existence represents. Or we can turn with thankfulness to God, who created us and sustains all of creation.

---

on (see the next footnote), in which we could only be observing a universe capable of supporting our type of life. This presupposes that there are many universes from which to choose. Alternatively, it is just a random statistical anomaly or unknown mechanism for the only universe there is to be capable of supporting life. The strong anthropic principle introduces the notion that the universe is in some way compelled to have some sort of life emerge within it. Of course, if there were a God, it would not be necessary for the universe to be fine-tuned, so it also assumes that galactic, solar, and biological evolution occurred in the way that scientists generally believe it did.

Response

I think a fascinating aspect of this argument is that it perfectly reveals the state of mind of the intelligent Christian. Kaita has a good Christian narrative of the selfishness of man, and his lack of gratitude for all the manifest blessings God has bestowed upon him. He sees in scientists a lack of appreciation for the regularity of the laws of physics. Kaita does not suffer from this lack of gratitude himself, or if he does, he at least appreciates the sinfulness of the situation.

He states that the immutability and simplicity of the laws of physics can only be ascribed to the existence of God. And notes that real life complexity and degradation means that God must be sustaining everything. This is the old trick of taking our observations and splitting them in two. One half (the orderliness) demonstrates that God made it that way, while the other half (the chaos) proves that God is needed to sustain everything.

This is not a trick that Kaita is pulling knowingly; it is a trick he pulled on himself by humbly taking on Christian values and ascribing only perfection to God. This is the essence of self-censorship: he does not even allow himself to interpret the evidence in any other way, or even to acknowledge that he has split the evidence at all. When an atheist points out that the universe appears to be a complex mixture of both orderliness and chaos, Kaita sees a lack of gratitude for different aspects of God. Criticism just makes you one of the nine lepers.

The point is that no matter what the universe was like, you would be able to split it into an orderly side (with gratitude to the Creator) and a chaotic side (with gratitude to the Sustainer).

The idea that it takes as much faith to believe in a creator as to believe that one is not needed is a misrepresentation of the atheist position. On the contrary, it takes no faith to admit that you do not know, but are not convinced by the arguments and evidence that you have seen. It takes a great deal to see a deity in Kaita's argument, and to link it to the God of the Bible based on verses like the one in Genesis while denying myriad other religions with similarly tenuous links is an altogether extraordinary act of faith.

In any event, the idea that the universe is comprehensible may not be so clear cut. There is no particular reason that the laws or constants of physics would change with time. The fundamental constituents of which we are aware seem to be somewhat stable, and if it were not so, we would presumably not be here to observe them. This is all the anthropic principle states, and it could equally be called a selection bias[3]. Kaita is focusing on

---

[3]Selection bias is a common statistical error. For example, if you wanted to find out

the word anthropic to accuse us of egocentrism, rather than wrestling with the underlying meaning of the concept.

His example of gravity as a simple and universal law is not compelling. Newtonian gravity is indeed a simple inverse square law, which has a physical basis. But it is also only an approximation, which breaks down near large masses. For this, we need Einstein's law of general relativity. Unfortunately, this contradicts the laws of quantum mechanics, and we do not yet have a model for when both laws are needed (for example, during the big bang and in black holes). Physicists are working on string theory to resolve this, but it would be hard to call this comprehensible or simple. It is an endearing human trait to work on something for years or even generations, and once solved to declare that the answer was obvious.

To stay with gravity a little more, we often teach physics with neat little example problems that have analytical solutions, that is solutions that can be described by equations[4]. Richard Feynman's famous physics lectures eschewed this approach because it is rarely useful in practice. For example, if you have two bodies orbiting each other you can find an analytical solution but with three or more, no such solution exists, and physicists must content themselves with numerical approaches. Feynman says:

> Each piece, or part, of the whole of nature is always merely an *approximation* to the complete truth, or the complete truth so far as we know it. In fact, everything we know is only some kind of approximation, because *we know that we do not know all the laws* as yet. Therefore, things must be learned only to be unlearned again or, more likely, to be corrected.

So, at least to some extent, mathematics only works to explain physics

---

the average height of the population and decided to use the local NBA team as your "random" sample, you would find the average height to be higher than other studies report. This example is obvious, but there are many times when it is much less obvious, and researchers working with data need constant vigilance. When we talk about it in terms of the anthropic principle, the bias could exist because we are simply unaware that we have taken a sample (of one) at all. We believe that the universe is all that there is, but it is possible that there are many and that observations are only made in those universes where life can evolve, that is universes with particular characteristics. The fact that we can observe the universe means that we have made a selection. A related example is that the age of the universe is such that enough time has passed for life to evolve, but not enough for us to have experienced heat death.

[4]An analytic solution is one where an equation describing the phenomenon can be solved exactly in the form of another simple equation. This is contrasted with a numerical solution, which is necessary when the equation describing the phenomenon cannot be solved exactly (far more common in practice). In this case, approximations must be calculated numerically. It is the difference between having the equation of a parabola $(y = ax^2 + bx + c)$ and a list of (x, y) coordinates.

because we force it to do so.

In the end, this argument is not evidence for God because we may split any conceivable universe into an orderly side (with thanks to the creator) and a chaotic side (with thanks to the sustainer). And once again, even if granted, the theist would have all their work ahead of them to link it to their chosen religion.

CHAPTER **9**

The Pale Blue Dot Revisited

Next up, we consider an essay by Jay W. Richards[1] and Guillermo Gonzalez[2] entitled "The Pale Blue Dot Revisited." In this chapter, Richards and Gonzalez do not directly argue for the existence of God.

The authors discuss the Copernican Principle, an idea that they say is "popular among modern scientists." This is the story in which "Copernicus demoted us by showing that ours was a sun-centered universe ... [H]e dislodged us from our place of centrality and, therefore, importance."

The authors assert that this narrative is false. "Historians of science have protested this description of the development of science for decades, but so far, their protests have not trickled down to the masses or the textbook writers." They go into what they claim is the real history involving Aristotle and Ptolemy as the main pre-Copernican thinkers, who did not consider the center of the universe to be a place of honor. It was the bottom rather than the center.

---

[1] Jay Richards is a Senior Fellow at the Discovery Institute, as well as the Center for Science and Culture, and the Center on Wealth, Poverty, and Morality. He is an Assistance Research Professor in the School of Business and Economics at The Catholic University of America.

[2] Guillermo Gonzalez is an Assistant Professor of Astronomy at Ball State University and a Senior Fellow at Discovery Institute's Center for Science and Culture. He received his PhD in Astronomy in 1993 from the University of Washington and has done postdoctoral work at the University of Texas, Austin and at the University of Washington. In 2004 he co-authored *The Privileged Planet: How Our Place in the Cosmos is Designed for Discovery* with Jay Richards.

They then argue that Copernicus, Galileo, and Kepler "saw the new scheme as exalting" the Earth, rather than demoting it.

In the last paragraph they make their point:

> The official story gives the false impression that Copernicus started a trend, so that removing the Earth from the 'center' of the universe led finally, logically, and inevitably to the scientific establishment of our insignificance. By sleight of hand, it transforms a series of metaphysically ambiguous discoveries into a grand narrative of materialism. None of these historical points answers the wider question of our significance in the scheme of things. But it does us good to remember that materialism does not enjoy the historical and scientific pedigree claimed by its adherents.

Response

For the purpose of this book, there is nothing to respond to here. They do not make an argument for the existence of God. The final sentence (quoted above) does not follow from the rest of the chapter (talking about sleight of hand!). It is notable though that the big challenge to religion comes not from scientists but from historians, so it is brave of these two to turn the spotlight in that direction at all. If humanity is capable of building a mythology around these relatively recent and relatively innocuous stories involving Copernicus, one can imagine that the stories surrounding Jesus might bear further scrutiny. I will do so in Section III.

To spell these points out further, let me examine the authors' central claim. They state that scientists and people in general ("the masses") see Copernicus as demoting humanity by the discovery that the Earth is not the center of the universe, but that Copernicus himself did not see it that way. He saw it as exalting humanity, lifting us from our Ptolemaic position at the bottom of the universe. They posit that this erroneous narrative has led us to promote materialism more than is warranted.

Firstly, it does not matter whether Copernicus saw it as a promotion or a demotion or was indifferent to heliocentricism. It is a brute scientific fact, regardless of how we feel about it. However, if we do have feelings about it, then our feelings are surely just as valid as Copernicus's feelings. The fact that he discovered it does not give him the right to determine how we feel about it. Now, I am a firm believer in honesty, so if we are misrepresenting him in our textbooks, then we should correct them. But this does not at all impinge upon either the science or how we end up feeling about it. We are forced to agree that the sun does not revolve around the earth (if we wish to be rational), but we are free to disagree about whether or not this is significant.

Secondly, their argument is a slippery-slope fallacy[3]. The authors state that this first step led "inevitably to the scientific establishment of our insignificance." It is hard to see why this would be so. If other science had shown that we were indeed significant, presumably the outcome would have been different. In fact, science does nothing either way, as our significance or lack thereof is not something that we can investigate scientifically. For example, we can understand the biological or evolutionary origin of the love our children have for us, independent of our feeling that we are significant to those children.

Thirdly, regardless of whether it was a promotion or a demotion, the Catholic Church resisted heliocentricity vehemently for theological reasons that ultimately proved false. It is difficult to understand why the authors avoided this part of the history, but the object lesson it contains should be ringing in their ears as they consider their advocacy of Intelligent Design.

Finally, the authors state that "it does us good to remember that materialism does not enjoy the historical and scientific pedigree claimed by its adherents." This sentence does not follow from their central claim and is erroneous in several ways.

Firstly, materialism is independent of heliocentricism, so this looks like a bait and switch. We could conceive of an earth-centered material world or a sun-centered world full of supernatural beings, so this substitution is invalid.

Secondly, the historical success of an idea is irrelevant to its truth; what matters is whether the evidence for it currently convinces us.

Thirdly, we accept materialism because of its empirical success. Its "scientific pedigree" is impeccable in the sense that no experiment has required us to reject it. We will return to this in Chapter 26.

Whether it "does us good to remember" such a manifestly erroneous non-sequitur I will leave to your judgment. Of most significance to this book is that the feelings of an ancient astronomer do nothing to persuade me of the existence of God.

---

[3] A slippery slope fallacy is one in which a person asserts that a first step in a progression will inevitably lead to all the steps happening. It is commonly used to argue against a relatively minor point based on the idea that it will lead to an extreme outcome far removed from the original position. Aristotle argued that one should seek the middle way, and that extremes in either direction tend to be problematic. The slippery slope fallacy argues against this, by implicitly asserting that things will always devolve to one extreme or other, and using this to argue against any small steps in the middle.

CHAPTER 10

Oxygen, Water, and Light

"Oxygen, Water, and Light, Oh My!: The Toxicity of Life's Basic Necessities" by Joe W. Francis[1] is considered next. Francis presents an argument from incredulity[2]. This is a known logical fallacy and will crop up several times over the next few chapters. The logic of the argument is that it seems unimaginable for complex life to have originated by natural processes (without a designer/creator). Therefore, there is a designer/creator. The unspoken assumption is that if complex life did evolve, we would know all about it. This elevates science to the level of religion, by ascribing to scientists a kind of omniscience that does not exist in reality. The temptation to make this argument is very understandable as the phenomena he describes are incredible.

Francis starts off by stating that "[e]very living creature is made of amazingly small and complex units called cells." Three vital elements of

---

[1] Joseph W. Francis is the Chairperson of the Department and Professor of Biological Sciences at Masters University. He holds a PhD from Wayne State University. Francis has published numerous scientific articles in medical and biological journals. His research interests include: microscopy, cellular immunology, invertebrate biology, and microbiology.

[2] The argument from incredulity is an informal logical fallacy, also known as an argument from ignorance. The unstated assumption is that if something is true, the person making the argument would be able to understand it. Since they cannot imagine how it could be true, it must be false. It is not hard to see that this is fallacious reasoning, but detecting an instance of it is not always as easy. It often goes along with the God of the Gaps argument that I discussed briefly in the footnote on page 23.

life are oxygen, water, and light. However, "all three of these substances are toxic to life. In fact, living cells fight a daily, moment-by-moment battle against the toxicity of oxygen, water, and light."

At this point, Francis dives with gusto into all the complexity associated with both utilizing and resisting this trio. It is admittedly fascinating.

After this overview, he says that

> the simultaneous evolution of several elaborate and complex protection mechanisms that are required to protect cells from some of the very basic necessities of life (namely, water, oxygen, and light), certainly complicates the origin-of-life problem.

On the other hand,

> the simultaneous existence of several complex protection mechanisms certainly is consistent with a creation or design in nature that was premeditated and constructed within a short period of time.

Francis sums up: "living organisms possess complex protection mechanisms built into each living cell, which appear to have protected life from its very first appearance on earth."

Response

It suggests a lack of tenacity for Francis to look at the current state of knowledge and then report back that researchers have not yet got it all worked out, so they might as well admit that only divine intervention can plug the holes.

Francis states that all this is "consistent" with design and creation in a "short period of time." What is he claiming here? That God made protons, neutrons, and electrons so that carbon and the other atomic species would have the properties to form and evolve life? Or that God had to assemble the first cells and then let it evolve from there? If so, what was that first life form? And how do we know it did not evolve from something else? Or did God have to keep tinkering to make things evolve? Or perhaps God just made it look like nature evolved when actually He had created it a few thousand years ago?

None of these is particularly satisfying. They are also wildly inconsistent with each other, so any claim of consistency is so broad as to be meaningless. It is consistent only in the sense that God (if He existed) could do anything, including make nature look like He was not involved at all. Far from being evidence of God, it is simply an acknowledgment that some mechanisms are difficult to understand.

However, science has made spectacular progress towards understanding the origin-of-life mechanisms, and it is fascinating. To me, it is far more satisfying than the morass hinted at in the previous paragraph, so I want to take the opportunity to discuss it, drawing on some of Francis's discussion points.

Francis discusses oxygen, which is useful precisely because it is reactive, but this reactivity can also be destructive.

> Cells handle this threat by making a *variety* of toxic-oxygen-binding enzymes, including a major type called superoxide dismutase (SOD), which binds and deactivates superoxide, the dominant toxic oxygen species (emphasis mine).

I emphasize the word "variety" because this is what is always seen, and what Francis himself admits several times in his essay. Far from irreducible complexity[3] (which we will come across more in the coming chapters), one always sees redundant complexity[4]. In other words, rather than complex mechanisms which would not function were anything missing, one always finds extraordinary redundancy and overlap in biological systems, characteristic of an evolutionary process.

Anyway, Francis goes on:

> [I]t appears that, very early in the evolution of life, two complex enzymes with very similar but distinct binding properties would have to appear simultaneously to allow cells to take up oxygen while at the same time protecting cells from the damaging effects of toxic oxygen.

---

[3]Irreducible complexity is a pseudoscientific term introduced by Michael Behe and is similar to specified complexity. The idea is that certain biological systems cannot evolve by successive small modifications through natural selection because the stages leading up to it are not useful. It is an appealing idea because it is so simple to understand and it seems like such a strong argument. However, the potential candidates for irreducible complexity have had viable evolutionary pathways proposed for them by researchers, which should not be possible if they really were irreducibly complex.

[4]Redundant complexity is what is always seen in practice in biological systems: multiple systems with overlapping function and considerable redundancy. So, in general, if one of the parts of a supposedly irreducibly complex system were to be removed, other components would fill in, perhaps with lower efficiency. The point is argued in a 1999 Philosophy of Science paper: Niall Shanks, Karl H. Joplin, *Redundant Complexity: A Critical Analysis of Intelligent Design in Biochemistry*. The paper is available at www.don-lindsay-archive.org/creation/shanks.html

He continues that "[m]any origin-of-life scenarios initially exclude molecular oxygen because of its activity and toxicity."

There is an implication here that researchers are creating wild speculation to fit their crazy theories. In point of fact, origin-of-life researchers are relatively confident that life began in an early earth environment that did not have any oxygen. The existence of oxygen in our atmosphere is an extraordinary anomaly that came about because cyanobacteria eventually evolved photosynthesis. Oxygen is so reactive that it tends to be mopped up by myriad molecules and elements such as silicon, aluminum, iron, calcium, and hydrogen. The history of oxygen in our atmosphere is an area of active research. We know that it took billions of years and that the ancient atmosphere contained mostly carbon dioxide, methane, and nitrogen. Many rocks contain molecules that could only have formed in the presence of oxygen, but the oldest rocks show no trace of them.

Study of rocks indicates that oxygen only appeared in our atmosphere three billion years ago when the level was 0.03% of today's levels. Though a small amount, this could only plausibly have come from life: a microbe had evolved the ability to carry out photosynthesis, which has oxygen as a waste product. This continued until the oxygen waste gradually saturated the ability of the earth to absorb it[5].

Scientists believe that early cyanobacteria were the first life forms to evolve photosynthesis. This led to the great oxygenation event, which in turn stimulated a dramatic increase in biodiversity (as well as a mass extinction of life that was not immune to oxygen). Scientists also believe that the chloroplasts found in plants (which all descended from green algae) came from ancient cyanobacteria, perhaps as a symbiont that was incorporated into the cell structure to evolve into a single organism, much like our mitochondrial DNA is thought to have done.

Francis goes on to say that "atmospheric oxygen plays a major role in filtering out much of the harmful ultraviolet (UV) light rays from the sun." Even today "UV light alters DNA in cells, ultimately causing mutation, cancer, or cell death." This damage is continually being repaired. "Many organisms possess up to four different kinds of DNA repair mechanisms." Again, we see the redundancy associated with evolutionary processes. In DNA the damage repair is quite astonishing: "UV light typically causes the double strand to stick together abnormally in one spot. The repair mechanisms recognize the sticky abnormal spot, cut it out, and resynthesize what was lost."

---

[5]For more on the history and research into Earth's oxygen, there is a very readable 2013 New York Times article, entitled *The Mystery of Earth's Oxygen* available at www.nytimes.com/2013/10/03/science/
earths-oxygen-a-mystery-easy-to-take-for-granted.html

It is true that any forms of life that existed in the early atmosphere would have experienced significant UV radiation. For this reason, Berkner and Marshall hypothesized in 1965 that life originated underwater[6]. In the 1980s, biologists found microbial life known as extremophiles, with an ability to survive in extreme environments including high radiation conditions, so this may open up an alternate path. On the other hand, DNA-based life, though ubiquitous now, was not the earliest self-replicating unit. Although there are several competing theories about this, the dominant one is that RNA-based life began first, a so-called RNA world. So complicated mechanisms in DNA-based cells are the result of hundreds of millions of years of evolution and are not relevant to the origin-of-life question.

In fact, it is a classic creationist argument to say that DNA, RNA, and proteins are needed to make proteins, and the probability of all three of these appearing out of nowhere is vanishingly small; therefore it must have been created by an intelligent designer. Everything is correct here except the conclusion. The more accurate conclusion would be that DNA-based cells were probably not the first form of life. With the former conclusion, we could have sat back with a self-satisfied smile secure in the knowledge that we had seen the hand of god. With the latter (which is what happened), we must search for a chemical pathway from which DNA-life could evolve. This led researchers to the discovery that RNA could fulfill all three roles, albeit with lower efficiency. More on this below.

Lastly, Francis discussed the toxicity of water.

> Water is destructive because it can break apart molecules by a process called hydrolysis. During hydrolysis water molecules force their way into spaces between atoms within molecules, breaking apart or preventing the formation of large molecular structures like proteins. In fact, protein synthesis in cells requires the removal of water, a dehydration reaction.

This presents a serious concern, especially for the RNA world hypothesis. Water seems to be essential for life, as are nucleotides, but water destroys nucleotides. However, there is so much evidence for the RNA world that most scientists think that a mechanism will be discovered to solve this problem. Scientists do not imagine that this bit required divine intervention, and nor should theologians, as it suggests a creation that *almost* worked but needed a couple of little pushes, like a domino run that fails a few times and needs restarting.

---

[6]L. V. Berkner and L. C. Marshal, AMS, 1965, *On the Origin and Rise of Oxygen Concentration in the Earth's Atmosphere*, doi.org/10.1175/1520-0469(1965)022<0678:IOPIVC>2.0.CO;2.

Interestingly, one solution for this is for life to have started on Mars, where certain minerals would be more common than on Earth. Another point, noted by Professor John Sutherland when he read an early draft of this essay, is that hydrolysis can be an advantage in that it allows recycling of inactive RNA molecules; biology continually synthesizes and breaks down its macromolecules to achieve homeostasis, that is, to regulate the concentration of molecules within the cell. So as long as the molecules are synthesized faster than they break down, hydrolysis is not an issue.

So how did life start? There are multiple steps involved, of course, and while we cannot be sure about all of them, many of them have been demonstrated to be at least plausible, and much of this path is widely accepted. Firstly a self-replicating reaction would be needed to kick things off. Once this happens in a way that is susceptible to mutations, one can imagine them spreading out across their environment. As the reaction spreads, and the environment shifts, the mutants that best suit each new environment dominate. A mixture of different forms appears. At some point, symbiosis emerges, and multiple species begin to cooperate. Inside clumps of symbionts, mutations that support the group over the individual are also successful, and specialization occurs.

Given this very broad framework, what could that initial reaction possibly have been? As I said, most researchers believe that RNA-based life did this. It is capable of being formed from simple compounds that might be found in an early earth atmosphere, storing information, and performing a replicating reaction. The steps to do this involve (1) the formation of the building blocks for RNA, (2) the assembly into RNA, (3) the discovery of an appropriately simple, self-replicating, RNA candidate and (4) the discovery of supporting metabolic processes. I will briefly touch on each of these four now.

First, we need the formation of the building blocks from a prebiotic atmosphere. RNA is built up from RNA nucleotides, which in turn are made up of a sugar, a base, and a phosphate. This reductionism caused a dead-end because chemists could not figure out how to join the base and the sugar. However, in 2009, John Sutherland, then at Manchester University, found a different chemical pathway that uses naturally forming intermediate molecules that are part sugar and part base. He extended this work when he moved to the University of Cambridge, and so far they have demonstrated ways to generate twelve of the twenty amino acids, two of the four nucleotides and a few other biochemical molecules[7].

---

[7]B. H. Patel *et al*, Nat Chem. 2015, www.ncbi.nlm.nih.gov/pubmed/25803468. www.sciencemag.org/news/2015/03/
researchers-may-have-solved-origin-life-conundrum.

Second, these need to be assembled into RNA. Again, this presents some interesting challenges. Some researchers believe that the vast variety of minerals available in the early solar system could react and bind with different molecules in diverse ways. There is some incredibly painstaking work going on in this area, figuring out how different amino acids react with various minerals, with the hope being that the right combination could be found to describe a building process. This may or may not succeed, but it is too early for Francis to dismiss these efforts as impossible or to proclaim that this required a divine intervention[8].

Third, RNA molecules that can self-replicate need to be found. It was discovered in the 1960s that RNA could fold like a protein, which suggested that RNA might be able to act as an enzyme, catalyzing the necessary reactions. In 1982, an RNA-based enzyme was indeed discovered in Tetrahymena thermophila, which was the first of many such discoveries[9]. This enzyme allowed RNA to cut itself out of a longer chain, in other words, support part of a type of sexual reproduction[10]. Biochemists are searching for self-replicating RNA, by evolving random RNAs. In 2011, Philipp Holliger at the University of Cambridge discovered an RNA enzyme through this process that reliably copies RNA sequences up to 95 letters long, almost half as long as itself[11]. Again these efforts represent remarkable and fascinating progress.

Lastly, RNA molecules would also need to metabolize. Co-factors are small helper molecules that attach to proteins to extend their capabilities. It turns out that RNA can and does use co-factors too. In 2003, Hiroaki Suga of the University of Tokyo created an RNA enzyme that could oxidize alcohol, by using a co-factor. Ronald Breaker of Yale University discovered that a natural RNA enzyme called glmS also uses a co-factor[12].

While the RNA world hypothesis is broadly accepted, there are numerous ways in which this may have happened. Some believe that the reactions could have occurred in a sequence of pools that ran into each other com-

---

[8]Smithsonian Magazine, 2010,
www.smithsonianmag.com/science-nature/the-origins-of-life-60437133.
[9]New Scientist, 2011, www.newscientist.com/article/
mg21128251-300-first-life-the-search-for-the-first-replicator.
[10]New Scientist, 1991,
www.newscientist.com/article/mg13217944-500-the-first-gene-on-earth/.
[11]Science, 332 (6026): 209, 2011 available at www.researchgate.net/publication/
51034023_Ribozyme-Catalyzed_Transcription_of_an_Active_Ribozyme.
New Scientist, 2011 www.newscientist.com/article/
mg21128251-300-first-life-the-search-for-the-first-replicator/.
[12]Science, 332 (6026): 209, 2011, www.researchgate.net/publication/51034023_
Ribozyme-Catalyzed_Transcription_of_an_Active_Ribozyme).
New Scientist, 2011, www.newscientist.com/article/
mg21128251-300-first-life-the-search-for-the-first-replicator/.

bining the various components in the right order. Others suppose that it started near deep sea vents. Some believe that multiple self-replicators may have appeared and gradually merged to form the Last Universal Common Ancestor (LUCA). Some think that Mars may have been a better environment for the initial phase.

All of the above (with the admittedly large gaps) was discovered through decades of painstaking research, and much more is needed. Would Francis and his ilk have us stop this work because they already know that God was responsible (although for which part, exactly)? And what will Francis do if (when) researchers have pieced together every last reaction, showing a plausible unguided chain from prebiotic earth to extant life forms?

This is the trouble with the God of the Gaps argument that Francis is presenting here. He is broadly accepting of the established science, but points to some of the difficult areas where it is not all worked out and says that must be (his) God's work. As more and more of the gaps get worked out, the need for his God disappears. I will note again that this, like the cosmological argument we met in Chapter 1, is evidence at best for deism, not theism. Given the above, I do not believe Francis makes his case, but even if he had, we would be no closer to any of the major religions.

CHAPTER 11

The Origin of Life

The next chapter we consider is Walter Bradley's[1] essay entitled: "The Origin of Life."

Bradley draws attention to Antony Flew, a well-known atheist philosopher who had a well-publicized conversion to deism at age eighty-one. Flew's reasoning, in his own words, is as follows[2]:

> My *one* and *only* piece of relevant evidence [for an Aristotelian God] is the apparent impossibility of providing a naturalistic theory of the origin from DNA of the first reproducing species ... [In fact] the only reason which I have for beginning to think of believing in a First Cause god is the impossibility of providing a naturalistic account of the origin of the first reproducing organisms (emphasis in the original).

Bradley quotes him as saying "super-intelligence is the only good explanation for the origin of life and the complexity of nature."

Bradley then asks rhetorically: "What is it about the origin of life that has so confounded scientists and persuaded atheists to become deists or

---

[1]Walter Bradley is another Fellow at the Discovery Institute, who has a B.S. in Engineering Science and a Ph.D. in Materials Science from the University of Texas in Austin.

[2]Richard Carrier, Internet Infidels, 2004,
infidels.org/kiosk/article/antony-flew-considers-godsort-of-369.html

theists?" This is a disingenuous statement on two counts. Flew was not a scientist (the majority of whom are not theists); and as I argued in Chapter 1 and will argue below, deism is closer to atheism than to theism. Theism is an altogether different matter, but Bradley offers us "deists or theists" as though they were interchangeable (Flew's reference to an "Aristotelian God" connects with deism as used here).

Bradley continues that the

> minimal functional requirements for a living system include processing energy, storing information, and replicating ... These biological operations are made possible by very complex molecules such as DNA, RNA, and protein.

His essay aims to provide "an overview of the molecular complexity that is essential to life" and to show why it is difficult "to ever adequately account for the origin of these remarkable molecules of life." You will notice that this is again an argument from incredulity.

He discusses that "DNA, RNA, and protein provide the necessary functions of life: namely, information storage, replication, and efficient utilization of energy," and then enumerates some issues with this for origin-of-life research, which I will discuss below.

Bradley summarizes by introducing Michael Behe's irreducible complexity and stating that this "would seem to" apply to origin-of-life studies.

> The necessary information, which expresses itself as molecular complexity, simply cannot be developed by chance and necessity but requires an intelligent cause, an intelligent designer, a Creator God.

Response

We need to be alert to the difference between an argument for deism and one for theism. Even if we granted everything in Bradley's essay, we would only have deism. The theist would not have advanced his cause in any meaningful way. The deist says that there must be some kind of powerful intelligence that got this all started. The atheist says that it is not clear what got all this started. While the theist makes specific claims about relationships with God, divine interventions, eternal life, virgin births, resurrections, etc.

Now, I would argue that the deist claim is too strong: a god who lit the fuse and walked away is broadly similar to one who is not there to begin with in all observable ways; the atheist merely remains skeptical that the deist knows enough to support their claim. In other words, an admission that we do not know or do not fully understand, and that we should continue to search, is more appropriate. Until convinced, we should remain skeptical.

The deism argument that Bradley is advancing is also vulnerable either to the discovery of a viable chemical path to life, which would completely destroy Bradley's argument (discussed in the previous chapter), or to the idea that there is an extreme selection bias going on (discussed in Chapter 8). Specifically, it is very challenging to distinguish between a god and a physical mechanism in the distant past, and we should be skeptical of someone who claims they can. Flew's argument is based on the impossibility of "the origin from DNA of the first reproducing species," but scientists do not believe that the first reproducing organisms contained DNA at all.

I want to go through Bradley's enumerated list of issues nonetheless because there are some interesting examples of the fallacy at play.

Firstly, Bradley discusses the famous Miller and Urey experiments from the 1950s, where they formed various amino acids, bases, and sugars from what were meant to be early earth conditions. Bradley states that their success

> was seriously undercut in the 1980s when it was determined that the early earth's atmosphere was never rich in methane, ammonia, or hydrogen, the chemical gases used in their experiments. *One cannot produce more than minuscule yields of amino acids and ribose sugar when one uses plausible prebiotic chemistry* (emphasis mine).

This shows the danger of making such assertions, as, after the publication of Bradley's essay, John Sutherland found an entirely plausible chemical pathway to form some of the necessary nucleotides by skipping the sugar phase altogether[3]. This is a quintessential example of why an argument from incredulity is fallacious.

Secondly, Bradley mentions that prebiotic earth would contain "other chemical reagents that react with the building blocks ... Unless such destructive cross-reactions could somehow be avoided, the emergence of DNA, RNA, or protein would be impossible." For this reason, scientists focus their efforts on the discovery of a mechanism to avoid the destructive cross-reactions. They do not rush reassuringly to god as Bradley appears to have done.

---

[3]Sutherland's work is discussed in a New York Times article entitled *Making Sense of the Chemistry That Led to Life on Earth*, available at www.nytimes.com/2015/05/05/science/making-sense-of-the-chemistry-that-led-to-life-on-earth.html

In this instance, several solutions have been hypothesized. The reactions could occur in a sequence of pools allowing each reaction to happen in turn. Or life could have begun in undersea vents, where nutrients and reagents could arrive sequentially. Another theory points out that the conditions on Mars might be better suited for those initial reactions. Once formed, the early molecules could travel to earth on meteor ejections (which are known to happen[4]). Or the first reactions could take place on a mineral or in clay, where specific reactions may be preferred. All of these and others are under serious scientific study. It seems premature for Bradley to dismiss it all, and all work like it, including hypotheses yet to be made.

Bradley's third challenge was difficult for me to understand. I will quote this section verbatim:

> A third problem is the assembly of the building blocks into the polymer chains. For example, amino acids can be joined (in chemical reactions) in a variety of ways, but only one type of joining of adjacent amino acid molecules (i.e., chemical bonds called peptides) gives a polymer chain that has the function of a protein. In a similar way, 3–5 phosphodiester linkages are needed, but 2–5 linkages dominate in the polymerization of polynucleotides, which is a primary step in the formation of DNA and RNA.

He provided no context or definitions beyond what I have quoted. After wrestling with it, this is what I believe he is trying to say: Firstly, amino acids are the building blocks of proteins. They have a carboxyl group (also known as a C-terminus (C for Carbon)) and an amine group (also known as an N-terminus (N for Nitrogen)). Proteins are formed by linking amino acids together in a chain through a sequence of peptide bonds (also known as amide bonds) which couple the carboxyl group of one amino acid to the amine group of another. Shorter chains (less than about fifty amino acids) are normally known as peptides, and longer ones are proteins. Bradley is saying that the peptide bond is necessary, but that various other chemical reactions could occur in practice, so what pre-biological mechanism could possibly allow only peptide reactions to occur? Bradley is implicitly asserting that no such mechanism could ever be discovered.

His second, related idea is that RNA and DNA are also chains. In these cases, they are formed by nucleotides (rather than amino acids) which are linked together with phosphoric acid in a phosphodiester bond (rather than

---

[4]The Meteoritical Society maintains a database of meteorites on Earth. 190 of them originated from Mars. The database can be found at www.lpi.usra.edu/meteor/metbull.php.

a peptide bond). Nucleotides have a sugar component with five carbon atoms in a ring, conventionally numbered $1'$, $2'$, ..., $5'$ (pronounced 1-prime, 2-prime, etc.). The phosphodiester bond links the $3'$ carbon atom of one sugar with the $5'$ carbon atom of a second to create the chains of DNA or RNA.

Bradley appears to be claiming that the linkage between $2'$ and $5'$ dominates. It is hard to make sense of this. In DNA, the $2'$ is not even a hydroxyl group and cannot participate in the reaction at all. In RNA, the bond happens with the $3'$ site even though the $2'$ is also a hydroxyl group. This small change dramatically increases the stability of DNA relative to RNA and makes DNA superior for information storage. The additional hydroxyl group makes RNA more flexible, able both to store information or to act as an enzyme (a catalyst role normally reserved for proteins). Regardless of these details, Bradley is presumably making a point about how difficult it is to make these molecules before life came about and asserting that no such reaction could ever be found. In fact, enormous progress has been made on this (see the previous chapter).

Bradley's handling of these intricate details feels like an attempt to blind with science. The Bible says that God "knit me together in my mother's womb," and from that whimsical image theists have been squeezed into smaller and smaller gaps until the above is considered evidence of God. In other words, despite the Biblical verse just referenced, we no longer view embryology as a divine intervention. So now Bradley is asking us to suppose that God's role was to ensure that an ancient chemical reaction involved the $3'$ site rather than the $2'$ site, when we do not even know the details of what the reaction was. This squeezing of God into smaller and smaller gaps is why even theologians reject this type of God of the Gaps argument.

A fourth challenge mentioned by Bradley is related to the handedness of amino acids and sugars. "Amino acids and sugars come in right-handed or left-handed versions (structures that are identical except that they are mirror images)." Living systems have only L-amino acids and so:

> How could we possibly get one hundred or more amino acids that are all Ls from a mixture of equal concentrations of Ls and Ds? This problem has been studied extensively, but the explanation remains elusive.

Once again the argument from incredulity shines through. Although in this case, Bradley is shading the truth a little since several plausible mechanisms have been proposed, predating his essay. In this example, circularly polarized light creates a small imbalance, and a simple chemical reaction amplifies this bias. In fact, amino acids in meteorites from space also show more of the left-handed variety, where no life is postulated, so once again this "problem" is just an exhortation to search harder for a mechanism.

Finally, Bradley says that beyond all of the above,

> the most challenging problem in the origin-of-life scenario is how to get the correct sequencing of amino acids in proteins and the correct sequencing of bases in DNA to give information that can provide biological function ... Functional DNA, RNA, or protein might be able to incrementally improve with replication mistakes acted on by selection, but this is meaningless in molecules that are not yet sufficiently complex as to provide at least minimal function. It is the molecular version of the old problem of which came first, the chicken or the egg[5].

In effect Bradly is summarizing the challenge of discovering the origin of life: what was the first abiogenesis event? It does indeed seem hard to get things going, and that is precisely what origin-of-life research investigates. But note that it "seems hard" is not in this case sufficient. And a great deal of headway has already been made on this front (see the previous chapter).

So we are left with a meretricious argument that evaporates into nothing at the slightest touch. In this case, the fallacy is that Bradley uses an argument from incredulity: Bradley is claiming certainty where it does not exist, and searching for God in arenas that have very little evidence available. And, even if you could get past this fallacy (perhaps the argument is so incredible that you are forced to ignore the logical error), there is a second fallacy of equivocation (the theist's God versus the deist's god) waiting in the wings. Deism is substantially closer to atheism than it is to theism. With two fundamental fallacies, it is clear that no theistic support can be gleaned from Bradley's argument.

---

[5] As an aside, the chicken and egg problem is easily solved: the egg came first. This is because the egg actually is the chicken, while the chicken lays a genetically slightly different egg. If the meaning of egg is not chicken egg, the answer is still that the egg came first. Eggs more generally long predate chickens.

CHAPTER 12

What Every High School Student Should Know about Science

Chapter twelve responds to Michael Newton Keas's[1] essay entitled: "What Every High School Student Should Know about Science." Keas does not argue for God directly but instead makes the case that our public schools should teach Intelligent Design as part of the science curriculum.

It is a common motif to argue that we should "teach the controversy," or "teach both sides," and what could be more reasonable than that? To cut to the chase on this point, let me say that you get to try to convince my children of something *after* you have convinced scientists of it. Of course, that is harder; that is why we do it that way. Creationism and Intelligent Design have not published anything in any reputable peer-reviewed journals, and certainly not the vast body of literature that would be needed to be classified as a field of science.

Despite this, Creationists and the Intelligent Design community, in general, have been extremely effective in bypassing the scientific process in terms of what is happening on the ground. I will not argue this in detail, but it is analogous to the difference between what theologians commonly believe (even quite conservative ones are well aware of some of the issues with the historicity and consistency of the Bible), and what pastors from

---

[1]Michael Keas is a Discovery Institute Senior Fellow in the Center for Science and Culture. He has a Ph.D. in the history of science from the University of Oklahoma. He is Professor of History and Philosophy of Science at the College at Southwestern.

the seminaries preach from the pulpit. In the same way, scientists are quite confident of their knowledge (there are thousands of peer-reviewed papers published every year that take evolution for granted or provide active support for it), but school teachers and the public, in general, remain isolated from this.

With this backdrop, I will now return to Keas's essay, responding to his points as I go. He states that "every high school student should know (1) what science is, (2) the various ways it is practiced, and (3) why it is important." He elaborates on these three and uses this discussion to promote his views of how to teach science.

Much of Keas's essay assumes that Intelligent Design is a valid scientific field. It is not, as I will discuss in Chapter 20 and Chapter 26. Here I will focus primarily on the issue of his syllabus suggestions.

What Science Is

Keas discussion on the first topic is only one paragraph long, stating that the question has "no conclusive answer, partly because of the amazing variety of ways science is actually practiced." He then says:

> Only Massachusetts and Kansas have proposed restricting science by a definition that only allows unguided natural causes to explain what is observed. Students should know why this restriction is controversial.

I disagree with Keas's last statement. This controversy has been invented by the Intelligent Design community and is not one that exists within the bounds of science. When prioritizing what science to teach our children, it is hard to imagine a circumstance in which this makes the cut. If Massachusetts and Kansas felt it necessary to affirm this point, it was presumably to defend against Design-based syllabus suggestions from the Intelligent Design community. Keas's proposal to include this in the science curriculum is nothing more than an attempt to circumvent the reason they affirmed it in the first place. In other words, faced with Intelligent Design syllabus suggestions, Massachusetts and Kansas defended its children vigorously and thoroughly, and this defense is now cited as evidence of controversy and therefore worthy of study.

It seems to me to be an omission for Keas not to define what science is. A simple Google search reveals a working definition of "the intellectual and practical activity encompassing the systematic study of the structure and behavior of the physical and natural world through observation and experiment." It may be possible to define it in terms of observation and inference, or in terms of hypotheses and models and fitting observations to these models, rejecting models that do not fit. While no doubt there are many nuances, these definitions would certainly get students started without undue fuss.

The Various Ways Science Is Practiced

Keas coins a new term that he believes all science students should learn. In his words: "Students must appreciate the variety of ways science is practiced, which I call *methodological pluralism*" (emphasis in the original). He defines this term extremely broadly, as we will see, but he did not convince me that the teaching of science requires any of it.

He first defines it in terms of what different science disciplines do:

> Laboratory scientists actively manipulate conditions, following the standard experimental method. Astronomers are typically restricted to passively peering into deep space, where celestial objects are beyond their experimental control. Geologists study a single large object (the earth) through methods and natural laws largely borrowed from other scientific disciplines (especially physics and chemistry). Astronomers and geologists sometimes use simulation models to understand large-scale, long-term changes in the objects they study. Many physicists study tiny subatomic particles that present unique investigative challenges. The 'scientific method' as presented in the introductory chapter of most science textbooks usually fails to recognize the methodological diversity of actual scientific practice.

From my perspective, the diversity of science is manifest and easily covered as a course progresses. What is fascinating and of significance is the commonality. In all these fields, the scientific method allows scientists to take observations and make inferences. Where possible, they fit their observations to a mathematical model or compare them with a simulation. This happens across all disciplines.

To say that astronomers peer "passively" into deep space is to misunderstand and misrepresent what astronomers do. Astronomers control their conditions every bit as tightly as Keas's "laboratory scientists" do. In this case, they do it by selecting which parts of the universe to look at, how to look at them (frequency range, exposure, etc.), and how to clean the data signal. Astronomers have to choose from a bewildering number of objects to look at, and in doing so make very deliberate scientific and experimental choices.

Similarly, to say that geologists "study a single large object" ludicrously oversimplifies the complexity of the Earth. Keas appears to be trying to undermine the sciences that draw conclusions that he does not like and elevate this artificial distinction to the level of something important for students. Scientists do not focus on these differences because the scientific method works brilliantly across all these disciplines and advances our knowledge everywhere.

Keas continues that students "should also recognize how different beliefs shape scientific practice. This is another form of methodological pluralism." He states that

> the ancient Babylonians produced the longest sustained scientific research program in human history (twenty centuries). Although their motivation was based in religion and astrology, their resulting mathematical astronomy wielded great predictive power.

He says that naturalism "amounts to atheism. Naturalism in science has guided many scientists to limit themselves to material causes to explain the natural world."

Keas is criticizing methodological naturalism and holding up the ancient Babylonians as an exemplar of how things should be done. However, this is a severely retrograde step. The triumph of the scientific revolution was that it was able to study nature as nature. That is why in a mere five centuries we have been able to advance so much more than the Babylonians did in twenty.

Even theistic scientists put aside their supernatural ideas to do science. This happens across all cultures and belief systems. Scientists have been able to collaborate around the world because of this central idea. It does not matter whether or not there is a god. The empirical fact is that this approach has been successful, so if there is a god, it/he/she has arranged matters so that we can study the world as though there were no god. It is difficult even to imagine how to implement Keas's ideas: "At this point, we believe God temporarily adjusted the laws of physics, and that is why we saw the anomaly," said no scientist ever.

Keas continues to expand his phrase's definition further, by introducing another distinction:

> [S]cience is devoted to two fundamentally distinct goals: 'how things work' and 'how things originated.' Each of these aims is

achieved through a somewhat different collection of investigative tools. This too is methodological pluralism.

Keas states that "[s]cientists who investigate 'origins' study presently existing things and use this evidence to construct various competing hypotheses on how natural things might have originated."

Scientists could hardly be expected to study things that do not exist. Scientists, including 'origin scientists,' may create something to study, but they would have to create it out of "presently existing things." Keas does not elaborate on what these different investigative tools may be, and given that scientists do not recognize this distinction it is again difficult to imagine why Keas would want to require our children spend time on this. The scientific method works well in both these arenas and often straddles them. For example, plate tectonics explains both "how things work" and "how things originated." Separating them confuses the issue and is artificial.

Next Keas discusses geologists who have "largely concluded that the earth is not eternal, but had a beginning and changed through unique stages over time." He claims that:

> This view was partly motivated by the Judeo-Christian view of history, with its notion of a unique beginning, unrepeatable development, and end. Real historical development replaced the ancient Greek idea of endless cycles. Both sacred and secular viewpoints provided analogies that guided early attempts to reconstruct the earth's history ... Such cultural legacies from the history of science deserve a place in science curricula.

Religion is a fascinating topic, and certainly was humanity's first attempt to understand the world around us. However, if the Judeo-Christian view of history happens to coincide with the scientific view in this instance, it is not of scientific interest. I think that the much more relevant contribution of Judeo-Christian thinking was the realization that God and nature were separate and therefore the latter could be studied without blaspheming the former. But this is merely a cultural backdrop in which the scientific revolution happened to emerge: it tells us nothing about the truth or effectiveness of either.

With our current vantage point, it is clear (even from Keas's writing) that we are using science to confirm or repudiate the religious claims rather than the other way around. We could equally point to the many areas in which Judeo-Christian thinking opposed the advancement of science. Geologists (and all other scientists) believe what they believe because they have made observations and inferences—the religious and cultural background of the development of these ideas is at best a curiosity.

Why Science Is Important

Finally, Keas states that:

> [W]e must convince students that science is important. Our understanding of 'how things work' helps us to better manage the earth's natural resources and to enhance human health. The scientific debate over the origin of the universe and life deserves special attention in science education *because it affects the way we view life and human purpose* (my emphasis).

Keas continues with his artificial split of 'how things work' versus 'how things originated.' His idea that we should study origins in science *because* it affects the way we view our purpose is outlandish. I do not know of anyone else who claims we should do science to influence our sense of purpose. It seems that Keas is applying a religious framework to science, and in so doing elevating science beyond its reasonable remit.

He refers to the awe-inspiring complexity of cells and then claims:

> Some students may attribute this apparent design to autonomous nature (naturalism). Others may conclude that this points to a designer beyond the realm of nature. Yet others may respond in other ways. The science instructor should help students develop their own opinions in a manner that takes science (and other scholarship) seriously.

So the science instructor needs to be versed with "other [non-scientific] scholarship" and be able to teach students about it? And support students in their conclusion that there is a designer "beyond the realm of nature"? If it is beyond the realm of nature, it is not in the realm of science. Trying to teach this in science is therefore not appropriate.

Keas next suggests some very specific curriculum ideas, such as the fossil evidence for the Cambrian explosion[2], which he states provides an "evidential challenge to Darwinism." He says "any complete theory of biological origins must examine fossil evidence." He also creates another distinction (also not recognized in science) between microevolution and macroevolution and picks two examples which demonstrate the former, but not the latter. He then states that:

---

[2]The Cambrian explosion was a relatively short period around 540 million years ago during which most major animal phyla appeared, or at least seemed to appear, according to the fossil record.

> [T]he large-scale macroevolutionary change necessary to assemble new organs or body plans requires the creation of entirely new genetic information. Leading evolutionary biologists know that this distinction poses serious difficulties for modern Darwinism. Students should too.

This sequence of statements is complete nonsense.

Firstly, if you take the fossil evidence seriously (which he says he does), you would find very stark evidence for (at the least) common descent. For example, Cynognathus[3] and other fossils are found in both Africa and South America, dating back to Pangaea when the continents were joined. After this, the fossils of the two continents diverge. This is consistent with common descent and is best explained by evolution (macroevolution to use Keas's term).

Secondly, his statement regarding leading evolutionary biologists is simply not true. There are several well-understood mechanisms that increase genetic information (for example, the merging of symbionts). Leading evolutionary biologists are unquestionably discussing various interesting aspects at the boundaries of their fields (as are all scientists), but that does not impinge upon the vast areas of knowledge that are well-established (which include evolution). Even the examples that Keas gives, such as the work of Stuart Kauffman, are advocating somewhat technical tweaks within the framework rather than a complete overhaul of evolutionary theory.

In the end, Keas promotes a "teach the controversy" approach. I cannot speak to the pros and cons of such an approach. But I can say that if controversies are wanted there are plenty to choose from within science, where both sides have significant scientific support which surrounds a genuinely unknown kernel. Keas's concern for science and students is revealed by his essay to be nothing more than an attempt to insert Intelligent Design into our children's science classes. As I said at the start of this chapter, you get to try to convince my children of something *after* you have convinced scientists of it. In no sense does his piece support the notion of god, so he has done nothing for his cause, or the cause of the book.

---

[3]Cynognathus was a 1.2 meter-long predator, closely related to mammals that lived about 240 million years ago. Fossils have been found in South America, Western Africa, South Africa, China, and Antarctica. Back then, these land masses formed the continent of Pangaea.

CHAPTER 13

Darwin's Battleship

On the subject of the Intelligent Design movement, we now consider Phillip Johnson's[1] essay entitled: "Darwin's Battleship: Status Report on the Leaks This Ship Has Sprung."

Johnson quotes his 1993 book *Darwin on Trial*, in which he gives an elaborate analogy:

> Darwinian evolution with its blind watchmaker thesis makes me think of a great battleship on the ocean of reality. Its sides are heavily armored with philosophical barriers to criticism, and its decks are stacked with big rhetorical guns ready to intimidate any would-be attackers. In appearance, it is as impregnable as the Soviet Union seemed to be only a few years ago. But the ship has sprung a leak, and the more perceptive of the ship's officers have begun to sense that all the ship's firepower cannot save it if the leak is not plugged. There will be heroic efforts to save the ship, of course, and some plausible rescuers will invite the officers to take refuge in electronic lifeboats equipped with high-tech gear like autocatalytic sets and computer models of

---

[1] Phillip Johnson is a retired UC Berkeley law Professor and author, often considered to be the father of the Intelligent Design movement, which is a very broad umbrella for any idea opposed to evolution, though Johnson's own motivation appears to be his Christian beliefs. He also co-founded the Discovery Institute's Center for Science and Culture.

self-organizing systems. The spectacle will be fascinating, and the battle will go on for a long time. But in the end, reality will win.

He now aims to give a status report. He says that:

> Science organizations regularly mischaracterize [Intelligent Design], calling it 'creationism in a cheap tuxedo.' They dream up conspiracies and make false accusations. They try to make sure that no one who is friendly to [Intelligent Design] is allowed to publish articles in the peer-reviewed literature and then use the lack of such articles to prove that [Intelligent Design] is not a science.

This juxtaposition of an accusation that "science organizations" dream up conspiracies next to a conspiratorial claim that they prevent Intelligent Design supporters from publishing is very amusing.

He states that "University presidents apparently feel so threatened by students questioning their biology teachers that they make strong statements declaring that [Intelligent Design] is 'not science.'"

The leak that Johnson sees is that "the Darwinian mechanism of evolution could not explain how the complex living world came about." He then says that:

> Harvard opened a new major research project especially to study the origin of life. This may be in response to the criticisms of the [Intelligent Design] movement ... If this is the case, it should be seen as a good thing by everyone. We in the [Intelligent Design] movement are proponents of good science. If our criticisms and questions lead to better research, we are unafraid of the results. In the meantime, our current concern is to keep evolutionary scientists honest about the current state of the evidence and to allow young people to understand why there is a controversy about the subject of evolution.

Response

To take an extreme analogy, a University president could equally make the "it's not science" claim about the flat earth society, another group that has failed to convince the scientific community to take its ideas seriously. What is needed is for better evidence and better science, not vague accusations against the establishment. It is emblematic of pseudoscientists to see in a vigorous rejection of their ideas a proof that there is a conspiracy going on, and therefore their ideas must be threatening and by implication correct. As Carl Sagan put it: "They laughed at Columbus, they laughed at Fulton, they laughed at the Wright brothers. But they also laughed at Bozo the Clown." In other words, being laughed at or being rejected does not imply that you are right.

It is remarkable that Johnson believes his criticisms "may" have resulted in more study of origins by scientists. Perhaps he is unaware that the reason for the rejection of the Intelligent Design movement as science is that it presumes to know more than is reasonable. What would be the point of studying origins naturalistically if it were assembled by an intelligent designer and did not come about naturalistically at all? If we knew what the Intelligent Design movement purports to know, there would be no point at all. Johnson's willingness to accept good science demonstrates that he is not as confident in his movement's ideas as he lets on. Perhaps he would argue that we could study it to find out which bits were naturalistic and which were done by god? In that case, such a study would be performed on a naturalistic basis—in fact, the precise opposite of what the Intelligent Design movement is recommending, which is to allow supernatural causes into science.

Johnson's essay is not an argument for god, and if it were, it would only be an argument for deism. The interesting part of this is how a movement so devoid of scientific rigor could have achieved so much. Perhaps there is something about the ideas that appeal to our evolved brains? Such discussions have been done elsewhere from both Christian and secular perspectives[2], and are not, I hasten to add, scientific discussions but social ones[3]. I will address Intelligent Design in Chapter 20 and Chapter 26.

---

[2] Karl Giberson's book *Saving Darwin: How to Be a Christian and Believe in Evolution* presents the history of the attack on evolution from a Christian perspective. Niall Shanks's book *God, the Devil, and Darwin: A Critique of Intelligent Design Theory* discusses the issue from a secular perspective.

[3] If you are interested in more discussion on Phillip Johnson's views, there are two excellent articles on the TalkOrigins website by Jim Lippard and Bill Hamilton entitled *Critiques of Anti-Evolutionist Phillip Johnson's Views*, available at www.talkorigins.org/faqs/johnson.html.

CHAPTER **14**

Debunking the Scopes "Monkey Trial" Stereotype

Next we consider an essay by Edward Sisson[1] entitled "Debunking the Scopes 'Monkey Trial' Stereotype."

An argument against evolution is not an argument for deism, and it definitely is not an argument for theism. However, Sisson now strays even further from arguments for God by discussing the Scopes trial. Whatever the merits or demerits of the Scopes trial are, they do not impinge upon the veracity of evolution, which in turn does not impinge upon the veracity of deism, which in turn does not impinge upon the veracity of theism. I am sorely tempted to stop this response here. But perhaps I will allow myself just a few comments.

History

Briefly, in 1925 the Butler Act was passed in Tennessee. It was "An Act prohibiting the teaching of the Evolution Theory in all the Universities, and all other public schools of Tennessee," and which stated:

> That it shall be unlawful for any teacher in any of the Univer-

---

[1]Edward Sisson studied at Pomona College in English, Philosophy, and Film making before transferring to MIT to earn a bachelor of science in Architectural Design. He then became a producer of experimental multi-media and avant-garde theater for about a decade, before getting a law degree from Georgetown University.

sities, Normals, and all other public schools of the State which
are supported in whole or in part by the public school funds
of the State, to teach any theory that denies the Story of the
Divine Creation of man as taught in the Bible, and to teach
instead that man has descended from a lower order of animals.

A Tennessee farmer named John Butler authored the bill to oppose the
teaching of evolution because such teaching was undermining confidence in
the Bible. The Tennessee governor, Austin Peay, signed the law to gain
support with the rural legislators. Note Peay's motive was not to improve
scientific literacy or to promote Christianity. His motives were political.

In response to this, the ACLU (American Civil Liberties Union) fi-
nanced a test case, in which John Scopes agreed to be tried for violating
the Act. The trial featured William Jennings Bryan for the prosecution and
Clarence Darrow for the defense. Scopes was convicted and fined $100. The
Tennessee Supreme Court reversed the conviction on a technicality (that
the jury should have fixed the amount of the fine), and the case was not
retried.

The law remained on the books until 1967 when a teacher (Gary L.
Scott) was dismissed for violation of the act. He sued for reinstatement,
citing his right to free speech. His termination was rescinded, but Scott
brought a class action lawsuit seeking a permanent injunction against en-
forcement of the law. The Butler Act was repealed by the Tennessee leg-
islature and Governor Buford Ellington within three days of Scott filing
suit.

Response

Sisson claims that:

> Whenever a challenge to the truth of Darwinian evolution arises,
> the scientific establishment and its allies trot out the Scopes
> monkey trial. It is their position that if the scientific estab-
> lishment has ratified a science textbook, such as the book from
> which Scopes taught evolution, the state should not engage in
> 'censoring' the material in that book.

A major problem with Sisson's claim is that the Scopes trial does not
make the slightest difference to the truth of evolution. If all record and
memory of the Scopes Trial were erased, it would not impinge upon science
at all. Or even upon the teaching of science. Sisson seems to believe that
the "scientific establishment" (as though it were a monolithic group) takes

Creationists, Intelligent Design advocates, and the legal system seriously as arbiters of truth. In fact, most scientists just get on with it and are vaguely bemused that there is a commotion going on outside the realm of science. Those who do engage, do so out of a personal interest in public scientific literacy and education. None of this makes the slightest difference to real science.

Sisson then goes on to argue that the Scopes trial was not a trial of Darwinian theory. Or even of the dispute between fundamentalists and modernists (that is, those who believe that evolution contradicts the Bible and those who believe the two can be harmonized). Sisson says "The statute merely barred the teaching of Darwinian evolution."

Reading the actual content of the statute (quoted above) makes me want to pinch myself. Modern readers surely find it hard to believe that such a law could ever have been passed. Butler himself was probably sincere but ignorant: it seems that he had heard that children were questioning the Bible because of evolution and he believed this to be unhealthy. However, it comes as no surprise that the passing of the law was done for political purposes, rather than out of any care for the well-being of the students (Governor Peay was currying favor with the rural legislators).

Sisson's statement that it "merely barred the teaching of Darwinian evolution" as though this is no big deal makes sense in the context of Sisson himself promoting the same agenda. The battle, of course, is lost, so now there is sudden concern that we teach the supposed controversy (see Chapter 12). But Butler and Sisson see the same trend of people falling away from their Christianity, and they diagnose evolution as the cause, so any attack on evolution seems warranted to them.

In my experience, I have come across people who believed that you could not be a Christian without rejecting evolution, and so they were not even interested in looking at Christianity since they knew a bit about science. And I know many Christians (indeed I was one) who are content to accept science as is. My rejection of Christianity came about because I found that the key stories of the Bible were not credible (which we will get to in Section III). It was the history, not the science, that posed the real threat.

The entire Intelligent Design movement, with its nebulous patchwork of ideas, seems to be trying to put Christianity on a firmer scientific footing. In this sense, they appear to want a stamp of scientific approval on the Bible. This means they put science ahead of the Bible as an arbiter of truth. It is an understandable desire, even if they would dispute it when put in such bald terms, because science has such a hegemony in society. However, to achieve scientific approval, they have to attack real science because it threatens their particular interpretation of their religion.

Sisson states that:

> Cambridge University astrophysics professor Sir Fred Hoyle, in
> his book critical of Darwinism, The *Mathematics of Evolution*,
> wrote that the scientific challenges to Darwinian evolution have
> 'never had a fair hearing' because 'the developing system of
> popular education [from Darwin's day to the present] provided
> an ideal opportunity for zealots who were sure of themselves to
> overcome those who were not, for awkward arguments not to be
> discussed, and for discrepant facts to be suppressed.'

This certainly sounds damning. However, it misses a central point,
which is that "popular education" is not the place for "a fair hearing." Nor
is a court of law. If education can, at the least, support a student to the
point where they can read and think for themselves, then a fair hearing
is virtually assured. The curious will read widely and learn voraciously.
Scientists love nothing better than to tear down an existing paradigm and
replace it with one of their own. If you are capable of writing a paper that
passes scientific scrutiny then its ideas will be disseminated, experts will
read it (with appropriate skepticism), confirm or repudiate it with experiments and calculations, and good ideas (ones that explain the evidence)
will advance. No-one will stop an interested student from reading some of
the more tenuous hypotheses out there, but one should equally not expect
a student to have sufficient expertise and knowledge to be able to assess
them. The notion that evolution has not had fair hearings is not true. They
occur in the halls of science not the courts of law or the schools.

Sisson then asks

> whether the rest of the world should wait for the science estab-
> lishment to catch up before deciding to reject paradigms that
> have hung on in our textbooks for years, despite manifold and
> rapidly accumulating flaws?

The answer to this question is yes, but Sisson evidently thinks otherwise.
He gives the example of eugenics, which used to be taught in schools.

> The hypothetical example of a state law mandating that doubts
> about the 'science' of eugenics be taught demonstrates that it is
> appropriate for the people who determine our school curricula
> not to be slavishly bound to adhere to whatever the scientific
> establishment espouses at any given time.

So rather than asking scientists and educationalists to come up with the best approach for teaching science, we should ask politicians to mandate particular curricula choices legally? The Butler Act under discussion was passed not to help our children, or to influence their education, but for the politicians involved to curry favor with a particular part of their constituency. I am surprised that Sisson does not remark on the obvious danger of this, or that his topic of choice (the Scopes Trial) is a glaring example of the need to do things differently. We will return to eugenics in Chapter 18, but its shameful inclusion in science text books was far more political than scientific.

Sisson then ominously implies that scientists are self-dealing here.

> Where tens of millions of dollars of funding, and the education of tens of millions of children, are at stake, the recipients of the funds and the purveyors of education deserve respect but should not hold the final say over their own funding and their own jobs. They are not as free from self-interested bias as they flatter themselves to be. Too often, to the parents, the science establishments' claim to be motivated only by the well-being of our children appears tainted by a self-interested desire that our children flatter their teachers' egos by believing everything their teachers believe. Indeed, Darwinians, who claim that all of life is motivated by an irresistible drive for survival, which necessarily means a drive for power, are poorly positioned to claim a special exemption from the very force they say rules life. To the contrary, we are justified in considering that they may be particularly susceptible to the operation of the very theory they advocate so vehemently.

Sisson is implying two areas of self-interest: control of funding and the desire to stroke their egos. Firstly, scientists do not hold the final say over their own funding and their own jobs, and if they did that would be a systemic governmental issue. Someone winning an argument does not automatically imply corruption, and it is hard to imagine a scenario in which scientists exchange large sums of cash and perform backroom deals over the exact details of the biology curriculum. Secondly, Sisson changes tack abruptly, sensing perhaps that the government conspiracy idea was not going to hold water, and says that scientists want to be believed unquestioningly because that will help their egos. If evolution were as weak as Sisson imagines, then scientists wanting to stroke their egos would be motivated to leave it out. This is a far-fetched scenario.

Nonetheless, Sisson doubles down by essentially stating that "Darwinians" lack a moral compass and are therefore prone to self-dealing. Apparently, evolution claims "that all of life is motivated by an irresistible drive for survival." I know of no-one who claims that the drive is irresistible. But Sisson feels "justified in considering that [Darwinians] may be particularly susceptible" to these evolutionary drives. I wonder if he thinks that cancer researchers are particularly susceptible to cancer? Again, I do not believe that he is correct in his view of the motives for including evolution in the syllabus. Speaking personally, I find the science of evolution exciting, fascinating, and relevant. That is my motivation for teaching it to my children.

At the end of the day, Sisson does not want evolution to be taught because it contradicts his interpretation of his faith. He seems to be under the misapprehension that if he undermines evolution, it will cause people to flock to Christianity.

To see why this is false, let me provide a tongue-in-cheek analogy. Suppose that Joe Bloggs is found dead, and the investigators come to the conclusion, based on the available evidence, that the butler did it. Suppose there is also a religion called Sissonism that has a holy text that implies that their God killed Joe Bloggs. If the Sissonists managed to find evidence that the butler had not done it, the investigators would not leap to the conclusion that the Sissonists' God had done it. They would look for another suspect, and the new theory would have to explain the evidence.

Now stretching this analogy even further, if we decided to teach about Joe Bloggs's murder in a criminology classroom, the Sissonists might be an interesting footnote, but their beliefs would have no bearing on the study of the details of the case. A teacher trying to get through all the circumstances of the investigation, the fascinating controversies, the evidence, the witnesses, and the ambiguities might be annoyed to find that a Sissonist lobby is insisting that he also cover Sissonism.

Sisson's essay has strayed far from the topic of evidence for God, so for my purposes, it is enough to say that he has not persuaded me of God's existence. Regarding the Scopes Trial, it should serve as a warning to keep politics out of the science curriculum, rather than the reverse.

Sisson's essay impugned the moral character of "Darwinians," which I found disappointing. As I reviewed early drafts of this essay, I realized that I had fallen prey to the same tendency to vilify Sisson and his agenda, so I am sympathetic with Sisson who probably feels that his sacred beliefs are under siege. I re-wrote large sections to remove assumptions and judgments about his motives, but it helped me appreciate how easy it is to respond with vitriol and how difficult it is to assume the best of intentions.

In some ways, I think this may be the most important lesson of this essay: how can we discuss the merits of an idea without attacking the people who oppose it? I felt an emotional reaction to what I perceived was an attack on my children's well-being. How ridiculous of me! Sisson is acting out of a desire for truth. We just disagree with each other on the solution. Solving this quandary in other areas of our lives is, I think, an important step to improving the discourse.

CHAPTER 15

How Darwinism Dumbs Us Down

Venturing into the philosophy of science, we now consider Nancy Pearcey's[1] chapter entitled "How Darwinism Dumbs Us Down: Evolution and Postmodernism."

Pearcey makes a series of philosophical arguments about Darwinism, naturalism, pragmatism, instrumentalism, constructivism, and postmodernism, and concludes that "naturalistic evolution is self-refuting," and that "Darwinism undercuts the very possibility of rational truth." She discusses that evolution "was welcomed by a group of thinkers who began to work out its implications far beyond science. They realized that Darwinism implies a broader philosophy of naturalism" and so they "began applying a naturalistic worldview across the board—in philosophy, psychology, the law, education, and the arts."

Pearcey explains the logic as follows:

> If humans are products of Darwinian natural selection, that obviously includes the human brain—which in turn means all our beliefs and values are products of evolutionary forces. Ideas

---

[1] According to her website: "Nancy R. Pearcey is editor at large of *The Pearcey Report*, as well as scholar in residence and Professor at Houston Baptist University. She is also a fellow at the Discovery Institute. Previously she was the Francis A. Schaeffer Scholar at the World Journalism Institute, where she taught a worldview course based on her book *Total Truth*, winner of the 2005 ECPA Gold Medallion Award for best book on Christianity and Society."

arise in the human brain by chance, just like Darwin's chance
variations in nature, and the ones that stick around to become
firm beliefs and convictions are those that give an advantage
in the struggle for survival. This view of knowledge came to
be called pragmatism (truth is what works) or instrumentalism
(ideas are merely tools for survival).

Pearcey discusses the work of John Dewey, a pragmatist

who had a greater influence on educational theory in America than anyone else in the twentieth century. Dewey rejected
the idea that there is a transcendent element in human nature,
typically defined in terms of mind or soul or spirit, capable
of knowing a transcendent truth or moral order. Instead, he
treated humans as mere organisms adapting to challenges in
the environment.

She states that the

pragmatists were among the first . . . to face squarely the implications of naturalistic evolution. If evolutionary forces produced
the mind, they said, then all beliefs and convictions are nothing
but mental survival strategies, to be judged in terms of their
practical success in human conduct.

She then laments how this "Darwinian logic continues to shape American thought." She states that William James applied pragmatism to religion: "we decide whether God exists depending on whether that belief has
positive consequences in our experience." She points out that choosing a
religion based on "whatever works for you" misses the essential point of
whether it is really true. On this, at least, we agree. She states that this
pragmatism is also applied to education:

[T]eachers are trained to be nondirective 'facilitators,' presenting students with problems and allowing them to work out
their own pragmatic strategies for solving them. Of course,
good teachers have always taught students to think for themselves. But today's nondirective methodologies go far beyond
that. They springboard from a Darwinian epistemology that
denies the very existence of any objective or transcendent truth.

Next Pearcey discusses how "postmodernism is simply the logical outcome of pragmatism." She presents the following anecdote:

I once presented this progression from Darwinism to postmodern pragmatism at a Christian college, when a man in the audience raised his hand: 'I have only one question. These guys who think all our ideas and beliefs evolved ... do they think their own ideas evolved?' The audience broke into delighted applause, because of course he had captured the key fallacy of the Darwinian approach to knowledge. If all ideas are products of evolution, and thus not really true but only useful for survival, then evolution itself is not true either—and why should the rest of us pay any attention to it? ... In short, naturalistic evolution is self-refuting.

Percey states that this is not "science versus religion," but "worldview versus worldview, philosophy versus philosophy." She quotes an evolutionist, Michael Ruse, who acknowledges the point, as saying "Evolution as a scientific theory makes a commitment to a kind of naturalism," which Pearcey interprets as "philosophy, not just facts." She also quotes Ruse as saying "Evolution, akin to religion, involves making certain *a priori* or metaphysical assumptions, which at some level cannot be proven empirically." She quotes Shapiro as saying "Darwinism is a philosophical preference, if by that we mean we choose to discuss the material Universe in terms of material processes accessible by material operations." Pearcey then states that:

Every system of thought starts with a creation account that offers an answer to the fundamental question: Where did everything come from? That crucial starting point shapes everything that follows. Today a naturalistic approach to knowledge is being applied to virtually every field.

She ends her essay by stating that:

[M]orality is always derivative, stemming from an underlying worldview. The culture war reflects an underlying *cognitive* war over worldviews—and at the core of each worldview is an account of origins.

Response

Her essay does not support her provocative title, and if it did, so what? The only thing that matters is the truth. Pearcey herself quotes a Lutheran theologian John Warwick Montgomery as saying "Truths do not always 'work,' and beliefs that 'work' are by no means always true." Quite so.

She has strayed from the goal of the book, namely arguing for the existence of God. If evolution were found to be false, scientists would look for alternative mechanisms. But her arguments do not even engage with the evidence for evolution. She finds some people who are evolutionists and then argues with other things those people say. She is writing an essay in support of belief in God, but instead spends her time arguing about what evolutionists believe "far beyond science." So her discussion does not cover a scientific reason for belief in God. It does not even cover a scientific reason for not accepting evolution.

For example, she claims that pragmatism stems inevitably from Darwinism, and then sets about trying to undermine pragmatism. This is a slippery slope fallacy since not all Darwinists are pragmatists. In other words, it is erroneous to argue against pragmatism and assume that you have thereby undercut evolution and therefore somehow bolstered a belief in God.

Pearcey says: "If evolutionary forces produced the mind, they said, then *all* beliefs and convictions are *nothing but* mental survival strategies" (emphasis mine).

If "they" said that, they were wrong. Evolution's production of our mind certainly does not condemn *all* beliefs and convictions. It means that we should be on guard against the logical fallacies to which our minds are prone. For instance, if the human mind has a tendency to ascribe supernatural causes (as our everyday experience would suggest), we should be leery of people who claim knowledge of supernatural beings when they do not have evidence. Or, if people are inclined to make slippery slope arguments we should keep an eye out for those too.

She argues that "Dewey *rejected* the idea that there is a transcendent element in human nature" and refers to a "Darwinian epistemology that *denies* the very existence of any objective or transcendent truth" (emphases mine). I cannot speak for Dewey (though I could not find support for Pearcey's claim), but I can say that this is a common misrepresentation of atheists. In general, it is false to say that atheists *believe* there is no god. Rather, they do *not believe* that there is a god. It is not an active belief or an active rejection; it is an assertion that those who believe there is a god have not made the case; that the evidence does not support the proposition. We would not *reject* the tooth fairy. We would simply not believe that there is one. The difference may seem subtle, but it is important because it determines the burden of proof. To prove that there is no tooth fairy is impossible. Yet none of us believe in one because the evidence is inadequate. So if you assert that the tooth fairy exists, then the onus is on you to demonstrate it.

Pearcey quotes someone at one of her talks as saying: "If *all* ideas are products of evolution, and thus not really true ...then evolution itself is not true either" (emphasis mine). This is a false dichotomy. Evolution has not prepared our minds only to accept what is true, or only to accept what is false. Our minds cannot be completely trusted, but also cannot be completely distrusted. In any event, it is our minds that evolved not our ideas (at least traditional biological evolution—we talk more loosely about ideas evolving, but we should not conflate the two if we wish to have a precise conversation in search of the truth). So, no, evolution is not self-refuting. We just need to step carefully, discuss openly, and follow the evidence with an awareness of the weaknesses our minds have.

She ends by discussing naturalism, which I discussed in detail in Chapter 4. Yes, we perform science naturalistically, and yes, that is what pragmatically has worked. But that does not mean science is about "philosophy, not just facts." It is simply that there is no evidence that anything else is there. The big revolution of science was that it was acceptable to admit that you did not know something: this admission is an invitation to try to find it out empirically. Until God presents himself for experimentation, we have no other recourse than naturalism.

Digging slightly deeper, we find that experiments have been done, for example on the efficacy of prayer for healing, and no positive result has ever been seen in a double-blind study. But theists always have an excuse for God's apparent indolence. These cases do show that science's supposed philosophical boundaries are not as rigid as Pearcey suggests: scientists test them but have found no reason to abandon them yet.

Pearcey states that "[e]very system of thought starts with a creation account that offers an answer to the fundamental question: Where did everything come from? ...at the core of each worldview is an account of origins." This is not accurate. Scientists are willing to admit that they do not know. Contrast this with the theist who presumes to know, and throughout the ages has preached the 'truth' with fervor, only to have to shift position as science uncovers contradictions in their position. The vast majority of scientists study the phenomenon in front of them without undue, scientific concern for the universe's origins.

Pearcey asserts that "morality is always derivative, stemming from an underlying worldview." This appears to contradict Copan's essay discussed in Chapter 2 which argued that God's existence could be proven by the existence of an absolute morality. On several occasions, Pearcey allows morality into the argument, with the clear idea that the Darwinist lacks the moral fiber of the theist.

Firstly, morality is not relevant to this discussion. The only question of importance is whether God can be shown to exist, which Pearcey has not attempted to do.

Secondly, the not-so-subtle subtext of Christian moral superiority is undermined by the actual evidence. Tell me your views on women, homosexuality, authority, and power in the church and then we can discuss moral issues in more depth and critique the idea of the theist's supposed moral superiority (I discussed this in much more detail at the end of Chapter 5). Or perhaps we can look at the matter statistically to determine relative morality. But this is a separate conversation, and should not distract us from the search for the truth.

In the end, this essay cannot be seen as evidence for the existence of God. A critique of evolution does not achieve this, as I have already discussed. But to critique something far beyond the science of evolution moves in the wrong direction. She laments the success of scientific ideas in society and does not seem to stop to consider that maybe these ideas are gaining ground because they are better than the alternatives she is offering. I took the time to read her essay in detail. I was open to her best shot. If she wants to win the hearts and minds of society, she needs to present more convincing proofs.

CHAPTER 16

Limits to Evolvability

In this chapter, I discuss an essay by Ray Bohlin[1] called: "Limits to Evolvability."

The thrust of Bohlin's argument is that microevolution is possible, but lots of it over time does not add up to macroevolution. He first asserts that there are limits to how far evolution can take things, based on the extant limits within a species and the existence of convergence.

He claims that there has been a "misuse of artificial selection." He says that "Darwin relied heavily on the analogy between artificial selection and natural selection." But then he points out that when breeders select for a particular trait, there are limits to how far they can go. "Chickens don't produce cylindrical eggs. We can't produce a plum the size of a pea or a grapefruit ... There are limits to change." Then he switches tack and argues that breeders

> plan and manipulate the process. Natural selection can do no such thing. Natural selection, by contrast, operates with no plan and is at the mercy of whatever variations come along. Trying to compare a directed to an undirected process offers no insight into evolution at all.

---

[1] Raymond Bohlin has a Ph.D. in molecular and cell biology from the University of Texas at Dallas. He is the Vice-President of Vision Outreach for Probe Ministries and a Fellow at Discovery Institute's Center for Science and Culture.

Next, Bohlin discusses the peppered moths and Galapagos finches' beaks and the degree of adaptation that they underwent. He says that there are

> many other documented examples of natural selection in the wild. But whereas limited change is possible, there are also limits to change ... The real issue is that examples such as the peppered moth and Darwin's finches tell us nothing about evolution.

Bohlin then argues that mutations do not produce real change. He states that mutations fill the role of a continual source of variation.

> These mutations fall into two categories, mutations to structural genes and mutations to developmental genes. [Bohlin defines] structural genes as those which code for a protein that performs a maintenance, metabolic, support, or specialized function in the cell. Developmental genes influence specific tasks in embryological development and therefore can change the morphology, or actual appearance, of an organism. Most evolutionary studies have focused on mutations in structural genes.

He gives the example of microbial antibiotic resistance and states: "All of these mechanisms occur naturally and the mutations simply intensify an ability the cell already has. No new genetic information is added."

Finally, Bohlin claims that natural selection does not produce new body plans.

> A fundamental question that now needs to be addressed is how sponges, starfish, cockroaches, butterflies, eels, frogs, woodpeckers, and humans all arose from single-cell beginnings without design, purpose, or plan. All such organisms have very different body plans. How can all these different body plans arise from mutation and natural selection?

He goes on to argue not just about the type of mutation, but about the rate of mutation:

> Susumo Ohno points out that 'it still takes 10 million years to undergo 1% change in DNA base sequences ... [The] emergence of nearly all the extant phyla of the Kingdom Animalia within the time span of 6–10 million years can't possibly be explained by mutational divergence of individual gene functions.'

Bohlin does not have any further discussion on the rate of mutation, or what the significance of this point might be and ends by saying: "There do indeed appear to be built-in limits to evolutionary change."

Response

If the reader is genuinely interested in the story of evolution, Richard Dawkins's book *The Greatest Show on Earth* presents the argument linking so-called microevolution and macroevolution in a very lucid fashion. Dawkins also shows the continuum between artificial and natural selection very clearly.

I will respond to Bohlin's claims but note that this is unnecessary for my purpose, as he presents no theist argument. At best a few evolutionary mechanisms are attacked ('maligned' would be a better word), but this is not the same thing at all: rejecting evolution as a mechanism does not turn you into a Christian or even require you to accept god.

Firstly, Bohlin supports the notion of limits to evolution because of convergence. He does not explain the exact link but simply asserts it. However, he does not seem to question that convergence is a result of evolution, which is strange because convergence is macroevolutionary in origin: creatures arriving at a new form, even if similar to other creatures arriving at a similar place down a different evolutionary path, constitutes a significant change (of species and/or body plan). Using an example of macroevolution to support his argument that macroevolution is impossible makes no sense. He is explicitly arguing that convergence results from evolution, so he cannot now introduce a different cause for convergence.

His second argument for the concept of limits is that the analogy between breeding and natural selection is not adequate. But the analogy, while it may have inspired the formulation of evolution as a theory, is certainly not the only reason to accept it. That requires far more science, and that science continues to support evolution (both micro and macro).

The argument that "natural selection [cannot plan and manipulate the process]" is equally invalid. Natural selection is entirely ruthless when it come to removing unsuccessful individuals from the gene pool. It is true that it is not planned or manipulated because it is not conscious, but by definition, it selects individuals that will survive in a particular environment which is identical to planning and manipulating apart from the intent.

Bohlin states that comparing "a directed to an undirected process offers no insight into evolution at all" but does not back this up. It is plainly not true since the analogy at the least demonstrates the plausibility of emphasizing a trait in a population, either through human whim or the exigencies of survival. In fact, scientists believe that the analogy is a good demonstration of the principles of natural selection.

Furthermore, chickens and plums both have relatively long lives, so we have observed relatively few generations, and therefore do not know if Bohlin is correct in his assertions. Certainly, changes of similar magnitudes have been seen in situations where many generations occur in a short period, such as E. coli.

Bohlin argues that the well-documented change in peppered moths is not a good exemplar of evolution. Again, he is wrong in his over-simplification. Kettlewell investigated the evolutionary mechanism of peppered moths in the 1950s. However, repetition of his experiment was difficult and led to general skepticism. It also became an argument popular with creationists, especially after Judith Hooper's 2002 book *Of Moths and Men: An Evolutionary Tale*. However, in 2012 (after the publication of *Evidence for God*), results from a new experiment were published[2]. The research involved the release of 4,864 peppered moths over the course of six years and is the largest trial of its type ever attempted. It confirmed Kettlewell's original investigation. The discussion section of the paper states that:

> Factors other than predation have often been argued to play a substantial role in the rise and subsequent post-industrial fall of melanism in [peppered moths]. Nonetheless, with this new evidence added to the existing data, it is virtually impossible to escape the previously accepted conclusion that visual predation by birds is the major cause of rapid changes in frequency of melanic peppered moths.

Bohlin did not have this paper available to him when he wrote his piece so we can forgive him this oversight, though it should be noted that the result was not a surprise to scientists in the field who were familiar with the extensive literature on the subject. It does show the weakness of a God of the Gaps argument: new information can undermine it.

Bohlin continues with the old claim: "No new genetic information is added." Bohlin does not define information precisely, which is a common issue with this claim. But it does not matter: by any meaningful definition of the word he is wrong. There are well-known examples of[3]

- an increase in genetic variety in a population,

- an increase in genetic material

- novel genetic material

- novel genetically-regulated abilities

---

[2]L. M. Cook, Biology Letters, *Selective bird predation on the peppered moth: the last experiment of Michael Majerus*, available at rsbl.royalsocietypublishing.org/content/8/4/609.

[3] The talkorigins website has an article on the "no new genetic information" claim made by creationists, available at www.talkorigins.org/indexcc/CB/CB102.html.

The authors in footnote 3 comment that if "these do not qualify as information, then nothing about information is relevant to evolution in the first place." Bohlin picks an example where mutation emphasizes traits that are already there. However, it is difficult to understand how this is not an increase in information. Information about the environment is communicated to the DNA of the bacteria through natural selection. There are also many examples of information increasing in different ways, or where entirely novel attributes are added. New Scientist debunked this myth in 2008[4], and more evidence has been added every year since then.

Bohlin's discussion on new body plans also involves an argument from incredulity. It seems that he is comfortable with the idea of a fin evolving gradually to a leg, but for the fin to be added initially required God. How then must we understand the fossil record, where all the intermediate steps are observed?

Bohlin's discussion on the rate of evolution is presumably a reference to the now out-dated notion that body plans evolved all of a sudden during the Cambrian explosion. Fossils that old are rare so it is difficult to build an accurate picture. However, older fossils have now been found, which again undermines Bohlin's argument with new information.

Of course, evolution does have its limits. Another New Scientist article[5] pointed out that "zebras with built-in machine guns would rarely be bothered by lions," yet somehow this innovation has not evolved. The reason is that these limits have more to do with trade-offs than genuine limits: the Intelligent Design community's artificial distinction between microevolution and macroevolution adds nothing to the discussion. The weight of evidence has wrung this concession (that evolution is happening) from the Intelligent Design community and only by carefully picking their data and ignoring real advances made in the science are they able to continue with their assertions.

Evidence for God offers us an article that suggests that the limits of evolution imply that evolution could not have occurred and that therefore we should accept divine intervention. It misrepresents the real science since the limits of evolution do not prove that macroevolution cannot occur. We accept macroevolution for myriad other reasons, and see no reason why microevolution cannot build up to macroevolution over time. But even if we were to reject evolution, we would not be required to accept the existence

---

[4]New Scientist, 2008, *Evolution myths: Mutations can only destroy information*, available at www.newscientist.com/article/
dn13673-evolution-myths-mutations-can-only-destroy-information.

[5]New Scientist, 2008, *Evolution myths: Evolution is limitlessly creative*, available at www.newscientist.com/article/
dn13639-evolution-myths-evolution-is-limitlessly-creative.

of God. As such, this essay does not persuade me that there is a divine creator.

CHAPTER 17

Evolutionary Computation

Next, I respond to the seventeenth chapter by Robert J. Marks II[1] titled "Evolutionary Computation: A Perpetual Motion Machine for Design Information?"

Marks takes a step away from arguing for God with his discussion of evolutionary computation. He says "[e]volutionary computing, on the surface, seems to be a candidate paradigm [for generating more information than is given]. As with all 'something for nothing' claims, this is not the case." He does not take the time to define information, which I regard as a significant and regrettable oversight. Mark's purpose here is to undermine an exemplar analogy that supports the notion of evolution. If he were to succeed, it would establish nothing. Many lines of evidence support evolutionary ideas, and this is not a particularly important one in the grand scheme of things. But even if he succeeded, as has been discussed, the dismantlement of evolution would leave scientists searching for another model. It would not constitute a proof of God nor any theistic claim.

So it seems that we can safely ignore Mark's contribution for the purpose of a discussion on the existence of God. However, the science is fascinating, and I want to be sure that I have picked through his argument in detail, so I will discuss it below.

Marks begins his essay with this paragraph:

---

[1] Robert Marks II is a Distinguished Professor of Engineering in the Department of Engineering at Baylor University.

> Evolutionary computing, modeled after Darwinian evolution, is a useful engineering tool. It can create unexpected, insightful, and clever results. Consequently, an image is often painted of evolutionary computation as a free source of intelligence and information. The design of a program to perform evolutionary computation, however, requires infusion of implicit information concerning the goal of the program. This information fine-tunes the performance of the evolutionary search and is mandatory for a successful search.

This paragraph seems to give evolutionists all that they need to make their case. Evolution was discovered first, and computer engineers decided to try out the principles as an optimization tool. It worked and is now a successful field in computing. That alone establishes that evolutionary principles work in at least some respects. This does not prove evolution, nor is it meant to do so. Didactically, it is a useful example of evolution, because it is easy to grasp, and students can even make their own examples and see it in action. Computationally, it is useful and therefore worthy of study divorced from its biological origins.

However, I must clear up one point because it is a straw man that is central to Mark's case. He says that "evolutionary computation ... requires infusion of *implicit* information concerning the goal" (emphasis mine). There is nothing implicit about it. A goal is central to evolutionary computing and to biological evolution. In computing, the goal needs to be structured mathematically, so that a candidate solution can be given a numerical score. In biology, the "goal" is the passing along of genes with all the complexity of the surrounding environment, competitors, reproduction, survival, and food (I put the word goal in quotes because goal implies intent, which is not evident in nature. We may talk about goals loosely, but it is shorthand for the idea that nature is dominated by creatures that are able to survive, and is lacking in creatures that are not able to survive).

Marks continues to make this point about the need for implicit information by performing a few combinatorial calculations, showing that one would not expect to be able to find these things by random sampling. All this demonstrates is something the biologists have been telling us for more than 150 years: that we need both random mutation *and natural selection* for evolution to work. Random sampling is not sufficient by itself.

Marks says:

> Searching an unstructured space without imposition of structure on the space is computationally prohibitive for even small problems. The need for implicit information imposed by design

heuristics has been emphasized by the *no free lunch theorems* (emphasis in the original).

This is just restating the above argument, but now bringing in the concept of free lunch theorems, with no further description or justification. One might be tempted to believe that this ostentation was an attempt to blind with science. The "no free lunch theorems" do not, in fact, emphasize anything of the sort. They refer to a set of technical theorems that state that learning algorithms cannot perform well in all conceivable environments. For example, a deep learning algorithm can learn to beat a human at Go or chess in a genuinely novel way, but they cannot learn to decrypt a public key cryptography scheme. We use evolutionary algorithms because they are successful in some environments, but the no free lunch theorems merely state that they will not be useful in all possible problems. We see this in nature too because there are limits to the kinds of solutions that evolution has found.

Marks continues with his central point:

> In the early days of computing, an engineer colleague of mine described his role in conducting searches as a *penalty function artist*. He took pride in using his domain expertise to craft penalty functions. The structured search model developed by the design engineer must be, in some sense, a *good* model (emphases in the original).

So Marks is arguing that an engineer is needed for evolutionary computing, and by implication biological evolution needs an engineer. However, the art is in translating the real world complexities against which the design will be tested into a mathematical model that can score a given design in a reasonable amount of time. The engineer is trying to simulate what nature does. In biological evolution, no engineer is needed because nature just does it directly: it is not necessary to simulate nature if nature is acting on the organisms directly.

Finally, Marks reasserts his central point.

> The added structure information needs to be implicitly infused into the search space and is used to guide the process to a desired result ... In any case, there is yet no perpetual motion machine for the design of information arising from evolutionary computation.

But he has failed to make his case. He has not demonstrated that evolutionary computation cannot generate information. Why else would we use it? Possibly it depends on his definition of information, but he did not share this with us. But if his definition does not include some of the novel advances that evolutionary computing has given us, it is unclear that his definition is meaningful.

Marks is trying to argue for the existence of God. But he has failed to show that his discussion on computational evolution impinges upon the veracity of biological evolution. He has not convinced us that the removal of biological evolution would require us to accept a creator. And he has not connected a creator to any of the specific claims that theists make. He would need to succeed in *all* of these to make the chain of arguments necessary to establish the existence of God, but he has not persuaded me of *any* of them. As such, I remain unmoved on the issue: this is not a reason to accept the existence of God.

CHAPTER 18

Science, Eugenics, and Bioethics

Chapter eighteen considers Richard Weikart's[1] essay entitled "Science, Eugenics, and Bioethics."

Weikart gives a brief history of eugenics, linking it to the study of evolution, and mentions some of the areas of recent research that need ethical consideration. The words "god," "God," "Jesus," "intelligent," "intelligence," "intelligent design" are not used anywhere in the whole chapter, and the word "design" is used once when talking about "designer babies." I struggled to connect his essay with the aim of the book, which is to provide evidence for God.

In any event, Weikart attempts a sort of "shame by association" strategy:

> Darwin argued that hereditary change together with natural selection would produce new species. Because eugenics was based on Darwinian theory, many eugenicists feared that modern institutions, such as medicine and social welfare, were spawning biological degeneration among humans. By softening the struggle for existence, modern society allowed the 'inferior' to reproduce. The purpose of eugenics was to reverse this degenerative trend so humans could foster evolutionary progress instead.

---

[1] Richard Weikart is Professor of History at California State University, Stanislaus. He completed his Ph.D. in modern European history at the University of Iowa in 1994. He is also a Senior Fellow at the Discovery Institute's Center for Science and Culture.

He also refers to eugenicists who were "propagating new ideas about sexuality" and "pressing for legislation to control reproduction" to promote

> a new ethic or new morality. Many early eugenicists based their ethic on evolution, calling eugenics 'applied evolution.' ... Often, their new morality was in conflict with traditional Christian morality.

There is a shameful history associated with eugenics, with the United States government forcibly sterilizing many thousands of people leading up to the second world war, and we should indeed acknowledge this as a cautionary tale.

However, Weikart's argument implies a unanimous creation of eugenics by the scientific establishment. 'If evolutionary thinking creates such evil, surely evolutionary thinking is wrong' appears to be the thrust of his argument. There are a couple of important points to be made in response to this.

Firstly, eugenics is not science, and the scientific establishment was far from unanimous in their support of it. Biologist Peter Kropotkin made this point as far back as 1912 at the first international eugenics congress in London:

> Who were unfit: workers or monied idlers? Those who produced degenerates in slums or those who produced degenerates in palaces? Culture casts a huge influence over the way we live our lives, hopelessly complicating our measures of strength, fitness, and success[2].

'Fitness' is not a moral measure or a measure of quality. It is simply a measure of survival in the environment. That is why a proportion of psychopaths remain in the population—they are successful at leeching off the goodwill of society. In any event, science, given its due course, came to the conclusion that reducing genetic diversity will result in inbreeding: the exact opposite of what eugenicists hoped to achieve.

Secondly, evolution inspiring an immoral idea does not mean that evolution is not true. The Bible has also inspired many horrible ideas, such as the Salem witch trials (Leviticus 20:27: "A man or a woman that is a medium, or is a wizard, shall surely be put to death: they shall stone them with stones. Their blood shall be upon them."). Evolution is judged

---

[2]Quoted in New Scientist, 2016, *Eugenic America: How to exclude almost everyone*, available at
www.newscientist.com/article/mg22930663-000-how-to-exclude-everyone. This is a book review of Adam Cohen's book *Imbeciles*.

true because of the evidence for it—we should not apply moral judgments to determine this. The Bible, on the other hand, purports to be a moral guide, so many of its immoral statements should lead us to question its origins (human or evil deity?). But the truth of the Bible should also be determined by evidence.

The real point here is that civil society is inept at assimilating scientific ideas[3]. Societal prejudices and hegemonies abuse science, rushing to draw conclusions that the data do not support, especially for political purposes. What is needed is more evidence-based, scientific thinking, not less.

Weikart then touches on what he sees as modern incarnations of eugenics:

> [N]ew reproductive technologies, such as in-vitro fertilization, amniocentesis, and genetic screening, have presented us with new prospects for a more individualized form of eugenics in the late twentieth and early twenty-first centuries ... Human cloning will likely be a reality in the near future, and with present heated debates over the morality of cloning and stem cell research, the history of eugenics is a cautionary tale. Scientists and physicians in the early twentieth century who supported eugenics often denied the validity of Christian (or any other) ethics on their research and even on their public policy proposals ... Many purveyors of genetic technologies today sound remarkably similar to earlier eugenicists. They claim scientific imprimatur for their views, reject ethical restrictions on their research, make health the highest arbiter of morality, and devalue the lives of the disabled. They promise great advances to help humanity, but they do not consider or understand that by destroying individuals they deem 'inferior,' they are perpetrating gross injustice.

I am a little disappointed that Weikart chooses to vilify scientists with such a broad brush as I do not think it advances this very relevant conversation. I believe we can all agree that we need ethical restrictions. The ground rules for this are that everyone should be allowed to voice their views. I need to convince people of a moral claim, and they need to convince me of theirs. Weikart may present his views and the reasons for holding them, and we may adopt them if we are persuaded or reject them if we are not. What we cannot have is someone claiming that their view has been revealed to them by God (or science or anything else) and therefore must be adopted by everyone regardless of whether they consent or agree.

---

[3] *Ibid*

I would dispute that there is such a thing as a valid "Christian ethic" in this context because the Bible does not anticipate modern medicine. Any such ethic will be the perspective of the person providing it rather than a representation of the view of the Bible, or of all Christians. Even if they quote scripture, it will be their interpretation of scripture as it pertains to an issue that scripture did not foresee. As such, it holds no more validity than any other ethic. I think most Christians will agree with this. If two Christians meet, there is a good chance that they will disagree on some ethical issues. They would not want the Christian ethics of the other imposed upon them, especially in opposition to their own Christian ethics.

Many challenging and fascinating conversations lie ahead of us. Of relevance to the wider book, Weikart's discussion does not persuade me that there is a God. Nor does he demonstrate that the Bible will help guide us through these ethical considerations. It may, or may not. Thoughtful people wrote it, but in a culture and context that may be hard to apply to contemporary situations. I will welcome his attempts and those of others, and I will consider their arguments as I am doing now, but I will not welcome an effort to foist views on me with which I do not agree. In any event, the kind of disparagement Weikart presented above is probably not the best way to convince anyone of his argument.

CHAPTER 19

Designed for Discovery

Examination of the second essay by Guillermo Gonzalez and Jay W. Richards (who also co-authored Chapter 9) is next.

Gonzalez and Richards present an original twist on the intelligent design argument. They say:

> Although scientists don't often discuss it, the degree to which we can 'measure' the wider universe from our earthly home—and not just our immediate surroundings—is surprising. Few have considered what science would have been like in, say, a different planetary environment. Still fewer have realized that pursuing that question systematically leads to unanticipated evidence for intelligent design.

They continue:

> Think of the following features of our earthly home: the transparency of Earth's atmosphere in the visual region of the spectrum, shifting crustal plates, a large moon, and our particular location in the Milky Way galaxy. Without each of these assets, we would have a very hard time learning about the universe. It is not idle speculation to ask how our view of the universe would be impaired if, for example, our home world were perpetually covered by thick clouds. After all, our solar system contains

several examples of such worlds. Just think of Venus, Jupiter, Saturn, and Saturn's moon Titan. These would be crummy places to do astronomy.

They go on to argue a similar point about our position in the galaxy. Had we been in a dustier spiral arm, we may never have seen the cosmic microwave background that "was the linchpin in deciding between two main cosmological theories of the twentieth century." They are referring to the steady state theory versus the big bang theory, which they say settles the debate on "one of the most fundamental questions we can ask about the universe: Is it eternal, or did it have a beginning?"

In other words, they continue, "we inhabit a planet privileged for scientific observation and discovery." This, they say, needs to be considered in the context of Earth also being a privileged place for life. "It is the connection between life and discovery that we think suggests purpose and not mere chance."

They then briefly mention fine-tuning:

> Physicists and cosmologists began realizing decades ago that the values of the constants of physics ... must be very close to their actual values for life to be possible. As a result, they began talking about the universe being 'fine-tuned' for life. And some have even begun to suggest that fine-tuning implies a fine-tuner.

However, Gonzalez and Richards say, "even in our fine-tuned universe, many other 'local' things must go just right to get a habitable planetary environment." They enumerate a partial list and then add:

> This evidence is becoming well-known among scientists interested in the question of life in the universe. Researchers involved in the Search for Extraterrestrial Intelligence (SETI), for instance, are especially interested in knowing what life needs. That knowledge would allow them to determine their chances of finding another communicating civilization. Unfortunately for SETI researchers, the probabilities do not look promising. Recent evidence favors the so-called Rare Earth Hypothesis (named after a book written by Donald Brownlee and Peter Ward in 2000). The theory posits that planets hosting simple life may be common, but planets with complex life are very rare.

They then acknowledge that "it's difficult to make a strong case for intelligent design based merely on the conclusion that habitable planets are rare." However, they

do think there is evidence for design in the neighborhood. For
...there is a suspicious pattern between the needs of life and
the needs of science. The same narrow conditions that make
a planet habitable for complex life also make it the best place
overall for making a wide range of scientific discoveries. In other
words, if we compare our local environment with other, less hos-
pitable environments, we find a striking coincidence: observers
find themselves in the best places overall for observing. For
instance, the atmosphere that complex life needs is also an atmosphere that is transparent to the most scientifically useful
'light.' The geology and planetary system that life needs is also
the best, overall, for allowing that life to reconstruct events from
the past. And the most habitable region of the galaxy, and the
most habitable time in cosmic history, are also the best place
and time, overall, for doing astronomy and cosmology. If the
universe is merely a blind concatenation of atoms colliding with
atoms, and nothing else, you wouldn't expect this pattern. You
would expect it, on the other hand, if the universe is designed
for discovery.

Response

Gonzalez and Richards make a brave attempt to defend Intelligent Design
in a novel way. They appear to be saying that it is unusual to have a planet
that supports life and it is unusual to have a planet that is good for science,
and so it is implausible to have both unless there is a designer who wanted
it that way.

There are several problems with this. Probabilistically, are these things
independent? There are two possible ways of looking at their argument.
One is that they are independent, and so the probability of two unlikely
events is just extra unlikely. The other is that they are inevitably correlated
and that this correlation is itself evidence of design.

The authors seem to be leaning towards the second interpretation ("The
same narrow conditions that make a planet habitable for complex life also
make it the best place overall for making a wide range of scientific discoveries ... you wouldn't expect this pattern"). But how can they know enough
about all possible universes to know that this is an unlikely combination?
Any talk of probability requires a model of the mechanism. They postulate
that it is unlikely to have both together, but based on what model? What
alternative life forms and what alternative universes have they observed to
know that this pattern is unusual? Simply having a low probability in a

particular model does not cause us to leap to the conclusion that God did it. There could be undiscovered mechanisms or selection bias involved.

Secondly, are they correct in saying that this correlation exists at all? Again, I think, they are postulating more than they can know. For example, if intelligent life originated in a dust cloud, the beings might have a good understanding of what we call dark matter while missing the cosmic microwave background. They could be looking at us pityingly, wondering at our state of ignorance that we cannot even determine what makes up most of the universe. If life evolved under the clouds, perhaps they just examine alternative frequencies of light. Astronomers do that routinely since visible light does not tell the whole story. We cannot take for granted that the visible spectrum is "the most scientifically useful 'light.'" In fact, it is likely that we evolved sensitivity to this light because it emanates from the sun, but scientifically, gamma rays, x-ray, ultraviolet, infrared, microwaves, and radio waves are all useful. When science became aware of this wider spectrum, we realized that our view of the universe was very limited, as though we were peering through a tiny slot when a much wider window was available.

Thirdly, scientists wrestle truth out of the world around us in cunning and ingenious ways. It is a little obnoxious to stand up now, and state how easy is all was. Scientific truth was found through the blood, sweat, and tears of generations of scientists. Had we been in a different location in the galaxy the challenges may have been different, but not necessarily significantly harder in the scheme of things. For most of human history, very little was known about the universe, and the primary lens for determining truth was religion. Humans gradually began to understand the world empirically, and the authors now tell us that the fact that we could do so is because God made it easy for us. But not so easy that He gave any clue of it through any of His books or prophets: quite the contrary. Empiricists through the ages have fought superstition and religious folly sometimes at the cost of their lives.

Fourthly, they are assuming that they know something about the nature of God and His motives. Indeed, if we are in a "privileged place for [scientific] discovery," then why is there no evidence for God? Does God want us to discover things, as Gonzalez and Richards seem to imply (though how could they possibly know)? If so, then why does He not want us to discover Him? The funny thing is that, in my experience, if you go down this line of questioning there will be no shortage of answers from apologists. The reason is that it is easier to invent answers, to assume knowledge of the mind of God, and to proclaim them as truth than it is to discover genuinely new things, the authors' central hypothesis notwithstanding.

They briefly mention the fine-tuning argument and state that "some [scientists] have even begun to suggest that fine-tuning implies a fine-tuner." I know of few scientists who make this claim, and even those that do are aware that they have strayed from the bounds of science. Such points are never made in scientific papers, even as speculation, because it is not a valid inference and is therefore beyond the remit of science. The inference is invalid because every intelligence we have witnessed scientifically is attached to a physical brain and is observed through the impact of physical actions. Not only this, but a "fine-tuner" could be some undiscovered physical mechanism and not be an indication of intelligence at all.

Gonzalez and Richards also express some interest in the SETI program. They allow that "planets hosting simple life may be common" and that "it's difficult to make a strong case for intelligent design based merely on the conclusion that habitable planets are rare." It is clear that they are in a fight that is gradually losing ground. Just a few chapters ago (Chapter 11), the improbability of life forming from nothing was thought to be an argument for God. Now it seems that Gonzalez and Richards have conceded that ground.

In the end, their argument does not convince me of the existence of God. There is a long chain of arguments required to get from what they think they have shown (that a combination of habitability and the ease of scientific discovery imply intelligent design) to what they are trying to show (that God exists). If any link in this chain is broken, their argument proves nothing yet they are in a position where every link in the chain is broken. It is not clear that we are in "the best place overall for making a wide range of scientific discoveries." If we were, it is not clear that this combined with habitability implies an intelligent designer. If it did, it is still not clear that this designer was in any way associated with any particular theist claim such as Christianity or belief in Odin.

CHAPTER 20

Intelligent Design

Design arguments are now described by William A. Dembski[1] in his essay: "Intelligent Design: A Brief Introduction."

Dembski introduces Intelligent Design (ID) as the study of

> patterns in nature that are best explained as the result of intelligence. Is that radio signal from outer space just random noise or the result of an alien intelligence? Is that chunk of rock just a random chunk of rock or an arrowhead? Is Mount Rushmore the result of wind and erosion or the creative act of an artist? We ask such questions all the time, and we think we can give good answers to them.

However, Dembski laments,

> when it comes to biology and cosmology, scientists balk at even raising such questions, much less answering them in favor of design. This is especially true of biology. According to well-known evolutionist Francisco Ayala, Darwin's greatest achievement was to show how the organized complexity of organisms could be attained without a designing intelligence. By contrast,

---

[1]William Dembski is a mathematician and philosopher and was a founding Senior Fellow at the Discovery Institute's Center for Science and Culture.

ID purports to find patterns in biological systems that signify intelligence. ID therefore directly challenges Darwinism and other materialistic approaches to the origin and evolution of life.

Dembski then admits that ID

has had a turbulent intellectual history. The main challenge facing it these last two hundred years has been to discover a conceptually powerful formulation of it that will fruitfully advance science ... For design to be a fruitful scientific concept, scientists need to be sure they can reliably determine whether something is designed.

He explains that it is the "fear of falsely attributing something to design only to have it overturned later that has prevented design from entering science proper."

Dembski argues that now "design theorists ... have formulated precise methods for discriminating designed from undesigned objects. These methods ... enable them ... to locate design in biological systems."

Dembski argues that:

Intelligence leaves behind a characteristic trademark or signature— what I [Dembski] call 'specified complexity.' An event exhibits specified complexity if it is contingent and therefore not necessary, if it is complex and therefore not readily reproducible by chance, and if it is specified in the sense of exhibiting an independently given pattern.

He notes that the

important thing about specifications is that they be objectively given and not just imposed on events after the fact. For instance, if an archer fires arrows into a wall, and then we paint bull's-eyes around them, we impose a pattern after the fact.

Dembski links his concept of "specified complexity" with Michael Behe's concept of "irreducible complexity," noting that the latter is a special case of the former, and therefore also an indicator of design.

One irreducibly complex biochemical system that Behe considers is the bacterial flagellum. The flagellum is an acid-powered rotary motor with a whip-like tail that spins at twenty thousand rpms and whose rotating motion enables a bacterium to navigate through its watery environment. Behe shows that the intricate machinery in this molecular motor—including a rotor, a stator, O-rings, bushings, and a drive shaft—requires the coordinated interaction of at least thirty complex proteins and that the absence of any one of these proteins would result in a complete loss of motor function.

According to Dembski, this is evidence for design. Dembski concludes that

> ID is more than simply the latest in a long line of design arguments. The related concepts of irreducible complexity and specified complexity render intelligent causes empirically detectable and make ID a full-fledged scientific theory, distinguishing it from the design arguments of philosophers and theologians, or what has traditionally been called 'natural theology.' ...ID, therefore, takes a long-standing philosophical intuition and cashes it out as a scientific research program ... Whether this program can turn design into an effective conceptual tool for investigating and understanding the natural world is for now the big question confronting science.

Response

Scientists regard Intelligent Design as a pseudoscience. In other words, it does not conform to the scientific method though it claims to do so. Dembski argues that we search for intelligence already in science (SETI, archæology, forensics, etc.) but we somehow are unwilling to do so in biology. However, the difference is quite clear: science does not search for nebulous signs of *intelligence*; it searches for signs of actions by an intelligent *agent* which it weighs against other hypotheses. The marks you leave on your surroundings are not because of your intelligence, but because of actions you take as a result of your intelligence. It is these actions that are amenable to scientific inquiry.

Extra-terrestrial intelligence is plausible since we know that intelligent beings have evolved once before, and so we can begin to hypothesize on what actions they might take. The presence of a person at a crime scene or of people living long ago is visible through their actions, which are comprehensible to us. But what agent and what action is Dembski proposing in his essay? Intelligent Design takes great pain not to specify either and therefore is outside the bounds of science.

Another aspect of this that Dembski glosses over is the concept of certainty. Dembski is a mathematician and so perhaps is used to the idea of proofs and drawing unassailable conclusions. Other sciences are not able to do this. They work on the basis of probability and uncertainty. In mathematics, you can create all your axioms and make reliable deductions. In other sciences, you test hypotheses empirically and induce a result. With SETI, archæology, and forensics we talk about probabilities and search for motives and competing explanations. No probability can be assigned to an undefined agent because we know nothing about it. Dembski asserts, for example, that the bacterial flagellum must have been designed by an intelligence and that no other possible mechanism known or unknown can account for it. This level of certainty does not conform to the scientific method. In fact, anyone can see that it is unreasonable when put in these bland terms.

The concept of the definition of god is vital not only to Intelligent Design but to the broader discussion of theism and atheism. Intelligent Design attempts to bypass this, by talking vaguely about intelligence, but this is not adequate. Any attempt to clarify the definition of god inevitably leads us to aspects and motives that are unknowable, or beyond our comprehension. If Dembski asserts that the bacterial flagellum *must* have been designed, the scientist would want to know why and how and by whom? In forensic science, if we discover evidence of a crime, we seek to understand motive and to build up a coherent case. In biology, Dembski is asking us to accept non-answers to our legitimate questions and abandon the search for the evolutionary origins of irreducibly complex biochemical systems.

Dembski defines specified complexity in unmeasurable ways (contingency, complexity, and specificity). This is the equivalent of asserting that water boils when it is hot—it is not scientifically meaningful without accurate measurements. He does not help us with a scale and method with which to measure these things or the threshold level which gives us specified complexity. Nor does he demonstrate that specified complexity requires intelligence. He is arguing from incredulity even though his terms are not defined (at least in the scientific sense). In fact, one could say that the concept of specified complexity, while contingent, is neither complex nor specified and so it shows no indication of intelligence! The preceding sentence is, of course, both facetious and illogical, but it makes the point that untestable and unmeasurable assertions and word games are not fertile soil for science. Specificity, in particular, is problematic in biological systems: how can anyone assert that anything that is observed was specified in advance? One cannot do this based on function because function changes through evolution. So what is Dembski's solution?

Dembski gives an example of the Carl Sagan novel *Contact*, later made into a movie. By Dembski's account, the

> researchers discovered a pattern of beats and pauses that corresponded to the sequence of all the prime numbers from 2 to 101 ... That got their attention, and they immediately inferred a designing intelligence.

This example is based on fiction, but it is also misleading. Firstly, what they are inferring is an evolved intelligent lifeform comparable with humans deliberately sending out a detectable signal, not just an intelligence. Not on the list of candidate hypotheses is that god did it, or that an intelligent star did it. The inference is far more precise. Secondly, were this really to happen, the first thing to look for would be terrestrial interference. We would need to be sure that no human was responsible, and that certainty would be difficult to obtain. We would also want to eliminate possible natural causes. Although it is beyond something we have experienced so far, it is not impossible for prime numbers to show up in nature. For example, periodical cicadas have a cycle that is 13 or 17 years, both prime numbers[2], and pulsating radio stars (pulsars) emit pulses with extraordinarily precise intervals[3]. Eliminating natural causes might not be as easy as Dembski imagines.

The other point that Dembski makes is related to Michael Behe's well-worn example of bacterial flagella. It is interesting to contemplate what he is asserting here.

Firstly, the various groups who are doing research into the evolutionary origins of flagella are presumably wasting their time and can stop, based on nothing more than an argument from incredulity and a subjective decision by Behe that the flagellum is contingent, complex, and specific *enough* to qualify as design.

---

[2] Periodical cicadas occur in the United States, and are remarkable for their prime number based life cycles, emerging only every 13 or 17 years depending on the species. They spend most of this time underground as juveniles feeding on the roots of deciduous forest trees. They then all emerge together as adults and are active for 4 to 6 weeks, mate, lay eggs and disappear for another 13 or 17 years.

[3] A pulsar is a highly magnetized, rotating neutron star or white dwarf that emits a beam of electromagnetic radiation that rotates with the star. This radiation can be detected when it is aimed at the earth, analogous to a lighthouse. The pulses come with a very regular period from microseconds to seconds, sometimes rivaling atomic clocks in their precision. When first detected, there was a great deal of effort to ensure that it was not man-made or an instrument error. The researchers nicknamed the signal LGM-1, short for "little green man." Though this was tongue-in-cheek, there was clearly the possibility that this regular signal represented some kind of extraterrestrial civilization. When a second such pulsating source was discovered in a different part of the sky, such ideas were abandoned.

Secondly, Dembski does not explicitly disagree with evolution, so is he saying that the world evolved in accordance with the picture presented by scientists, except for now and then when something got stuck, and God had to intervene? But then what does this intervention look like? Are there bacteria floating about successfully reproducing, but unable to propel themselves efficiently through the fluid? Suddenly something happens, but what? Perhaps God takes one of them and tweaks its DNA code so that its offspring will produce a flagellum? Then this God-made mutant's descendants gradually take over the whole bunch? But the tweak needs to be very subtle so that the intervention cannot be detected, and the bacteria leading up to this moment need to look convincingly similar even in the structure of their DNA because that is what is observed. In fact, it seems that God would have gone to great pains to make His intervention indistinguishable from evolution. At this point, we should realize that God is a superfluous assumption in this discussion, and we should simply search for a natural mechanism.

There are other possible ways that God could have done this, of course, but Dembski avoids discussing it. But no matter how He did it, it is clear that His intervention is meant to be undetectable since we do not see any dramatic step changes in our fossil record, DNA studies or any other scientific investigation. Did God get careless when he made the bacterial flagella? Or are Dembski and Behe endowed with a unique ability to detect God where no-one else can? Regardless, God is going to a great deal of effort to hide Himself. This is a common theological theme: elaborate motives are ascribed to God to explain why His actions are indistinguishable from His non-existence.

If you are interested in some of the remarkable work on the evolution of the flagellum, there are many detailed articles on the subject[4].

When I was a Christian, I had theological reasons for disagreeing with Intelligent Design. Paul, talking about evangelizing in 1 Corinthians 2:2, said: "For I determined not to know anything among you, except Jesus Christ, and him crucified." Apparently, however, for proponents of Intelligent Design, there is now another way to demonstrate God's existence. We can use science. Or perhaps "human wisdom" as Paul puts it in the same passage. This shows that Intelligent Design proponents do not believe the Bible to be as well designed as it might have been: Dembski's theories have superseded Paul's advice. A more cynical view of this situation is that science is the current hegemony, and so Dembski is attempting to get a

---

[4]For example, an excellent article on the subject is *Evolution in (Brownian) space: a model for the origin of the bacterial flagellum*, by N J Matzke, 2003 (updated in 2006). The article can be found at www.talkdesign.org/faqs/flagellum.html.

"Science Approved" stamp on the front of his Bible. Of course, science does no such thing. But theologically the Intelligent Design movement always seemed to me to be putting science ahead of the Bible.

Finally, Dembski says that Intelligent Design

> takes a long-standing philosophical intuition and cashes it out as a scientific research program ... Whether this program can turn design into an effective conceptual tool for investigating and understanding the natural world is for now the big question confronting science.

There are many big questions confronting science, but this is not one of them. "Design" fails as a scientific framework for the reasons I have discussed: it focuses on a nebulous intelligence rather than the actions of an intelligent agent; it relies on certainty rather than the relative probability of multiple hypotheses (deduction rather than induction); and it relies on poorly defined and unmeasurable concepts (god, contingency, complexity, and specificity) to make untestable assertions. It also seems to me to be weak theologically, at least from a Christian perspective. In other words, I believe Dembski is wrong, and no design has been detected in nature. He, therefore, has not proven the existence of any supernatural designer (god), and even if he had, he would not be able to link it to any specific theistic claim (God).

CHAPTER 21

Intelligent, Optimal, and Divine Design

But is intelligent design always optimal? We look at this question by considering Richard Spencer's[1] essay: "Intelligent, Optimal, and Divine Design."

Richard Spencer attended the Nature of Nature Conference at Baylor University in 2000 in which he heard speakers talk about intelligent design as though it were synonymous with optimal design. He believed this to be wrong and made a comment to that effect. He then crafted this comment into an essay, which the editors included in *Evidence for God*[2].

Spencer saw a challenge in the incompatibility of divine design and the apparent lack of optimization in nature. He, therefore, created a narrative to explain it. To me, it is clear that his hypothesis exists to explain why God's design is indistinguishable from what we would see if there were no God. In other words, Spencer is plugging a hole that only exists if you assume God's existence. Without evidence for God, his discussion has no foundation or even any meaning.

Spencer starts with the following:

> If something has been intelligently designed, people often expect
> to see structures that are perfectly crafted to perform their indi-

---

[1] Richard Spencer is a retired Professor of electrical and computer engineering at the University of California, Davis.

[2] *Intelligent, Optimal, and Divine Design*, by Richard Spencer can be found at www.namb.net/apologetics/intelligent-optimal-and-divine-design. There is a postscript that explains the origin of the essay.

vidual tasks in the most elegant and efficient way possible (e.g., with no extra components). This expectation is incorrect not only for human design but also for divine design.

Spencer attributes imperfect divine design to

the use of secondary agents (including physical laws), the reuse of common design elements, the adaptive nature of biological organisms, and the fact that we don't fully know the purposes of the Creator.

It is unclear to me how anyone can know so much about divine design. What possible vantage point could we have that would allow us to assess divine design in this way? Nonetheless, I will go through Spencer's four reasons for imperfect divine design: (i) Secondary agents; (ii) reuse of common design elements; (iii) adaptive systems; and (iv) unknown purposes. The divine reuse hypothesis is particularly interesting because there is a scientific prediction involved that is testable as we shall see.

Secondary agents

Spencer observes:

In human design, we frequently have to do things in ways that are suboptimal simply because the complexity and magnitude of the overall task preclude spending time and attention on each detail that would be required to execute an optimal design ... This limitation does not, of course, affect divine design.

Nonetheless, a similar limitation does affect divine design. It arises whenever design employs secondary agents.

Spencer then gives an example of designing a microprocessor with a computer-aided design (CAD) tool, which he then notes might be a better design in many senses, undermining his point a little.

In any event, he continues:

In the same way, but for different reasons, God usually makes use of secondary agents to accomplish his work. Such secondary agents include physical laws since these laws do, at least sometimes, define or help to define structures in nature. For example, there are physical laws and properties of matter that determine the physical structure of certain objects, and once the laws and properties are in place, God does not need to individually create each atom, cell, or higher-level object. Having created physical laws, God is constrained by them unless he specifically chooses to suspend them. As a logical possibility, God is, of course, free to suspend the physical laws he has instituted. Yet I don't know a single unequivocal example in which he has done so. This is not to deny miracles. I am simply saying that I don't know of any examples of miraculous structures in nature, and that includes biological structures.

He does not specify what "secondary agents" God uses apart from physical laws. I certainly cannot think of any. So what is Spencer claiming? His vagueness here means there are multiple possible scenarios, but none that I can see help his cause. Is he saying that the world looks as though it were created through natural causes because God chose to do it that way? In this case, he is left positing an explanation for why God made it look like He does not exist. If all we need is one positive demonstration of God's existence, why is Spencer focusing on this area which seems devoid of God's influence, even if it was because God used "secondary agents"?

And observe the statement "God usually makes use of secondary agents." Are we to suppose that Spencer has witnessed God in multiple universes with a variety of creation styles, and from his observations, this is "usually" how God does it? Apparently not, because Spencer then says he has never seen any unequivocal case of God intervening in nature at all. To the apologist, this may indicate that God chose to use a secondary agent. To the scientist, God is an unnecessary assumption in this scenario. This does not disprove God's existence, but it certainly does not prove it either. The ball remains firmly in the theist's court.

Reuse of common design elements

Next, Spencer says:

> Given that God uses secondary agents to bring about physical structures, we can expect to see certain patterns and processes repeated in many places and used in different ways, even though the design may not be optimal for each *individual* application. In addition, any designer, divine or otherwise, is certainly free (and likely) to reuse structures and to implement similar functions in similar ways, although this will not always be the case. The appearance of similar structures in many different systems,

particularly when those structures are not optimal for each situation, is frequently cited as evidence for macroevolution ... But it is also exactly what you would expect to see for a system constructed using secondary agents under divine control.

Again, evolution is the natural law that drives this, and that is how it looks. But Spencer "expects" that this is just what a divine being would do. Once again the apologist is left explaining why God acts in a way that is indistinguishable from a Godless nature. Also, God's use of secondary causes does not exonerate him from poor design since he must have made all the secondary causes too. If God is omnipotent and omniscient then for Him to think through all the consequences of creating and using physical laws would presumably constitute no effort at all.

There is another crucial point that I need to make on the "divine reuse" hypothesis[3]. Spencer claims that divine reuse and evolution would both account for the observed structural similarity across different systems. That may be true qualitatively, but it is not so quantitatively. Here Spencer is making a claim that is amenable to empirical testing, and so we should look at the similarities more carefully and see whether we can distinguish between these two hypotheses.

One can look at a particular gene that occurs across different species (for example, the gene for hemoglobin A) and deduce a family tree based on how many differences there are. Identical genes are more closely related than genes separated by one mutation, which in turn are more closely related than genes separated by two mutations, etc. So the gene gives you a family tree. The significance of the tree will depend on the hypothesis you are testing, but the existence of the tree is an empirical fact.

One can then do the same for many different genes (fibrinopeptide B, cytochrome C, etc.). So you will end up with many family trees, one for each gene.

In the "divine reuse" hypothesis, there would be no expectation that different, independent genes have the same family tree. For instance, if God reused an element of a kangaroo's hemoglobin A gene in a sheep, He would not be required to perform a similar reuse for the fibrinopeptide B gene. He might or he might not. In the evolution hypothesis, the expectation would be that all the different genes have the same family tree since the tree would arise from common descent.

---

[3]Richard Dawkins, *The Greatest Show on Earth*. I have written an essay on this called *Evolution's Most Remarkable Prediction*. Available at glentonjelbert.com/evolutions-most-remarkable-prediction. "Most remarkable" might be hyperbole, since there are many more in this vein.

Note that there are many possible trees. For example, if we had ten different mammals and no other restrictions, we would expect there to be more than a million different possible trees, so each gene we examined would be like rolling a million-sided die. The divine reuse hypothesis says that we would get different results for each different gene: just a random throw of the die. Evolution says that each time we roll this million-sided die, it will come up with the same family tree: the one implied by common descent. In other words, evolution is making a far stronger and more specific prediction than the divine reuse hypothesis.

This experiment has been done multiple times, so the results are in and, of course, all the different genes reveal the same family tree which is what evolution predicted. The theory of evolution was developed before we knew about DNA, so this confirmation is truly remarkable. On the other hand, we should reject the divine reuse hypothesis based on these results. I am sure that a creative Intelligent Design advocate will eventually devise an appendage to the hypothesis that tries to account for it, but we should favor the simpler explanation. And we should note that if divine reuse is the cause, then the divinity in question has gone to extraordinary lengths to make it look like evolution.

Adaptive systems

Spencer continues that adaptive systems "may appear to be less than optimal" because they are "inherently wasteful. In order to be able to adapt to different conditions, the system will virtually always have components that are not being used in a given situation." This means that:

> [E]ngineers like [Spencer] who design adaptive systems expect to see many components that appear to be wasted or left over from some previous use. Although the appearance of such structures is commonly used to argue that evolution is not under intelligent control, in fact, it is a necessary consequence of adaptive systems. Moreover, since adaptive systems are not infinitely malleable, . . . this feature of adaptive systems provides evidence for microevolution but not for macroevolution.

This line of reasoning is also inadequate when one looks at specific designs. For example, many people choke to death each year because our food intake is connected to our air intake and we can easily envisage a person designed in such a way that this weakness does not exist. So either God designed humanity this way, or this feature changed through adaptation. But such a significant change would constitute macroevolution. In other words, the built-in choke hazard is a design flaw that is unrelated to our adaptability, so either God designed it poorly, or macroevolution occurred. Either way, the adaptive systems argument falls flat as an excuse for suboptimal design.

Unknown purposes

Finally, in tacit acknowledgment that the above is inadequate, Spencer falls back on the old idea that the design is done for reasons beyond our comprehension. He says that "we are rarely in a position to fully understand all of the design objectives and constraints." The challenge with all this is related to the loose definition of God. Spencer ascribes attributes to God to pull together an argument but eventually has to admit that he does not know what God would do and why. This is theistic agnosticism—the belief that God exists, but cannot be known—and is often the end point of any theistic attempt to describe God. Terms like omnipotent, omniscient, unchanging, and ineffable are just ways of expressing ignorance. Such terms can have no real meaning[4].

Spencer goes on to quote Francis Collins[5] approvingly:

> It seems to me we should not make the mistake of assuming that God's perfect will for us is biological perfection, any more than we should assume that God's perfect will for us is the absence of suffering. It is those occasions when things *aren't* perfect that we often learn the most, and when our closeness to God, which is a higher goal even than our own happiness, is most likely to come about. And so perhaps God in a merciful way speaks to us *through* our imperfections, and we shouldn't neglect the significance of that. The underlying assumption that we should all be genetically perfect doesn't necessarily make sense to me.

Spencer agrees "wholeheartedly" and mentions in passing that we must

> also remember that the world we are observing is *not* the original creation. It is a corrupted version of the creation ... [T]here is still an unknown factor to deal with since we are not able to observe the original creation at this time.

---

[4]This point is made very clearly and in much more detail in George H. Smith's book *Atheism: The Case Against God*.

[5]Francis Collins is a well-known geneticist who headed the Human Genome Project.

Collins, who is a serious scientist (he headed the Human Genome Project) and an earnest Christian, rejects Intelligent Design and Creationism. If you have accepted faith in Christianity, then you need some way to understand the poor design. Collins does this with theistic evolution which excuses God by allowing a secondary cause (evolution, that is macroevolution by Spencer's definition) and by making it not be a priority for God, which removes the issue, at least when discussed in the abstract. In practice, I cannot imagine what "closeness to God" is brought about by watching your baby choke to death on a grape, for example, for either baby, parent or anyone else. However, if you have not accepted theism, then no contradiction exists at all. So the entire discussion sits squarely inside the realm of theism, rather than acting as evidence for theism. It is brought up by both Spencer and Collins to shore up defenses against an apparent contradiction. But for the atheist, this is a non-issue: we are looking for (and not finding) a reason to accept faith in the first place.

Spencer then suddenly brings in the creationist fall. This seems strangely esoteric. Did Adam and Eve have a built-in choking hazard? If so, then the poor design existed before the fall, and God must take the blame. If not, then what mechanism changed Adam and Eve's breathing orifice? Did God do that, or did the devil tinker with our design, or was there some very rapid evolution in the course of a single generation? All of these scenarios are beyond the remit of observations and reason, and so can only be believed irrationally. It is difficult to take this kind of argumentation seriously. I cannot understand this comment as it does not seem to fit in with the rest of his argument.

Ultimately, Spencer has proffered no evidence for belief in God. He has merely attempted to defend the implications of a belief in Intelligent Design. He has failed to make this defense, and the logic of *reductio ad absurdum*[6] would dictate that we now reject the belief. Collins rejects Intelligent Design and squares his belief in God with an acceptance of science in a different way. It is the original belief in God that is concerning us here, and Spencer's essay fails to make the case.

---

[6] *Reductio ad absurdum* is a logical and mathematical method for proving an assertion. The assertion is assumed false; this assumption is used to deduce other propositions and a contradiction is found. The contradiction means (assuming no other logic flaws in the deduction process) that the original assumption is false and therefore the assertion is true. In this case, belief in Intelligent Design contradicts the obviously bad designs that we see, and so the belief should be abandoned. This is a little glib, but it is the argument that Spencer was trying to break down by finding logical flaws. His lack of success would seem to mean that the rejection of Intelligent Design stands. However, I am content for now with a far lesser proposition, which is that Spencer has not convinced us of the existence of God.

CHAPTER 22

Molecular Biology's New Paradigm: Nanoengineering Inside the Cell

Young molecular biologist, Bill Wilberforce[1] wrote a chapter entitled: "Molecular Biology's New Paradigm: Nanoengineering Inside the Cell" which we will now consider.

Wilberforce describes some of the advances made in the biological sciences and the equipment used to determine the contents of a biological system, using analogies (over-simplified for my taste). He states that the

> mechanism by which these tools read DNA is beyond the scope of this essay, but the important point is that these tools of molecular biology have revolutionized the way we understand living systems. Before these tools existed, scientists thought cells were rather simple, just a blob of protoplasm (i.e., a chemical soup), surrounded by a thin membrane. But after pointing these new tools at various forms of life, scientists have realized

---

[1] According to the notes at the back of *Evidence for God*, "Bill Wilberforce is the pen name of a young molecular biologist. He has been trained at one of the world's top institutions and is beginning to publish his own research ideas in leading journals." He is hiding his identity out of some kind of fear of ostracization. Personally I think a person should have the courage of their convictions, which may include the courage of changing your mind. This secrecy indicates that he does not publish these ideas in scientific journals.

that there are a lot more parts 'under the hood' than they had originally expected.

Wilberforce then gives an example of

one particular protein, namely, kinesin heavy chain. This medium-sized protein, formed from a pair of identical chains (each with about one thousand amino acids), normally operates with a smaller partner protein called kinesin light chain.

Kinesin can walk along microtubules in the cell, taking hundreds of steps per second and dragging cellular cargo across the cell.

Nerve cells present a particularly striking example of how important kinesin transport is for proper cellular functions. Our longest cells, which stretch from our lower back to our toes, are found in the sciatic nerve. Much of what is needed to keep the ends of these nerve cells alive comes directly from the blood in our toes. But some things must come all the way from the beginning of the cells in our lower back. If we had to wait for these things to randomly diffuse their way down to the end of our toes, we would have to wait for years! Instead, we rely on the active transport of kinesin to supply the ends of our nerve cells with the necessary components.

For Wilberforce, such a component implies intelligent activity, and he laments the way biologists brush this idea aside. "In any other field, things that look like they have been carefully engineered are presumed to be engineered."

He concludes:

What seems therefore to be the likely outcome of molecular biology's fantastic revolution is a growing awareness that living things, including us, are best explained as objects of intelligent nanoengineering. This awareness will no doubt follow the normal course that new ideas follow. First, it will be ignored. Then it will be ridiculed. Next, it will be grudgingly tolerated. Finally, it will be said, 'Well, we knew that all along!'

Response

I sense there is a conflict within the author. The essay seems to be admiring science but is also undermining it. I, of course, do not know whether this is deliberate or why he would do so. But consider a statement like this: "Before these tools existed, scientists thought cells were rather simple, just a blob of protoplasm . . . surrounded by a thin membrane." What nonsense! Scientists have appreciated how complex cells are for a long time, certainly before anything that could reasonably be called a "new tool." But here Wilberforce is planting a seed that seems to say that in the old days when we invented evolution, we did not understand anything. And now that we have begun to understand the complexity, we lack the insight or courage to draw the obvious conclusion.

In reality, Wilberforce misrepresents the situation. The biggest issue is that these tools in fact dramatically confirm predictions made by evolutionary theory. Several journals specialize in aspects of evolution, and many more have evolution as a significant factor. BMC Evolutionary Biology, The Journal of Evolutionary Biology, and The International Journal of Organic Evolution are producing hundreds of peer-reviewed articles per year. Much of this work is open access, meaning that you can find the full articles on-line. This emphasizes the scope of the problem facing the Intelligent Design community: all these experiments and simulations that are naturally interpreted by evolution would need to be re-interpreted. Intelligent Design does not even have a framework for doing so. In other words, there are no meaningful predictions coming out of the Intelligent Design movement that can be tested.

In the previous chapter[2], we met a more specific claim than any made by Intelligent Design (that the similarity of genes is because God reused genetic material) and found that it failed empirically, thanks to experiments made possible by "new tools": the precise opposite of Wilberforce's thesis.

Wilberforce brings up kinesin, stating that it is an elaborate cellular machine that suggests there was an intelligent nanoengineer behind it. He fails to mention that kinesin is one of many such cellular mechanisms for transporting large biochemicals about the cell. In fact, when such transport occurs in living cells it is believed that multiple different mechanisms all work at the same time. In other words, this cellular machine shows every sign of redundant complexity, the hallmark of evolution. Also, kinesin transport only occurs in eukaryotes—far down the evolutionary chain. So are we supposed to believe that god popped this little mechanism into the cell to help out all the other transport mechanisms, long after life had begun? Wilberforce is silent on this.

Wilberforce ends with a confident assertion that it looks to be engineered so it must be and that gradually everyone will come to this fringe view. He does not acknowledge that this is the view from which human-

---

[2]Chapter 21, in the section "Reuse of common design elements" on page 137

ity has slowly emerged. Nor does he acknowledge that the thousands of papers produced every year by scientists using these "new tools" are continually whittling away at the unknown, finding natural causes for things confidently adduced as proof of god in the past. Science does not see kinesin transport as insurmountable; quite the opposite. Where Wilberforce throws up his hands in despair at the challenge and exhorts everyone else to do so too, scientists continue undaunted vaguely bemused by the claims of Intelligent Design advocates. Wilberforce asserts that there is no possibility of a natural explanation, which seems to me to be a rather grandiose claim.

The concept of searching for intelligence is fundamentally flawed, as I discussed in Chapter 20 on page 129. Rationally, we can search for evidence of the activity of an intelligent agent, but without an agent, there is no disprovable hypothesis. The unknowable gods proposed by the world's religions do not serve. In any event, it would be circular to assume they exist when searching for proof of their existence. Rationally, we will always search and go on searching for natural causes for any unknown, preferring to admit that we do not know than to give the non-explanation of an ill-defined, supernatural being.

It should be abundantly clear that nothing in any religious text is supported by or supports this discussion since the authors knew nothing of the results of these new tools. Wilberforce wishes to assert that there is an intelligence out there somewhere, which he will label god and then suddenly switch it out with the God of the Bible. This is all the worse if he is unaware that he is doing it. In other words, the existence of kinesin transport and other biological macromolecules prove nothing about God. Scientists are not forced to assume that they required an intelligent designer.

CHAPTER 23

Panning God: Darwinism's Defective Argument against Bad Design

---

The next article by Jonathan Witt[1] presents a very different take on the design argument.

Witt begins:

> The metaphor of cosmos as 'watch' (a time-piece) captured the imagination of Enlightenment thinkers, confronted as they were with fresh insights into the laws governing motion both near and far. Despite the advance of science since the Enlightenment, the metaphor of the cosmos as a watch persists.

He then admits that the "universe is watch-like" because of the fine-tuning of the physical constants. But "all metaphors break down if pressed far enough, and this one breaks down pretty quickly."

> Think of the morally compromised gods of Mount Olympus meddling in the affairs of their various mortal offspring, ... or the holy God of the Bible, father and shepherd and husband of his people. With none of these conceptions of the deity is

---

[1] Jonathan Witt is a Senior Fellow and Senior Project Manager with Discovery Institute's Center for Science and Culture. He has a Ph.D. in English and Literary Theory from the University of Kansas.

the world construed primarily as a precision instrument meant to function so perfectly its Maker need never pay it any mind. Whenever the Deity is construed as a personality, and not merely as a non-sentient organizing first principle, he is depicted as interested in the world itself, as a Creator who delights in the work of his hands.

Witt then complains about "Darwinists" who argue that the universe does not appear to be designed very well and so there cannot be a God. They equate "the Designer's ongoing involvement in creation with incompetence." Witt cannot see their point: "What if the Designer is more like a spirited dramatist than a fastidious watchmaker?" Then their complaints would show them up as Philistines. The problem is that "the Darwinists have already smuggled this issue into the debate by assuming that, if there were a Designer, he could only be a detached and hyper-tidy engineer."

Witt then quotes a Dawkins passage, in which Dawkins discusses an aspect of design that offends a "tidy-minded engineer." Witt says that "Dawkin's obsession with neatness" is worthy of a deity that "might serve nicely as the national god of the Nazis, matching Hitler stroke for stroke," which, if nothing else, is in accordance with Godwin's law[2]!

Response

Witt shows very neatly here why we require evidence *for* God, not evidence *of* God in a discussion about God's existence. The latter assumes that God exists and hypothesizes all kinds of attributes for Him to explain observations. Witt's essay unwittingly demonstrates that any behavior can be explained in this way. Such an approach might be necessary if we already knew that God existed and we were seeking to understand Him. But, if we wish to be rational, we need evidence for his existence *before* we believe it. We also need a willingness to change our minds if our reasons are shown to be inadequate.

To understand this problem more fully, consider that I may claim I have a God in my pocket. I cannot show her to you because she wants you to have faith. But she makes it rain, so every time it rains it is evidence of her existence (and goodness). This obviously will not do. We need evidence for her existence before we start imagining roles for her, and in a book entitled *Evidence for God*, it does not seem unreasonable to expect some.

---

[2]Godwin's law is an internet adage that states that eventually any online discussion will result in a comparison involving Hitler.

The arc of the argument and Witt's apparent outrage are somewhat amusing to me. Genesis 1:31 says: "God saw everything that he had made, and, behold, it was very good." Psalm 139:13–14 says: "For you formed my inmost being. You knit me together in my mother's womb. I will give thanks to you, for I am fearfully and wonderfully made. Your works are wonderful. My soul knows that very well." Romans 1:20 says "For the invisible things of him since the creation of the world are clearly seen, being perceived through the things that are made, even his everlasting power and divinity; that they may be without excuse."

Given all this, it is not hard to see why people might believe we should be looking for evidence of good design. Even Witt admits it when he talks about the fine-tuning of the universal constants. But when atheists point out that some design is not all its cracked up to be, Witt simply changes his God's attributes and the analogy he is going to use.

And, no doubt, if we point out that God's involvement appears to be very capricious; in fact, that there is the appearance of randomness and callousness around every corner; things that occur that do no-one any good, that bring no redemption, that appear to fulfill no grand plan, and appear to lack any kind of good stage management (to use his drama analogy), then Witt will either fall back on God's mysteriousness or switch metaphors once again and accuse us of being unappreciative of some other, new divine attribute.

Atheists do sometimes point out some of the challenges that occur when belief in God is assumed, but this is not central to atheism and is a fool's errand because, as Witt's essay shows, it is like trying to grasp a slippery eel. The central issue is that the arguments that theists use do not persuade atheists—nothing more and nothing less. There is no unifying belief or common understanding beyond this. Of course, there are atheists with myriad other beliefs, but those beliefs are not what make them atheists. What makes them atheists is that they are not theists.

There are two further noteworthy points in Witt's essay. Firstly, he is willing to pick one of several versions of God to make his point. He is saying that several conceptions of God support the notion of ongoing divine involvement, so it is reasonable to have that as a divine attribute. These conceptions of God are mutually exclusive and do not exhaust all the Gods humanity has believed in over time. So at least one of the Gods on which Witt bases his notion of involvement is fictional. Thus, if they were all fictional, his argument would remain unchanged. This demonstrates that he is assuming that which he is trying to prove. It demonstrates that he is not presenting evidence *for* God, but evidence *of* God. The attribute of God's involvement in the world, as described by Witt, is indistinguishable from a world in which God does not exist at all.

The second is his apparent antipathy towards science. He misrepresents scientists as reifying the metaphor of the watchmaker and therefore drawing wrong conclusions. In fact, science uses metaphor primarily as a teaching aid, not as a way to search for truth[3]. He accuses science of being antithetical to art and aligned with the Nazis (I still laugh at this: it smacks of desperation). He says:

> Why, after all, should the Designer's world read like a dreary high school science textbook, its style humorless, homogeneous, and suffocating under the dead weight of a supposedly detached, passive voice?

> At the aesthetic level, this assumes that the panda's maker could not have been thinking (as artists do) of the whole work. It is the same mistake Darwinists make again and again.

> The criticism of Shakespeare is akin to the Darwinist's overly tidy treatment of vision or the panda's thumb. In each case the critic analyzes the work narrowly, ignoring the larger context, be it ecological, aesthetic, or otherwise.

To me, this misses that scientists are often some of the most passionate people around, wrestling truth out of a mysterious world and that scientists actively seek to understand the broader context. I personally love reading science textbooks and cannot identify with Witt's description. Witt does not need to vilify science for his point so why does he do so? I could only guess, but I do not think it helps his argument.

In summary, Witt's speculative essay (his use of the words "what if" is a giveaway) presents nothing that would make a rational person want to become a theist. He is guessing, as even he would probably acknowledge, at things that he does not and cannot hope to know. I find myself no closer to accepting the existence of God as a result of it.

---

[3] Ironically, it is Intelligent Design that rejected evolution based on a wrong application of the watchmaker metaphor—see for example William Paley's 1802 book *Natural Theology*. In the amazon page for this book (available at `a.co/eBOASjZ`), it says: "In *Natural Theology*, William Paley set out to prove the existence of God from the evidence of the beauty and order of the natural world. Famously beginning by comparing the world to a watch, whose design is self-evident, he goes on to provide examples from biology, anatomy, and astronomy in order to demonstrate the intricacy and ingenuity of design that could only come from a wise and benevolent deity." Now that this analogy has proven inadequate, Witt suddenly tells us that "Darwinists" are the ones who misapplied it!

CHAPTER 24

The Role of Agency in Science

Here we will consider Angus Menuge's[1] essay entitled: "The Role of Agency in Science."

Menuge writes a philosophical attack on materialism. He says:

> The very idea of agency is problematic for scientific materialism, according to which everything that happens can be explained by the undirected behavior of matter. An event can occur as the result of a lawful regularity or because of chance or because of a combination of law and chance, but if matter is all there is and matter has no goals, then the appearance of goal-directed behavior is difficult for the scientific materialist to explain.

He spends most of his essay attacking eliminative materialism, especially as put forward by Paul and Patricia Churchland, which, he says, is that agency is just an illusion.

He says that eliminativism is unpopular, even among materialists, who mostly "believe in naturalism of the mental: intentionality and other problematic mental categories are real but can be shown to be compatible with materialism." Menuge says that there are two main problems:

---

[1] Angus Menuge is a Professor of Philosophy at Concordia University in Wisconsin, specializing in Philosophy of Mind, Scientific Methodology and Apologetics.

(1) there is good reason to think agency cannot be understood in purely materialistic terms; (2) if human agency is simply declared part of nature, then the naturalist has abandoned materialism by allowing the existence of directed causation and in that case can no longer exclude the possibility of nonhuman (and possibly divine) agency active in nature.

Summing up, Menuge says:

Agency is the Achilles' heel of scientific materialism. If materialists eliminate agency, they undermine the rationality of science. But agency also fails to reduce to materialistic categories. So, if we want to preserve the rationality of science and follow the evidence wherever it leads, we must conclude that agency is an irreducible causal category. And that is precisely the claim of intelligent design.

Response

Menuge is not arguing for the existence of God directly, but rather that the existence of agency (in humans) implies a breakdown of materialism that can only be solved by admitting Intelligent Design into science. He even allows that "only empirical data can decide whether design is manifest in biology, cosmology, and elsewhere." There are several issues with this idea.

Firstly, "agency" is not well enough defined by Menuge, but for any reasonable definition, it is something that occurs in nature over a broad spectrum. The agency that a chimpanzee has is different from ours only by degree, and we can easily envisage a chain of animals and organisms in which their agency decreases bit by bit. Even towards the bottom, the search for food and the urge to reproduce is a type of agency. In fact, even if we limit it to human agency, it is something that we observe emerging from the fertilized egg (which has none) to the grown adult. It is something that has clear evolutionary benefit, so it, like vision, could evolve materialistically. It is difficult to see why Menuge believes this needs special treatment.

Secondly, agency has never been credibly observed outside of material beings. If we remove someone's brain, we do not expect them to exhibit agency. We have no means of explaining agency with anything other than physical agents, and attempting to do so, for example with a soul, achieves nothing because the unknown does not explain the unknown. So the existence of agency based on agents cannot rationally require us to search for agency in the abstract. Rationally, it is quite the opposite: if every example we have ever seen of agency needs a physical agent, it would be foolish to suppose they can be separated, which is what Intelligent Design does.

Thirdly, as has already been discussed in Chapter 20 on page 129, there is no effective way to search for Intelligent Design, absent a known designer, and the designer that is implied by Intelligent Design is unknowable. It does no good to assume there is a God since that is assuming what Intelligent Design is trying to show. We are always better off positing an unknown mechanism. The probabilistic arguments require a probability, and a probability can only be calculated if there is a known mechanism. At best they show that a specific mechanism is unlikely to explain a particular phenomenon.

Fourthly, the claim that goals cannot be matter based is asserting what he is trying to show. But, in fact, matter is capable of very complex, emergent behavior of many different sorts, so this amounts to an argument from incredulity.

Fifthly, it is hard to imagine anyone seriously basing their belief in God on the existence of human agency, in the absence of any other evidence (and even more so any specific theistic claims), so this argument is, at the least, not convincing evidence for God.

In discussing eliminative materialism, Menuge argues:

> Any worldview capable of defending the rationality of science must be one that allows scientists to have identifiable reasons. Since intelligent design allows intelligent and goal-directed causes as part of nature, it is in the right position to do this.

This is a logic error: even if both sentences were true, it would not follow that Intelligent Design was useful, true, good or valid[2]. In fact, it is none of these, or at least it has not been shown to be any of these. Menuge

---

[2] I will spell out the logic error with the use of a simple analogy. Menuge's claim is: "Any worldview capable of defending the rationality of science must be one that allows scientists to have identifiable reasons. Since intelligent design allows intelligent and goal-directed causes as part of nature, it is in the right position to do this."

Now consider this claim: "Any umbrella capable of defending us against rain must be one that does not have any holes in it. Since cell phones do not have any holes in them, they are in the right position to protect us from rain."

The analogy should be clear: Menuge has slipped from the general ("one that allows scientists to have identifiable reasons," or "does not have any holes in it") to the specific ("intelligent design . . . is in the right position to do this," or "cell phones . . . are in the right position to protect us from rain"). So the logic does not hold up.

There is a very real question of whether the first claim is true, but analysis would first involve understanding it unambiguously. Unfortunately Menuge glossed over his definitions here, so further scrutiny of this would be speculative.

raises some valid points in his discussion of eliminativism but then tries to shoe-horn in Intelligent Design which spoilt the effect for me[3].

In his discussion of "naturalism of the mental," Menuge argues that "there is good reason to think agency cannot be understood in purely materialistic terms." He says that the most "fundamental" problem is that of "giving an illuminating materialistic account of functions." But this is the equivalent of saying that truth can only exist when it is meaningful. It may be (and probably is) the case that the interaction of our agency and our brain function is simply too complex to be illuminating currently. However, scientists are mapping and simulating simpler brains, so this issue may be solved at some point. This demonstrates that Menuge is just presenting a version of the god of the gaps argument.

Menuge also says:

> The second problem for naturalism is that if there is even one case (the human one) in which the evidence shows that agency is an irreducible feature of reality, then materialism is false, and agency is a legitimate causal category for scientific explanation.

But our agency is plausibly reducible to the functioning of our brains, and no evidence exists refuting that, so this syllogism does not advance his case.

In short, Menuge fails to show a conflict between the existence of materialism and agency and fails to show how agency can be disconnected from the material. He cannot assume it because that is what he is trying to prove. His essay, therefore, does not present any evidence for God or even for the failure of materialism.

---

[3]Menuge is arguing that there is intent in nature. However, in displaying his own intent, he undermines his credibility. If you are trying to persuade someone of a specific position, then your statements need to be checked rather closely for bias. A disinterested arbiter is always nice to have. In this discussion, it is difficult because religion is so tightly interwoven with identity, and so something as benign as checking the accuracy of someone's claim or announcing that an argument is not persuasive is seen as an attack.

CHAPTER 25

The Scientific Status of Design Inferences

Examination of Bruce L. Gordon's[1] essay "The Scientific Status of Design Inferences" is next.

Gordon attempts to impose the validity of design studies on science through a discussion of the philosophy of science, in particular models of scientific explanation. He says:

> Even if we grant that [methodological naturalism] has been a fruitful strategy for science, we must still ask whether it is methodologically required by science ... [P]erhaps there is a perfectly rigorous *method* for ascertaining when such restrictions *cannot* be applied if a correct explanation for something is to be given. Would such a principled decision, subject to a strict and objective methodology, not also conform to the canons of scientific explanation? (emphases in the original)

He briefly describes three models that have been proposed by philosophers of science to represent a scientific explanation: the deductive-nomological model, the causal-statistical model, and the pragmatic model[2]. He then argues that methodological naturalism is not an explicit constraint on these

---

[1]Bruce Gordon is a Senior Fellow at the Discovery Institute. He is an Associate Professor of the History and Philosophy of Science at Houston Baptist University.

[2]I do not think it is necessary to delve into the details of these models of scientific explanation to understand and respond to Gordon's essay. All that need be understood is that these are different models of scientific explanation. For the in-

three models, and attempts to show that design inference conforms to these models.

> Since design inferences satisfy all three models of scientific explanation, there seems little reason to bar their legitimacy as a mode of scientific explanation. Indeed, when generating scientific conclusions in cryptography or forensics, the design inference is not controversial.

Response

The notion that a design inference is not controversial needs to be answered. Apart from the last sentence quoted above, Gordon approvingly notes that:

> William Dembski points out, drawing design inference is already an essential and uncontroversial part of various scientific activities ranging from the detection of fabricated experimental data, to forensic science, cryptography, and even the Search for Extraterrestrial Intelligence.

This is a very misleading idea. As I have noted in Chapter 20 on page 129, science searches for the *actions* of an intelligent *agent*; this is a very different thing from a search for design in the abstract. Cryptography, forensics, and the others involve the detection of the actions of an agent.

It has been pointed out before me that Paley's analogy of finding a watch and supposing it to be made by man because of its design and purpose is also misleading[3]. We suppose it to be made by man because we know that man makes watches. We could even find a single cog, with no idea of the purpose and suppose it to be made by man because of tool marks or other knowledge about man's manufacturing capabilities. We could even envisage this working with the ruins on a different planet, where we know nothing about the alien species involved. In such instances, we find that things are designed if we cannot find the object in nature. This makes the task of finding something in nature to be designed impossible in principle.

Gordon also briefly discusses Dembski's specified complexity criterion. "It is an essentially probabilistic concept ... [I]f an event is genuinely one of *specified* small probability, then the proper conclusion is that the cause of

---

terested reader, however, a good essay is available at `plato.stanford.edu/entries/`
`scientific-explanation`.

[3]In fact, in Chapter 23, we saw Witt trying to pin this analogy on "Darwinists."

that event is intelligent agency" (emphasis in the original). It is this idea that Gordon links to the deductive-nomological model.

However, the challenge with all such probability calculations is two-fold. Firstly, a probability calculation can only be performed when a mechanism is known. A low probability may only mean that the proposed mechanism is unlikely to be the correct one. Some other as yet unknown mechanism may have a far greater probability, and the wise will acknowledge their ignorance of this and keep looking for more probable causes. Secondly, a low probability event may occur by chance, especially if there are enough repeated occurrences. For all we know, a low probability event may be evidence for an infinite number of universes, with our witness of this one being a selection bias. In other words, low probability events mean we should admit our ignorance and look closer; not that we should make bold proclamations.

I will not delve further into Gordon's discussion on the philosophy of science since most philosophers of science do not accept his arguments. The reason is that the concept of design provides no explanatory power at all. We will get into this point more in the next chapter. If Gordon's arguments are correct, it is an indication of flaws in the models of scientific explanation. But the previous paragraph shows a fundamental flaw in Gordon's argument, which I suspect is the more likely explanation. I would be surprised if this kind of abstruse reasoning convinced anyone of the existence of God. It certainly does not persuade me.

It remains the case that Intelligent Design does not prove anything, and if it did, it would not show anywhere near as much as its adherents claim. No extant being would be necessary (god might be long dead); no supernatural being would be required (we could be part of a simulation). You would still have the problem of infinite regress: who designed the designer? And no linkage to any religion or sect can be established, at least given the holy writings we have. Gordon's tenuous argument does not prove anything.

CHAPTER 26

The Vise Strategy: Squeezing the Truth Out of Darwinists

Ending the section on science is another essay by William A Dembski: "The Vise Strategy: Squeezing the Truth Out of Darwinists."

For me, Dembski's essay is the low point of the book. The notion that "Darwinists" should have their heads stuck in a vise, with its shades of the Spanish Inquisition, and its implication that scientists are evading questions and confusing the public is repugnant as well as misleading. Dembski proposes to "subject [Darwinists] to a sustained line of questioning about what they mean by each of these five terms: *science, nature, creation, design,* and *evolution.*" The essay then consists of one side of a legal drama, in which Dembski writes the questions out for our Intelligent Design lawyer hero, leaving the answers to the readers' imaginations. Presumably, we are meant to see in our mind's eye the floundering Darwinist withering under Dembski's penetrating cross-examination. He seems to have missed the fact that evolutionists have so far won the hearts and minds of the scientific community and that biologists are very open about the science around this.

Nevertheless, at the risk of normalizing his scenario, I will submit to the questions, as has been done countless times before by many far better qualified than me to do so. If you are interested in the truth, and the reasons why scientists accept evolution there are many excellent books to read, such as Bill Nye's *Undeniable* and Richard Dawkins's *The Greatest Show on Earth.* Either book shows up Intelligent Design for the intellectually vapid and scientifically trite nonsense that it is.

What follows is every question put by Dembski is his essay along with my head-in-the-vice response.

Dembski: Is it fair to say that you regard intelligent design as not a part of science? Would you agree that proponents of intelligent design who characterize it as a "scientific discipline" or a "scientific theory" are mistaken?

Me: Yes.

Dembski: Would you characterize intelligent design as a 'pseudoscience'?

Me: Absolutely.

Dembski: Would it be fair to say that, in your view, what makes intelligent design a pseudoscience is that it is religion masquerading as science? If ID is something other than science, what exactly is it?

Me: No. What makes it pseudoscience is that you know what conclusion you are going to draw in advance. It is a bunch of scientific-sounding ideas meant to enable you to draw conclusions that are not warranted. It is an idea in search of supporting evidence, rather than the other way around. It is a theory that does not make any predictions. It is an assertion of certainty on matters that are not, in fact, well-understood. I am not convinced that it is "religion" since the statements of belief are so vague as to be meaningless. For example, what does it mean to have design without a designer? The reticence to define terms and the tendency to talk in generalities are also part of it.

Dembski: Are you a scientist?

Me: Yes.

Dembski: Do you feel qualified to assess whether something is or is not properly a part of science? What are your qualifications in the regard? [*Take your time here.*]

Me: Not necessarily. There are probably interesting boundary cases where things get subtle. I have a Ph.D. in physics, but I think the cases that are far from the boundary are obvious regardless of your qualification. By analogy, you do not need to be a car mechanic to recognize that a steering wheel is a part of a car while a tree is not. But some components might be harder to distinguish.

Dembski: Have you read any books on the history and philosophy of science?

Me: Yes.

Dembski: [*If yes:*] Which ones? [*e.g., Herbert Butterfield, Ronald Numbers, Thomas Kuhn*]

Me: I do not remember reading those. I am certainly not an expert on the philosophy of science.

Dembski: Would you agree that in the history of science, ideas that started out as 'pseudoscientific' may eventually become properly scientific, for example, the transformation of alchemy into chemistry?

Me: No, obviously not. Science is a search for truth, even if that truth is admitting ignorance. Pseudoscience seeks to justify a predefined conclusion with scientific-sounding ideas. They might seem similar at first glance, but they are not. Alchemy did not become chemistry. Chemistry started when people began to behave more scientifically and rejected alchemy as an approach.

Dembski: Is it possible that ID could fall in this category, as a transformation into a rigorous science of something that in the past was not regarded as properly scientific? [*If no, return to this point later.*]

Me: Since I do not agree with your original premise, your question makes no sense. Yes, ID is similar to other pseudosciences (worse generally since something like homeopathy at least can be subject to testing), but no, it cannot evolve into science without rejecting its foundational basis. The premise is flawed. We never find intelligence; we find the results of the actions of intelligent agents. We do not see design because of purpose or complexity; we find it because of tool marks or other indications that it is not natural. Finding design in nature is a contradiction in terms: you would be looking for nature that does not look like nature.

Dembski: Are there precise criteria that tell you what belongs to science and what doesn't?

Me: No.

Dembski: [*If no:*] Then on what basis do you preclude ID from being science? In that case, isn't your exclusion of ID from science purely a subjective judgment? How do you rule it out as non-science if you have no criteria for judging what's in and what's outside of science?

Me: It looks like you changed from "precise criteria" to any criteria. As I said, I am sure there are marginal cases out there, but this is not one of them. It is a logical fallacy to say that since I cannot apply my criteria to every case, I, therefore, cannot apply it to a specific case. Intelligent Design is one of the easy ones. If I asked you if you can solve every mathematical equation on earth, I suppose you would answer no. Therefore you do not know what 1+1 is. The fallacy is clear.

Dembski: [*If yes:*] Please list all the criteria you can think of that demarcate science from non-science. [*Take your time with this.*] Are you sure these are all of them? If you are not sure these are all of them, how can you be sure that your criteria are the right ones? Do these criteria work in all cases? Do they tell you in every instance what's inside and what's outside the bounds of science? Are there no exceptions?

Dembski: [*If yes:*] Tell me about the exceptions. [*After several of them:*] Are there any more exceptions? Is that everything? [*Take your time with this.*]

Me: My answer to the yes fork would have been similar.

Dembski: Let's consider one very commonly accepted criterion for what's inside and what's outside of science, namely, *testability*. Would you say that *testability* is a criterion for demarcating science? In other words, if a claim isn't testable, then it's not scientific. Would you agree with this?

Me: Not really. That would exclude mathematics and string theory for example. Most theories are not directly testable. We test predictions made by the theory.

Dembski: Would you give as one of the reasons that ID is not science that it is untestable? [*Return to this.*]

Me: I guess it is a factor, but it is not the biggest problem that ID faces.

Dembski: Let's stay with testability for a bit. You've agreed that if something is not testable, then it does not properly belong to science. Is that right?

Me: No. Testability is important, but it does not demarcate the boundaries of science.

Dembski: Have you heard of the term *methodological materialism* (also sometimes called *methodological naturalism*)?

Me: Yes. [Aside: I discussed methodological naturalism in Chapter 4. Methodological naturalism is the principle that science should restrict itself to considering material causes].

Dembski: Do you regard methodological materialism as a regulative principle for science? In other words, do you believe that science should be limited to offering only materialistic explanations of natural phenomena?

Me: Yes.

Dembski: [*If you experience resistance to this last question because the Darwinist being questioned doesn't like the connotations associated with 'materialism' try:*]

Dembski: This is not a trick question. By *materialistic explanations* I simply mean explanations that appeal only to matter, energy, and their interactions as governed by the laws of physics and chemistry. Do you regard methodological materialism in this sense as a regulative principle for science? [*It's important here to get the Darwinist to admit methodological materialism—this is usually not a problem; indeed, usually they are happy to embrace it.*]

Me: There are examples where scientists have been willing to perform experiments that attempt to detect non-materialistic phenomena (such as the AWARE study[1] seeking to identify out-of-body experiences (see Chapter 3)), so the boundary may not be as rigorous as you imply. But I am fine to accept that we are primarily studying the natural universe.

Dembski: Could you explain the scientific status of methodological materialism? For instance, you stated that testability is a criterion for true science. Is there any scientific experiment that tests methodological materialism? Can you describe such an experiment?

Me: I would say that testability derives from materialism, not the other way around. Materialism is more fundamental. Without materialism,

---

[1]Investigators in the United Kingdom wanted to test reports of out-of-body experiences. They suspended boards from the ceiling of resuscitation units with figures on them facing upwards and not visible from the floor. The idea was that "anybody who claimed to have left their body and be near the ceiling during resuscitation attempts would be expected to identify those targets." There have been no positive results so far.

we would not necessarily expect testability. The test is every experiment ever performed, which affirms materialism by their results in every instance. In fact, scientists have performed many experiments attempting to disprove materialism (such as the efficacy of prayer), and they have all failed. After hundreds of years of the success of materialism, it is starting to seem like a pretty robust system, but as I said, scientists continue to push the boundaries where there are testable predictions.

Dembski: Are there theoretical reasons from science for accepting methodological materialism? For instance, we know on the basis of the second law of thermodynamics that the search for perpetual motion machines cannot succeed. Are there theoretical reasons for thinking that scientific inquiries that veer outside the strictures of methodological materialism cannot succeed? Can you think of any such reasons?

Me: You have it backward. We believe the second law of thermodynamics because we have not found any examples of perpetual motion. These laws describe reality. If they did not, they would not be laws. It is not that reality is conforming itself to the laws. If we discovered a perpetual motion machine, we would have to reject thermodynamics. Thermodynamics has simply been extremely successful at describing the universe. It has got to the point where people do not seriously expect it to be overturned. The same applies to evolution, in fact. Similarly, methodological naturalism is accepted because of its success.

Dembski: A compelling reason for holding to methodological materialism would be if it could be demonstrated conclusively that all natural phenomena invariably submit to materialistic explanations. Is there any such demonstration?

Me: Of course not, and this badly misunderstands the way science is done. There is no proof for any physical theory—it stands or falls empirically. If a theory's prediction turns out to be false, we reject it (or at least we refine the conditions for its acceptance, which is what happened with the Newtonian theory of gravity, for example). If it succeeds, we keep searching, but gradually build up our confidence that the theory is worth accepting.

Dembski: [*Suppose here the success of evolutionary theory is invoked to justify methodological materialism—that is, so many natural phenomena have submitted successfully to materialistic explanation that it* *constitutes a good rule of thumb or working hypothesis. In that case, we ask:*]

Dembski: But wouldn't you agree that there are many natural phenomena for which we haven't a clue how they can be accounted for in terms of materialistic explanation? Take the origin of life. Isn't the origin of life a wide open problem for biology, one that gives no indication of submitting to materialistic explanation?

Me: I would not phrase it so strongly. I am certainly happy to admit our ignorance, but I think there are many clues for materialistic explanations for all natural phenomena. There are several plausible pathways for the origin of life under investigation. Scientists could publish a paper tomorrow that demonstrated a plausible materialistic path to self-replicating organisms from primordial matter. The fact that such a thing could happen means that it is premature to say that it cannot. It is an open problem, but one in which materialistic explanations have already made plenty of headway (as discussed in Chapter 10). But finding an example from the ancient past where data is scarce and saying that it *cannot* be explained materialistically is asserting more than is reasonable. You would need a better example than that.

Dembski: [*If they claim that it isn't an open problem, continue:*]

Dembski: Are you claiming that the problem of life's origin has been given a successful materialistic explanation? If so, please state the "theory of life's origin" comparable to the neo-Darwinian theory of biological evolution. Can you sketch this widely accepted theory of life's origin? How does it account for the origin of biomacromolecules in the absence of the biosynthetic machinery that runs all contemporary living cells? Furthermore, how does such a theory provide a materialistic explanation for how these biomacromolecules came together and organized themselves into a living cell in the first place?

Me: You mean that your theory explains all this? I would love to hear your explanation, remembering that explaining the unknown with the unknowable does not constitute an explanation at all. Anyway, materialistically, this is all work in progress, and I do not think there is any reason to throw up our hands and stop these efforts, especially given how much knowledge has yielded to our materialistic approach so far.

Dembski: Would you agree, then, that methodological materialism is not scientifically testable, that there is no way to confirm it scientifically, and therefore that it is not a scientific claim? Oh, you think it can be confirmed scientifically? Please explain, exactly how is it confirmed scientifically? I'm sorry, but pointing to the success of materialistic explanations in science won't work here because the issue with materialistic explanations is not their success in certain cases but their success across the board. Is there any way to show scientifically that materialistic explanations provide a *true* account for *all* natural phenomena? Is it possible that the best materialistic explanation of a natural phenomenon is not the true explanation? If this is not possible, please explain why not. [*Keep hammering away at these questions until you get a full concession that methodological naturalism is not testable and cannot be confirmed scientifically.*]

Me: We have already covered this ground. Theories are tested empirically by testing their predictions. To give an illustrative juxtaposition: Materialism and thermodynamics have never broken down, despite testing. Materialism and thermodynamics would be rejected if an experiment showed that they did not work. But no experiment can show that they will always work in all future experiments: that is an unrealistic expectation of science. For example, scientists have tested the efficacy of healing by prayer and by homeopathy experimentally. Were these to have returned a positive, statistically significant result, we would have grounds to question materialism. But it has never happened. Of course, the theist then dismisses this result, saying that naturally, God would not want to be tested! Hammer away as much as you like, but methodological naturalism has been tested extensively with every experiment ever performed. It cannot be "confirmed scientifically" by your definition, but neither then can any other scientific theory.

Dembski: Since methodological materialism is not a scientific claim, what is its force as a rule for science? Why should scientists adopt it? [*The usual answer here is "the success of science."*]

Me: The success of science.

Dembski: But if methodological materialism's authority as a rule for science derives from its success in guiding scientific inquiry, wouldn't it be safer to say that it is merely a *working hypothesis* for science? And as a *working hypothesis*, aren't scientists free to discard it when they find that it "no longer works"?

Me: Yes. Just like thermodynamics or relativity or any other theory. I would not use the word "merely" given the enormity of the success of all these endeavors, but I cannot force you to appreciate them, and I certainly would not put your head in a vise. I also would question if its success has been in "guiding scientific inquiry." That may or may not be the case, but it is not as important as the empirical results and fulfilled predictions.

Dembski: It's sometimes claimed that the majority of scientists have adopted methodological materialism as a working hypothesis. But have *all* scientists adopted it? Is science governed by majority rule?

Me: I do not know. Certainly all the good ones. Science is not governed by majority rule. It is guided by what works in practice. I know of no scientific papers or theories that postulate anything beyond materialism.

Dembski: If [*as the Darwinist will by now hopefully have admitted*] methodological materialism is not a scientific claim, how can it be unscientific for ID theorists to discard it as a working hypothesis for science? In the absence of methodological materialism as a regulative principle for science, what else is there that might prevent ID from being developed into a full-fledged science? You claimed earlier that ID is not testable. Is that the reason you think ID cannot be developed into a full-fledged science?

Me: I think I have shown that methodological naturalism *is* a scientific claim, as it follows the same pattern as other theories that are not in dispute. However, ID theorists are welcome to reject it and see where it gets them. Just do not expect to be allowed to indoctrinate your ideas to our children as though they were established science. Testability is part of it, in the sense that no testable predictions are coming out of ID, but the lack of explanatory power and the warrantless rejection of naturalism also feature.

Dembski: But how can you say that ID is not testable? Over and over again, Darwin in his *Origin of Species* compared the ability of his theory to explain biological data with the ability of a design hypothesis to explain those same data. Moreover, Darwin stressed in the *Origin* that "a fair result can be obtained only by fully stating and balancing the facts and arguments on both sides of each question." How, then, can you say that ID is not testable when Darwin clearly claimed to be simultaneously testing a design hypothesis against his own theory?

Me: Can you give me an example of a testable prediction made by ID? I cannot speak authoritatively about Darwin, but perhaps he added that sentence to mollify hysterical people who wanted to put his head in a vise? I know of no prediction made by ID, but I would love to see such a prediction tested. I cannot see how such a prediction is even possible based on the core premises of ID, but perhaps you can enlighten me. On the other hand, evolution was proposed before we knew about DNA and tectonic plates, for example, and have been bolstered remarkably through these discoveries. Meanwhile, the claims of Intelligent Design have been gradually whittled away by new discoveries.

Dembski: Let's talk about creation and creationism a bit. Is it fair to say that you think ID is a form of creationism? Why do you think that?

Me: No. It is more like the other way around. ID is a nebulous catch-all.

Dembski: Does ID try to harmonize its scientific claims with the Bible? If so, please indicate.

Me: ID does not make any scientific claims of which I am aware.

Dembski: Is it fair to say that ID is not in the business of matching up its scientific claims with the Genesis record of creation or any other system of religious belief? If otherwise, please indicate.

Me: It is fair to say that since ID makes no scientific claims.

Dembski: Is it fair to say that ID is not *young earth creationism*, also known as *scientific creationism* or *creation science*? [*The important thing with this line of questioning is to get the Darwinist to agree that ID is not creationism in any conventional sense.*]

Me: Yes. They are not the same thing, despite obvious similarities.

Dembski: Is it possible to hold to ID and not be a Christian, Jew, or Muslim? Is it possible to be a Buddhist and hold to ID? Is it possible to be a Hindu and hold to ID? [*The answer in all these cases is yes, and there are respected scientists from all these systems of religious belief who hold to ID.*]

Me: Sure. Anything is possible. Those scientists have not published any scientific paper supporting ID or even proposing any predictions from ID, so the fact that they are scientists is irrelevant. When they do science, they put aside their ID beliefs.

Dembski: Is it possible to hold to ID for philosophical reasons that have nothing to do with conventional belief in God? In other words, can one hold to ID and not believe in God, much less a creator God?

Me: Sure. Anyone can hold onto any belief.

Dembski: Would you agree that Aristotle, who held to an eternal universe and an inherent purposiveness within nature (i.e., a purposiveness not imposed on nature from the outside), did not have a conventional belief in God but would today properly be regarded as an ID advocate? Are you familiar with Antony Flew's recent embrace of intelligent design despite his rejection of conventional belief in God (for instance, he explicitly rejects personal immortality)?

Me: I am not an expert on either person's beliefs. However, belief in some form of design was certainly the norm before the scientific revolution. I discussed Flew's beliefs in Chapter 11. More significant, then, is why this essay is in a book called *Evidence for God*? You have just conceded that all the essays in this book that affirm Intelligent Design are not, in fact, evidence for god.

Dembski: Your main beef with ID, therefore, seems to be not that it holds to a religious doctrine of creation but rather that it takes material causation to be an incomplete category of scientific explanation. Is that true or is there any other criticism that you think is more significant? If it is true, how can you claim that ID is creationism? Creationism suggests some positive account of an intelligence creating the world, but your problem with ID seems to be its denial that a certain category of causation can account for everything in nature.

Me: That is certainly part of it. However, the bigger issue is that there is no concrete proposal being put forward with ID. At least creationism gets that far, which is better and more scientific in many ways. Of course, when the predictions of creationism are falsified, they find ways of slipping out of it, which is the hallmark of pseudoscience. But ID does not even get that far. Out-of-body experience studies and homeopathy are making falsifiable predictions, though its adherents do not accept the falsifying results, again marking them as pseudosciences. ID is claiming special knowledge that it does not have, in the sense that it (1) rejects all conceivable materialist explanations, even those that have not yet been discovered, and (2) does not provide any particular instance where the materialist model breaks down.

Dembski: Are you merely a methodological materialist or are you also a metaphysical/philosophical materialist? In other words, do you pretend that everything happens by material causation merely for the sake of science, but then bracket that assumption in other areas of your life (say on Sundays when you go to church)? Or do you really hold that everything happens by material causation—period? If the latter, on what grounds do you hold to metaphysical materialism? Can that position be scientifically justified? How so? If you claim merely to be a methodological materialist, then whence the confidence that material causation is adequate for science? [*This cycles back to previous questions.*]

Me: I am a methodological materialist. When I was a Christian, I believed that nature was obtainable through science, but that there may be other forms of knowledge. I am now simply not persuaded by the arguments for other forms of knowledge. This is similar to other scientific theories. I accept the efficacy of thermodynamics and relativity, but if they were shown to be incorrect, I would accept whatever replaced them. I do not think it likely, but I am an empiricist. Materialism works, so we will go with it. However, I am willing to explore the edges with something like the AWARE study mentioned earlier, so my offer stands: give me a prediction from ID, and we will test it. But do not expect me to welcome this or any other crazy idea into the halls of science until they have been thoroughly tested.

Dembski: What is the nature of nature? Does nature operate purely by material causation? If not, how could we know it?

Me: I do not know, but there is no evidence of it operating any other way so far.

Dembski: Consider the following riddle (posed by Robert Pennock): "If you call a tail a leg, how many legs does a dog have?" Wouldn't you agree that the answer is four? Calling a tail a leg doesn't make it one. Accordingly, wouldn't it be prejudicial to define nature as a closed system of material entities in which everything happens by material causation? Wouldn't you agree that nature is what nature is, and it is not the business of scientists to prescribe what nature is like in advance of actually investigating nature?

Me: I would agree: the answer is four. If by "material causation" you mean naturalistic causation, I would say far from being prejudicial it is tautological. I agree that nature is what it is, and scientists should seek to understand it. We should not lightly seek explanations beyond nature, and it is not clear that such a thing is possible since beyond nature means beyond everything we have ever experienced. If we can measure something, even something intermittent, then we can do science on it. If we cannot measure it, then it is beyond the realm of science.

Dembski: Let's return to the issue of testability in science. Do you agree that for a proposition to be scientific it must be testable? Good. Would you agree, further, that testability is not necessarily an all-or-nothing affair? In other words, would you agree that testability is concerned with confirmation and disconfirmation, and that these come in degrees, so that it makes sense to talk about the degree to which a proposition is tested? For instance, in testing whether a coin is fair, would finding that the coin landed heads twenty times in a row more strongly disconfirm the coin's fairness than finding that it landed only ten heads in a row? [*Keep hammering on this until there's an admission that testing can come in degrees. Examples from the history of science can be introduced here as well.*]

Me: As mentioned earlier, I do not think that testability is the ultimate decider for all science, but empirical results are certainly a vital part of it. If by degrees, you mean statistical certainty, then yes, many experiments can be set up this way (though this is probably not universal).

Dembski: Okay, so we're agreed that science is about testable propositions and that testability of these propositions can come in degrees. Now let me ask you this: Is testability symmetric? In other words, if a proposition is testable, is its negation also testable? For instance, consider the proposition "it's raining outside." The negation of that proposition is the proposition "it's not the case that it's raining outside" (typically abbreviated "it's not raining outside"—logicians form the negation of a proposition by putting "it's not the case that..." in front of a proposition). Given that the proposition "it's raining outside" is testable, is it also the case that the negation of that proposition is testable?

Me: You are conflating ideas here. We have a theory, and that theory makes testable predictions. The prediction can be determined to be true or false (within the bounds of statistics). If false, the theory is rejected. If true, the theory is not rejected, but not necessarily accepted either. In this sense, a theory can never be proved, though it can be disproved. So, yes, testability is symmetric, but that does not apply to the scientific theories that generate testable propositions.

Dembski: As a general rule, if a proposition is testable, isn't its negation also testable? [*If you don't get a firm yes to this, continue as follows:*]

Dembski: Can you help me to understand how a proposition can be testable but its negation not be testable? To say that a proposition is testable is to say that it can be placed in empirical harm's way— that it might be wrong and that this wrongness can be confirmed through empirical data, wouldn't you agree? Testability means that the proposition can be put to a test, and if it fails the test, then it loses credibility, and its negation gains in credibility. Wouldn't you agree? [*Keep hammering on this until the point is conceded.*]

Me: Please see my previous answer, as it is indispensable. If a theory makes a prediction that is false, then the theory is false. If a theory makes a prediction that is true, it continues to survive, but it is never truly safe. More broadly, you can prove existence, but you cannot prove non-existence.

Dembski: Doesn't it then follow that whenever a proposition is testable, so is its negation, with a test for one posing a test also for the other?

Me: That is correct by definition.

Dembski: Let me, therefore, ask you, are the following propositions scientific and, as a consequence, testable: (1) Humans and other primates share a common ancestor. (2) All organisms on Earth share a common ancestor. (3) Life on Earth arose by material causes. Are the negations of these propositions, therefore, scientific and testable? If not, why not?

Me: If I were to land a rocket on Pluto, would it experience gravity? We assume so because gravity is a theory that has been tested extensively in other areas and its predictions found to be true. Evolution is a theory that has been extensively tested and never been falsified. It makes complex predictions such as the ones you gave, but the task of testing them is daunting. However, evolution has been so successful that we think those statements to be as likely as experiencing gravity on Pluto, though both are hard to verify directly. There are many parts of this, such as DNA studies that, though they came long after evolution was proposed, validated evolution remarkably. Statement 1, for example, though proposed before DNA was discovered, made it possible for us to predict that there would be more overlap in the DNA of more closely related species, and this is indeed the case. So we do not reject the theory.

In fact, staying with statement 1, we observe that humans have twenty-three pairs of chromosomes, while the great apes have twenty-four. Evolution and logic tell us that the most likely explanation for this is if two chromosomes fused together to form one at some point in our recent evolutionary history. This is a very precise prediction, and so scientists searched through the three billion base pairs of our DNA looking for tell-tale signs of such a fusion. It turns out that Chromosome 2 came from a recent, end-to-end fusion of two ancestral chromosomes. We can see this because there are vestigial telomeres and a vestigial centromere in the middle of Chromosome 2. Telomeres are normally found only at the two ends of chromosomes, and normally chromosomes only have one centromere. If you had two adjacent chromosomes, you would have this sequence:

- First telomere from Chromosome A,
- —(other DNA)—,
- Centromere from Chromosome A,
- —(other DNA)—,
- Second telomere from Chromosome A,
- First telomere from Chromosome B,
- —(other DNA)—,
- Centromere from Chromosome B,
- —(other DNA)—,
- Second telomere from Chromosome B.

What you see in Chromosome 2 is:

- First telomere from Chromosome 2,
- —(other DNA)—,
- Centromere from Chromosome 2,
- —(other DNA)—,
- Vestigial telomere,
- Vestigial telomere,
- —(other DNA)—,
- Vestigial centromere,
- —(other DNA)—,
- Second telomere from Chromosome 2.

This demonstrates that Chromosome 2 is an end-to-end fusion of two previous chromosomes, in striking fulfillment of the prediction of evolution.

Dembski: Let's focus on the third of these propositions, namely, that life arose by purely material causes. How is it tested? How would its negation be tested? If its negation is not testable, how can the original proposition be testable? Wouldn't it then be just like arithmetic— simply a necessary truth and not something in contact with empirical data?

Me: It is extremely difficult to test because we do not know how it happened. We have some ideas that can be tested in the laboratory. Perhaps some day we shall see an example of this in the early stages on another planet. Perhaps this knowledge is forever lost in the mist of time. However, we should continue to search for mechanisms, and, in fact, many proposed steps have been demonstrated to be plausible (see Chapter 10). This is not a proof, and probably evolution cannot be disproved through this either. We accept evolution for a whole bunch of reasons. This, however, is one of the predictions of evolution, so we accept it as reasonable, but also admit that we do not know the details for sure. One of the challenges with ID is that it claims to know about an origin event like this with certainty.

Dembski: Let's now turn to evolution. Back in 1989, Richard Dawkins remarked that those who don't hold to evolution are "ignorant, stupid or insane (or wicked, but I'd rather not consider that)." Is Dawkins right?

Me: I would not put it in such bald terms. It is a very complicated subject, on which there is a great deal of misinformation and willful ignorance. I always like to understand why people have the beliefs they have. But I also understand the frustration that scientists have when experiments like the above example of Chromosome 2 are ignored. It really takes a bizarre mental contortion to understand the above experiment and not accept evolution.

Dembski: Evolutionists distinguish between common descent (also known as universal common ancestry) and the mechanisms of evolution. Common descent is a historical claim. It says that all organisms trace their lineage back to a last universal common ancestor (sometimes abbreviated LUCA). Do you hold to common descent? Why? Please be as detailed as you can in describing the scientific evidence that leads you to that belief.

Me: Yes. This was considered a matter of straightforward observation as far back as the ancient Greeks, who could see it in the fossil record, as we can today. Of course, we now also have DNA evidence and the context of tectonic plate theory that support the theory further. It has never been shown to be false. I discussed very striking evidence for this in Chapter 21 and in the above discussion on Chromosome 2.

Dembski: No doubt you have heard of the Cambrian explosion. Isn't it the case that fossil evidence reveals most extant animal phyla first appear over a period of 5 to 10 million years in the Cambrian rocks without evident precursors?

Me: Not really. The limited fossil record shows the explosion over 20 to 25 million years, but evidence is accumulating gradually of metazoa in the Precambrian period. It is certainly a puzzle, but it is unlikely to be one that is unsolvable, as scientists are working on several plausible theories. If ID has any specific predictions about the Cambrian explosion, perhaps you can share them? However, I again note that you are using an example from the distant past where evidence is scarce.

Dembski: Consider an octopus, a starfish, an insect, and a fish. To what phyla do these belong? Is there solid fossil evidence that these share a common ancestor? If so, please provide the details. [*Watch for a snow job; no compelling evidence exists.*]

Me: I am sure you can look up their phyla for yourself, and I am not familiar with the fossil evidence for these creatures (though I would imagine such fossils are rare since most of them do not have bones). They are, however, all eukaryotes, which is somewhat compelling. The real answer either has come or will come through DNA methods similar to those discussed in Chapter 21. I am not an expert in this area, but I can imagine it would be difficult to find common genes across such different animals.

Dembski: Do you regard the Cambrian explosion as providing a challenge to common descent? If not, why not?

Me: Absolutely. It is a fascinating challenge. It does not disprove it, of course, since there are several possible ways of reconciling it, and, as an ancient event, the records are scarce. I suspect it will be resolved eventually, but science is nothing without the excitement of the search for truth.

Dembski: Let's turn next to the mechanisms of evolution. What are the mechanisms of evolution? [*Get as many out of the evolutionist as* *possible. Natural selection and random mutation will be at the top of the list, with genetic drift, lateral gene transfer, and developmental factors also receiving mention.]* Are these all of them? *[Take your time. Wait until the Darwinist admits that these are all he or she can think of.]*

Me: Symbiosis and Parasitism may also deserve mention: creatures once symbiotic later merged into one. This is how our mitochondrial DNA came to be, for example. I suppose there are many others.

Dembski: So you're not sure that these are all the mechanisms that drive the process of biological evolution. Is intelligence a mechanism? If you can't be sure that you've got all the relevant mechanisms of evolution, how can you rule out intelligence as a factor in biological evolution?

Me: Intelligence is not a mechanism, at least by any reasonable definition of mechanism.

Dembski: Okay, you're convinced that the neo-Darwinian mechanism of natural selection and random genetic change is the most important factor in biological evolution. Why is that? What is the evidence that it deserves this place in evolutionary theorizing?

Me: That is how things are observed to evolve in the laboratory, through DNA studies, and through studying the fossil record. But other mechanisms are also important.

Dembski: Are you familiar with the molecular machines that are in all cells and without which cellular life would be impossible (the one that has been most discussed is the bacterial flagellum, a miniature, bidirectional, motor-driven propeller that moves certain bacteria through their watery environments)?

Me: Yes.

Dembski: Are you familiar with the writings of James Shapiro (who is on faculty at the University of Chicago) and Franklin Harold (who is an emeritus professor at Colorado State University)? Shapiro is a molecular biologist, Harold a cell biologist. They both claim that there are no detailed Darwinian accounts for the evolution of molecular machines like the flagellum. Do you agree with their assessment? Are there any other evolutionary mechanisms that yield a detailed, testable scenario for the origin of such molecular machines?

Me: I am not familiar with their work, but I do not dispute it. There is lots of work on the evolutionary origins of such molecular machines, but, while plausible, it remains difficult to test[2]. Of course, if you already know that such work is futile I would love to hear how you know about work that has not been completed.

Dembski: Theodosius Dobzhansky, one of the founders of the neo-Darwinian synthesis remarked toward the end of his life that nothing in biology makes sense except in the light of evolution. Do you accept this statement?

Me: Yes.

Dembski: But isn't it the case that for systems like the bacterial flagellum, evolutionary biology has no clue how they came about? [*If the Darwinist balks, keep pressing for detailed evolutionary accounts of such complex molecular machines.*] So was Dobzhansky wrong?

Me: I would say that biologists have a pretty good idea[3]. I still agree with Dobzhansky. You seem to think that we either have a detailed account or no account, a fallacy known as a false dichotomy.

Dembski: Earlier you expressed reservations about ID being testable. Do you also share such reservations about the testability of evolutionary theory? No? Could you explain how evolutionary theory is testable? What sort of evidence would count against evolutionary theory?

Me: Again, it is the predictions of theories that are testable. ID makes none. Evolution makes many, some hard to test and others testable. Evidence that would count against evolution includes any out-of-place fossil; any non-naturalistic mechanism; if species did not get more complex over time. We see common species in the fossil record across the continents dating back to Pangaea, and then divergence in the species after the continents divided. We see extensive natural variation within species, which if it did not exist would count against

---

[2] As mentioned in Chapter 20, there is an excellent article on the subject: *Evolution in (Brownian) space: a model for the origin of the bacterial flagellum*, by N J Matzke, 2003 (updated in 2006). The article can be found at `www.talkdesign.org/faqs/flagellum.html`.

[3] If you are interested, more articles on this are: New Scientist, 2008, *Evolution myths: The bacterial flagellum is irreducibly complex* (available at `www.newscientist.com/article/dn13663-evolution-myths-the-bacterial-flagellum-is-irreducibly-complex`); the more detailed article mentioned in the previous footnote; the Wikipedia article on the evolution of flagella (available at `en.wikipedia.org/wiki/Evolution_of_flagella`).

evolution. We see ring species. We see gradual shifts in DNA as we move further back on the phylogenetic tree. We see genes independently implying the same tree of life. There are hundreds of papers published every year on this.

Dembski: The evolutionist J. B. S. Haldane once remarked that what would convince him that evolutionary theory was wrong was finding a rabbit fossil in Precambrian rocks. Would such a finding convince you that evolutionary theory is wrong? And wrong in what sense? Would it show that common descent is wrong? If such a fossil were found in Precambrian rocks, why not simply explain it as an evolutionary convergence?

Me: The point is that animals do not appear suddenly within the fossil record. Similar animals lead up to and away from it.

Dembski: Suppose, for the sake of argument, we accept common descent. In that case, why should we believe that natural selection and random genetic change are the principal mechanisms driving biological evolution? Is that claim testable?

Me: As discussed earlier, this theory is accepted because it makes accurate predictions, for example in the laboratory. Our understanding is improving, but at this point, we expect tweaks rather than rejection because it, like thermodynamics, has survived so much for so long. It is theoretically possible for these theories to be falsified, but no-one thinks that likely anymore.

Dembski: Do you accept that there are other mechanisms involved in biological evolution besides natural selection and random genetic change? If so, how do biologists know that the totality of these mechanisms account for all biological complexity and diversity? Is the claim that these mechanisms account for all of biological complexity and diversity itself testable? Have you tested it? How so? How can it be tested? If it should be tested and disconfirmed (as can always happen to testable propositions), then what is the alternative hypothesis that correspondingly is confirmed? Wouldn't it have to be a design hypothesis? If not, why not?

Me: We cannot expect the levels of certainty and exhaustiveness you seem to be looking for from science. More mechanisms may very well be discovered, and some may be rejected. But at this point that is likely to occur within the framework of evolution. Suppose we falsified evolution experimentally. That is a risible hypothetical at this stage, but let us go with it. As per my discussion above, this would show us that evolution is an invalid theory, like the aether. We would then have to wait for a new theory to take its place, and in the meantime accept our ignorance. It would not be design because that is not a scientific theory. By all means, try to falsify evolution. That is the scientific method. And, by all means, make predictions with ID for the world to test. But it is a false dichotomy to suggest that a rejection of evolution would result in us embracing pseudoscience. By analogy, if we discovered that a particular medicine was not efficacious, we would not automatically assume that homeopathy was the cure.

In the end, Dembski's legal drama is unable to give Intelligent Design the scientific footing he so desperately seems to want for it. This is particularly sad because he jettisoned the main thrust of this section of his book: he admitted that Intelligent Design did not prove God, and in so doing undercut the efforts of many of his fellow authors. He is right that, even if true, Intelligent Design is not evidence for God. It is not even evidence for god (deism). But it still is not science.

Part III

The Question of Jesus

CHAPTER 27

Did Jesus Really Exist?

Valuable though a discussion on science is, we have seen that it ultimately leaves us unsatisfied regarding evidence for god. In the previous chapter, Dembski was willing to jettison the idea that Intelligent Design is evidence for god in his eagerness to have it admitted into the halls of science. This severely undercuts the entire previous section.

The section on science made some serious errors: many of the chapters presented arguments from incredulity or arguments from ignorance or god of the gaps arguments, in which some gap in our knowledge or understanding was thought to point to the existence of god. It is hard to see how this works, as it appears to allow materialistic processes on either side of the gap and leaves god only a smattering of work to do. It also seems to postulate that no materialistic process will ever be discovered to fill this gap—this is being undermined over and over again and underplays how much scientists have already found.

The authors were desperate to include "design" as an allowable part of science, but this misses at least two important points: (1) we never see design or intelligence in the abstract; we only ever see the actions of intelligent agents; intelligence has never been credibly observed without attachment to something material; (2) we determine if something has been designed by an intelligent agent by considering whether it could have arisen naturally; to search for design in nature is therefore a contradiction in terms.

Finally, even if we granted the above, we would only get as far as deism.

This is just as far from any specific, theistic claim as atheism is: to say that the bacterial flagellum required an intervention and therefore we must accept the resurrection of Aristeas of Proconnesus[1], or any other historical claim is nonsensical.

The book now turns to the question of Jesus, switching from deism all the way to Christianity, or at least some subset of it. From my perspective, a close examination of the specific, historical claims made by religions presents a far greater existential challenge to them than the scientific discussion does. I am not interested in sophistry: I just want to know what is true; what can we realistically know. As such, I will respond chapter by chapter to each of the fifteen essays in this section and the nine essays in the next which considers the question of the Bible. We begin by considering Paul L. Maier's[2] essay entitled: "Did Jesus Really Exist?"

Evidence for God is going to build the case for the resurrection of Christ step-by-step over the next few chapters, culminating in Chapter 35. As such, each chapter does not necessarily contain evidence for God on its own, but I will consider the claims and evidence each provides nonetheless. Maier starts with the claim that Jesus was an actual historical figure. He presents evidence from the Bible, from Christian writing, from Jewish writing such as Josephus, and secular writing such as Tacitus. He comments that:

> Skeptics should focus instead on whether or not Jesus was *more* than a man. That, at least, could evoke a reasonable debate among reasonable inquirers rather than a pointless discussion with sensationalists who struggle to reject the obvious.

Response

This essay does not present evidence for God. I could quibble with some of the evidence he presents. For example, the "many messianic predictions

---

[1] Aristeas was a Greek poet and miracle-worker in Asia Minor around the seventh century BCE. Herodotus reports in *The Histories* being told that Aristeas entered into a fuller's shop and dropped dead. The fuller shut up the shop and went to tell Aristeas's family what had happened. The report of the death spread through the town, but was gainsayed by a traveler who had met Aristeas on the road to Cyzicus and spoken with him. The family went to the fuller's shop, but when it was opened, Aristeas was not found, dead or alive. Seven years later Aristeas reappeared in Proconnesus and wrote the poem called The Arimaspeia. Two hundred and forty years after his death, Aristeas appeared in Metapontum in southern Italy to command that a statue of himself be set up. He had, apparently, been traveling with Apollo in the form of a raven since his death. It is not clear to me how the credibility of this story is enhanced by the discovery of the bacterial flagellum.

[2] Paul Maier is the Russell H. Seibert Professor of Ancient History at Western Michigan University and an author.

in the Old Testament" are not exactly impressive since the New Testament authors are all too aware of them as they write their stories, often stating baldly that something "took place to fulfill what was spoken through the prophet"[3]. There is no evidence that Herod the Great (who died in 4 BCE anyway) tried to terminate the young Jesus (more on this shortly). But I do accept that Jesus was an historical figure, so I am happy to concede this point and will discuss this more below.

I should comment that Maier's statement that there could be "a reasonable debate" as to "whether or not Jesus was *more* than a man" concedes more than he might expect. The notion that Jesus is God is an extraordinary claim, and as such needs unassailable evidence. If the point is still up for debate, then the rational position is to assume it is not true until the case is made. So this simple concession, in fact, is an excellent exemplar of the atheist position, at least as it pertains to Christianity. The atheist position also incorporates the view that other religions present equally unconvincing evidence, with which most Christians would agree.

There are ample reasons to accept that Jesus of Nazareth existed[4]. To me, the biggest reason is the sheer weakness of the link between him and the rest of the Bible. If the story were going to be invented from scratch, Jesus would not have come from Nazareth, as it is inconvenient for the early Christian writers. This is a simple point, but let me first set a little context.

Paul, writing first, is remarkably short on biographical details: he makes no mention of Nazareth, Jesus's parables, Jesus's miracles, healings or casting out of demons, any of his Galilean ministry, the passion in Jerusalem, Calvary, Bethlehem, Galilee, the transfiguration, the triumphal entry, the cleansing of the temple, the interrogation by the Sanhedrin, the conflict with the authorities, the garden of Gethsemane, the thieves crucified with Jesus, the weeping women, the time or place of the crucifixion, Judas and his betrayal, Pilate, the trial, his rejection in favor of Barabbas, or the tomb[5].

---

[3]Verses that show an awareness of relating an event in order to fulfill some specific prophecy include: Matthew 1:22, 2:5, 2:15, 2:23, 4:14, 8:17, 12:17, 21:4, 27:9, Luke 4:21, 18:31, 24:44, John 12:38, 13:18, 15:25, 17:12, 18:32, 19:24, Acts 1:16. Notable by its absence is any Old Testament reference to the resurrection of the Messiah (the best that is offered is the story of Jonah, in which Jonah does not actually die).

[4]Bart Ehrman, *Did Jesus Exist?: The Historical Argument for Jesus of Nazareth.* This is well worth a read if you are interested in the various mythicist views out there (including that of G. A. Wells), and want to understand why they are not accepted among academics.

[5]G. A. Wells, *Cutting Jesus Down to Size: What Higher Criticism Has Achieved and Where It Leaves Christianity.* The scholarship of Wells is excellent, as Bart Ehrman acknowledges, but his conclusion that Jesus of Nazareth was not the person Paul was referring to is probably a bit of a stretch. Certainly it is not widely accepted among

The first of the gospels to be written was Mark. Much can be said on the gospels, but of relevance to us now is that Jesus came from Nazareth, though, according to Old Testament prophecy, was meant to come from Bethlehem[6]. Early Christians would surely wonder about this, and neither Paul nor the writer of Mark resolved the issue. The writers of Matthew and Luke, writing independently from each other (though with a copy of Mark in front of them), decided to set the record straight.

I should also note that these gospels may be a genuine attempt to record stories circulating at the time. Luke certainly set out to do so, though Matthew seems a little looser with his facts. In any event, it is possible for legends to grow through the gradual reification of speculation. In other words, a listener of something speculative firms it up a little before passing it on. It is hard to tell. But, with the above context, the facts of the Nazareth-Bethlehem link can now be set down in a very straightforward way.

Matthew has Mary and Joseph living in Bethlehem in their own house[7]. There is no mention of inns, innkeepers, stables or mangers. The wise men see in the stars (astrologically) that a king is to be born and head out to find him (there is no other reference to this star in or out of the Bible). Then a star leads them, ultimately positioning itself directly over the house[8]. Despite this, Herod is not able to find Jesus himself, so he decides to kill

---

scholars (see previous footnote).

[6]Micah 5:2:

> But you, Bethlehem Ephrathah, being small among the clans of Judah, out of you one will come out to me that is to be ruler in Israel; whose goings out are from of old, from ancient times.

Matthew 2:6 references it, again very aware of the prophecy as he relates the story. Of course, Micah goes on to say in verses 10–15:

> "It will happen in that day", says Yahweh, "that I will cut off your horses out from among you, and will destroy your chariots. I will cut off the cities of your land, and will tear down all your strongholds. I will destroy witchcraft from your hand; and you shall have no soothsayers. I will cut off your engraved images and your pillars out from among you; and you shall no more worship the work of your hands. I will uproot your Asherah poles out from among you; and I will destroy your cities. I will execute vengeance in anger, and wrath on the nations that didn't listen."

It is no wonder that they were expecting a military leader, but the switch from literal to figurative is sometimes hard to track.

[7]Matthew 1:24, 2:1, 2:11.

The phrase in Matthew 1:24 in the original Greek says that Joseph "took his wife to himself." This is understood to be part of the marriage ritual where the husband takes the wife into his home. The NIV adds the word home to make this clear. The phrase is not a reference to sexual relations, as is made clear by Matthew 1:25.

[8]Matthew 2:9

all the young boys in the slaughter of the innocents[9]. There is no external evidence for this, though Josephus, for example, kept close track of Herod's various atrocities. The family flees to Egypt (not a trivial journey), but that supposedly ties in with Hosea 11:1. After Herod dies, they come back, but decide not to go back to their home, choosing rather to go to Nazareth, which Matthew claims is also prophesied although the words 'Nazareth' and 'Nazarene' do not, in fact, appear in the Old Testament, and there is no extant prophecy of the sort[10]. No other source corroborates any of this, not even the rest of the Bible.

Luke, meanwhile, has Mary and Joseph living in Nazareth[11] and tells us that they were made to go to Bethlehem by a census[12]. There is no evidence of this census: Quirinius had one in 6 CE, but Luke says that it occurred during the reign of Herod the Great who died in 4 BCE, ten years earlier. Also, Romans, ever pragmatic, did not expect people to travel to a different city, especially not one related to their ancient Jewish ancestry[13]. They counted them where they lived. The idea is not credible and is uncorroborated. Anyway, the family heads to Bethlehem and lays Jesus in a manger, where shepherds visit him. Then they head peacefully back to their home in Nazareth, via Jerusalem, which Luke believes is of central theological importance (he changes Mark's resurrection location from Galilee to Jerusalem, for example). There is no mention of wise men, Egypt or any kind of slaughter.

So Matthew changes their home from Bethlehem to Nazareth with an uncorroborated slaughter of the innocent and an improbable detour to Egypt. Again there are theological motivations for this, as Matthew was trying to establish Jesus as the new Moses[14]. Luke tells us that this Nazarene family just happened to have Jesus in Bethlehem because they were briefly visiting there thanks to an uncorroborated census. This establishes that there likely was an historical Jesus of Nazareth because if he were invented from scratch, they would presumably just have had him come from Bethlehem. But the cost is the credibility of both authors. Neither story is plausible, and the two accounts are irreconcilable.

Could the birth narratives be cobbled together somehow? I cannot see how at least not with any integrity. But the more important question is

---

[9]Matthew 2:16
[10]Matthew 2:23
[11]Luke 1:26
[12]Luke 2:1–4
[13]Luke 2:4
[14]Bart Ehrman, *Did Jesus Exist?: The Historical Argument for Jesus of Nazareth.* Exodus 1 and 2 tell the story of how Moses escapes a similar slaughter of the innocent by the King of Egypt.

why. Why would you try? Why would you invent hypothetical scenarios to attempt to resolve the dissonance? The only reason I can think of to try would be if you knew that the Bible was the word of God already, which in turn would presuppose that God existed in the first place. I accept that Jesus of Nazareth was an historical character. But it seems that if the Old Testament said something that might apply to the Messiah, then for the early Christian writers that thing *must* have happened to Jesus, whether or not it did. The example of his birth narrative is just the first of many that we will discuss as this book goes on.

But this is far more than I am trying to establish here. I am merely arguing that I am unpersuaded by the evidence for God in each of these chapters, and the existence of a man called Jesus leaves me unconvinced of the existence of God.

CHAPTER 28

The Credibility of Jesus's Miracles

In this chapter, we will respond to an essay by Craig Blomberg[1] entitled: "The Credibility of Jesus's Miracles."

Blomberg begins by describing and arguing against some common objections to miracles: science, philosophy, and the similarity to other religious stories. Having dismissed these, he asks "what are positive reasons for *believing* in them?"

Blomberg answers that:

> [T]hey are deeply embedded in every layer, source, and finished Gospel in the early Christian tradition. Jewish sources likewise attest to Jesus's miracles. Faced with the opportunity to deny the Christian claims that Jesus performed such amazing feats, Josephus and the Talmud instead corroborate them, even though they don't believe he was heaven-sent. The rabbis often made the charge that Jesus was a sorcerer who led Israel astray, much like certain Jewish leaders in the Gospel accounts (Mark 3:20–30) accused Christ of being empowered by the devil.

Blomberg then argues:

---

[1]Craig Blomberg is a Distinguished Professor of the New Testament at Denver Seminary in Colorado, specializing in the New Testament.

[T]he nature of Jesus's miracles contrasts markedly with most of those from his milieu. There are a fair number of exorcisms and healing accounts from Jewish, Greek, and Roman sources but none where a given wonder-worker consistently and successfully works his miracles without the use of magical formulas, paraphernalia, or proper prayer to God or the gods. The more spectacular miracles over nature have fewer parallels in the Greco-Roman world.

Blomberg dismisses apocryphal Christian miracles as "quite frivolous compared to those in the canonical Gospels." He also states that:

The closest parallels to the miracles of Jesus are in fact in the Old Testament. Feeding the multitudes with miraculously supplied bread, God's sovereignty over wind and waves, Elijah and Elisha raising people from the dead all appear as crucial background for understanding the New Testament texts. If anything, such parallels should inspire confidence in the reliability of the New Testament accounts.

In any event, Blomberg notes that:

[N]othing in Christian theology requires one to argue that only the *biblical* miracles ever occurred. Nothing in the Bible requires us to imagine that God uses only his people to work the supernatural, and both demonic inspiration and human manufacture can account for other preternatural works ... Historians should not and need not have a more credulous attitude towards biblical miracles than toward extrabiblical ones. When we apply the same criteria of authenticity to both, the biblical miracles simply enjoy more evidential support.

Response

In this kind of discussion, we need to be aware of circular reasoning. We cannot suppose that a god or a demon accounts for some of the miraculous accounts *and* that the miraculous accounts are evidence for a god or a demon. If we knew one, we might get to the other. We have not had any evidence of supernatural beings, so if this is to be presented as such, we need to look at the credibility of the miraculous accounts on their own. For example, we cannot, as Blomberg did, have "demonic inspiration ... account for other preternatural works."

In general, it is difficult to imagine *any* account being sufficient to convince us of any supernatural event. Blomberg attempts to describe and dismiss this argument as follows:

> While not alleging that miracles are impossible, the claim now is that the probability of a natural explanation will always be greater than that of a supernatural one. Phenomena could mislead, witnesses could be mistaken, and besides, explanations of events must have analogies to what has happened in the past. But it is not at all clear that any of these arguments mean that the evidence could *never* be unambiguous and the witnesses unassailable. And if every event must have a known analogy, then people in the tropics before modern technology could never have accepted that ice exists!

You will see from the above quote that Blomberg does not do this topic justice. He ignores the strongest part, which is that witnesses could be mistaken. If someone you knew well and trusted completely told you that they had seen someone walking around town, who you believed to have died a couple of days previously, you would assume that there was a misunderstanding somewhere. Either they or you got something wrong. His argument about people in the tropics not accepting that ice exists is also misleading. It would, in point of fact, be a very healthy, natural, and correct level of skepticism not to accept the idea of solid water without proof. Now, in this instance, the claim is a true one, and many analogies could be used to help persuade: solids exist, solids burn into gases, liquids evaporate, etc. But belief in claims of the miraculous need far more substantial evidence.

It is notable, indeed, that evidence for miracles has dried up since those days. This was noticed long ago and explained away in various ways. Some claims of miracles continue, but, in an age of ubiquitous technology, there is a notable dearth of evidence. Take any miracle and search for rock bottom. In every case I have encountered, the evidence evaporates away. In the normal course of events, we should dismiss the biblical accounts in the same way. The only reason not to, is if you already know there is a God who is somehow linked to these accounts. If you know this, then first present the evidence for it.

It is often at this point that we are told that we need to have faith. But faith is not a valid way to obtain knowledge—only reason fills this role. What is faith anyway? Hebrews 11:1 tells us "Now faith is assurance of things hoped for, proof of things not seen." This could be paraphrased as wishful thinking. Hoping for something does not make it true, and believing things "by faith" has not been seen as a positive thing since the scientific revolution. In any event, faith is not evidence, and this essay is supposed to be providing us with that[2].

Blomberg also assures us that miracles "are deeply embedded in every layer, source, and finished Gospel in the early Christian tradition." This is simply not true. Paul himself does not mention *any* of Jesus's miracles apart from the resurrection, and there are several times even in the gospels when Jesus is reported to say "An evil and adulterous generation seeks after a sign, but no sign will be given it but the sign of Jonah the prophet." (Matthew 12:39, 16:4, Luke 11:29).

The implication is that the miracle stories come later (recall that Paul is the earliest Christian author). This also makes sense of Jesus telling the people he healed not to tell anyone (Mark 7:36, 8:30, Matthew 8:4): it would help listeners understand why they had not heard about these healings before; once the stories of miracles became common, such statements would not be needed. If you envisage stories spreading among a group before being recorded, it makes perfect sense. Similarly, James, the three letters of John and the apostolic fathers[3] do not mention or even suggest that Jesus worked miracles.

Josephus has three references of importance to Christianity. One mentions James the brother of Jesus, the second mentions John the Baptist (though not in connection with Jesus), and the third mentions Jesus directly, including his "surprising deeds" and his resurrection. The words in this last section cannot be seen as independent evidence since they are clearly Christian in origin, and most scholars see it as a Christian interpolation into Josephus's authentic material about Jesus. For example, Paul L. Maier, who wrote the previous chapter, elsewhere affirms this view[4].

So it comes down to the biblical accounts and an assessment of their credibility. In the preceding chapter, I discussed the birth stories from Matthew and Luke. Just this story completely destroys the credibility of those authors. Anyone able earnestly to tell you a story so transparently incoherent is not credible: you should question everything else they say. In those stories, it is not the miracles that are problematic (though they are). It is that the authors are relating stories that blatantly patch an issue

---

[2] See George Smith's book *Atheism: The Case Against God* for a more in-depth discussion on faith versus reason.

[3] The apostolic fathers are Clement of Rome, Ignatius of Antioch, and Polycarp of Smyrna. They were first- and second-century theologians and apologists, who were thought to have known some of the twelve apostles, or to have been influenced by them.

[4] Paul L. Maier, *Eusebius: The Church History*. This contains an appendix on Eusebius's citation of Josephus on Jesus. He argues that the passage that mentions Jesus cannot be entirely authentic because "no Jew could have claimed Jesus as the Messiah who rose from the dead without having converted to Christianity."

(the Nazareth-Bethlehem discrepancy), and do so using narratives that are not credible. You are looking at an author who has an incentive to believe something latching onto and relating a story that an objective observer and historian would not credit.

Blomberg claims that:

> The closest parallels to the miracles of Jesus are in fact in the Old Testament. Feeding the multitudes with miraculously supplied bread, God's sovereignty over wind and waves, Elijah and Elisha raising people from the dead all appear as crucial background for understanding the New Testament texts. If anything, such parallels should inspire confidence in the reliability of the New Testament accounts.

This last sentence is incomprehensible, as Strauss noted as far back as the 1800s (in a different context). Wells puts it like this[5]:

> Strauss also holds that some New Testament stories resulted from a desire to represent Jesus as equaling or even outdoing the achievements of important Old Testament figures. Thus he had to supply food miraculously, and even to raise the dead, otherwise he would have been inferior to Elijah and Elisha. Strauss (1840, section 100) gives, as an example of the latter feat, Luke's story of how Jesus, happening to meet the funeral procession of the only son of a widow, took compassion on her and restored him to life. No other gospel gives the story, even though, according to Luke (7:17), the report of the incident 'went forth ... in the whole of Judea and all region round about.' Now Elijah had raised a widow's only son from the dead (1 Kings 17:17–24) and Elisha performed a similar miracle (2 Kings 4:14–37). The evangelist is clearly anxious to show that the new prophet is in no way inferior to them; hence the bystanders are represented as saying: 'A great prophet is risen among us' (7:16).

In other words, it is clear that this kind of parallel should not "inspire confidence" at all.

Another issue with the credibility of the biblical accounts is that we do not even really know who the authors of the gospels are[6], but it is clear that they are not eyewitness accounts. Luke 1:2 admits as much when he

---

[5] G. A. Wells, *Cutting Jesus Down to Size: What Higher Criticism Has Achieved and Where It Leaves Christianity.*

[6] Bart Ehrman, *Jesus, Interrupted: Revealing the Hidden Contradictions in the Bible (and Why We Don't Know About Them).*

refers to the "eyewitnesses" in the third person. The earliest gospel, Mark, is revised by Luke to serve a theological purpose. Whatever else this shows, it at least means that even at the time of writing, the author of Luke did not regard Mark as completely reliable. For an example of this compare Mark 16:7 with Luke 24:6–7. In the former the angels say to Mary:

> He goes before you into Galilee. There you will see him, as he said to you.

Matthew 28:7 copies this. Luke 24:6–7, however, edits it:

> Remember what he told you when he was still in Galilee, saying that the Son of Man must be delivered up into the hands of sinful men.

Wells comments:

> The discrepancies in the gospel accounts of the resurrection events are not mere muddle but arise because one evangelist pursues theological purposes alien to another. For Luke, Jerusalem is of great theological importance, and in order to place the appearances there he amends the Markan narrative at two points.

Apart from the above, Luke 22:32–33 omits Mark 14:28 "However, after I am raised up, I will go before you into Galilee." If Luke was willing to 'correct' Mark (as Luke presumably saw it), it tells us that Luke did not regard Mark as uniformly reliable.

Another argument against the gospels being eyewitness accounts comes from Strauss quoted by Wells:

> Strauss realized that a very powerful argument against the ascription of the gospels to eyewitnesses is the presence in them of so-called literary doublets. Mark, for instance, includes accounts of two miraculous feedings, of the five thousand [Mark 6:30–44] and of the four thousand [Mark 8:1–13]. The sequence of events, and even the vocabulary, is in both cases remarkably similar . . . That two separate incidents are involved is hard to believe, since in the second the disciples—who are reported as having recently witnessed the first—have so completely forgotten it that they think it impossible for food to be supplied to thousands in a desert place (Mk. 8:4). The doublet is best explained by assuming that a tradition of one such feeding existed, before Mark wrote, in two slightly different written forms,

and that the evangelist, who drew on those written sources, incorporated both because he supposed them to refer to different incidents. If he supposed this, he obviously could not have been present as a witness of such a miracle.

Blomberg finishes his essay by quoting "one of the most meticulous historians among contemporary biblical scholars" as saying:

> Put dramatically but with not too much exaggeration: if the miracle tradition from Jesus' public ministry were to be rejected in toto as unhistorical, so should every other Gospel tradition about him.

Again, I would say that rather than actively reject, we should simply not accept. We do not know how accurately the Jesus of the Bible reflects the historical Jesus. But we do know that so far no miracle *anywhere* has sufficient evidence to accept it. We also know that the credibility of the Bible is not only short of extraordinary but weak. We are looking for evidence for God and Blomberg's essay does not provide any. In fact, his article highlights important reasons to be skeptical.

CHAPTER 29

The Son of Man

Darrell Bock[1] presents an essay entitled "The Son of Man" which we will now consider.

Bock discusses the usage of the term "Son of Man" as it appears in the Bible. He concludes that:

> [T]he Son of Man is a title Jesus used to refer to himself and his authority. He revealed its full import towards the end of his ministry. But the title referred to Jesus as the representative of humanity who also engaged in divine activity. It was a way of saying I am the One sent with divine authority who will also be the representative of humanity. In this context, all of Jesus's ministry and work, including his suffering on the cross for sin, takes place.

Response

It seems to me that this is an esoteric theological discussion that defends a predefined position. Read honestly, Bock's essay does more to damage the reputation of Jesus as God than it does to establish it, as I will discuss

---

[1] Darrell Bock is a New Testament scholar and research Professor at Dallas Theological Seminary in Dallas, Texas.

below. Bock seems to take for granted the existence of God and the credibility of the Bible, which are the specific areas under dispute. Hence, Bock is not arguing for the existence of God.

Bock immediately hits upon one of the problems of Jesus's use of the phrase. It means a human being, and that is how it is used throughout the Old Testament. In fact, its use in Numbers 23:19 explicitly states that God is not a "son of man." It is thought that Jesus's use of the term refers to Daniel 7:13, where the NIV has the footnote: "The Aramaic phrase *bar enash* means *human being*. The phrase son of man is retained here because of its use in the New Testament as a title of Jesus, probably based largely on this verse."

But Daniel 7 is explicitly a dream that Daniel had, so it should not be afforded any special attention. Also, the phrase used in 7:13 is "there came with the clouds of the sky one *like* a son of man" Note the words "like" and "a." So Daniel is saying that there was someone who looked like a human and descended on a cloud in glory. So if Jesus claimed to be the son of man, then he claims to be is saying that he *is* human. He says that he is the son of man, not that he is like a son of man[2].

Interestingly, historians who have looked at this have drawn several reasonably reliable conclusions, none of them supportive of Bock's position.

Firstly, Jesus's use of the term "Son of Man" supports the view, widely accepted among historians, that Jesus was an apocalypticist, believing that the end times were imminent[3]. He was wrong, and the end times did not arrive.

Secondly, Jesus sometimes refers to himself as the Son of Man, but sometimes seems to refer to someone else[4]. Though Christians often suggest that Jesus was referring to himself in the third person, Ehrman argues convincingly that Jesus believed that in the near future a cosmic figure known as the son of man would arrive to herald in a new age. Later Christians began to believe that Jesus was himself the son of man and adjusted some of his sayings to make this explicit. In other words, Jesus

---

[2] Jesus uses the phrase "the son of man" (not "like a son of man") 28 times in Matthew, 13 times in Mark, 25 times in Luke, and 12 times in John. In Acts the phrase is used once, said by Stephen describing his vision just before he is stoned. In Hebrews is it used once, quoting Psalms, referring to a human being. In the Revelation it is used twice, but in the phrase "like a son of man." It is not used elsewhere in the New Testament.

[3] Bart Ehrman, *Did Jesus Exist?: The Historical Argument for Jesus of Nazareth.* He makes the case for this forcefully, including his statements in Mark, his association with John the Baptist, the circumstances leading to his crucifixion, and the apocalyptic beliefs of the early church. I will discuss this in more detail in Chapter 33.

[4] Mark 8:38: "For whoever will be ashamed of me and of my words in this adulterous and sinful generation, the Son of Man also will be ashamed of him, when he comes in his Father's glory, with the holy angels."

probably did not call himself the son of man at all.

Bock's essay attempts to show that Jesus claimed to be God. I do not particularly dispute this point. Jesus, as he is portrayed in the Bible rather than the actual historical Jesus, probably claimed to be God, especially in the later Gospel of John (we will come back to this in the next two chapters). But he also claimed in Matthew 16:28 that "there are some standing here who will in no way taste of death, until they see the Son of Man coming in his Kingdom." This is yet more evidence that Jesus was a deluded apocalypticist, who thought the end times would be within the lifetime of some of his disciples. It is also not a claim to *be* the son of man, but rather that the son of man would soon arrive.

Once again, the theologian is put on the defensive and is required to redefine what "tasting death" and "coming in his kingdom" actually mean. Jesus is a bit vague on his meaning, deliberately it seems at least sometimes[5]. This makes space for the creative theologian to find symbols, signs, pointers, allusions, and meaning everywhere. But such sophistry misses the fundamental point: what is the initial reason to believe? Bock presents none.

---

[5] After Jesus tells the Parable of the Sower in Mark 4:1–8, he is alone with his disciples who ask him what it means, and he responds (Mark 4:11–12):

> "To you is given the mystery of God's Kingdom, but to those who are outside, all things are done in parables, that 'seeing they may see, and not perceive; and hearing they may hear, and not understand; lest perhaps they should turn again, and their sins should be forgiven them."'

A less inclusive message is hard to find.

CHAPTER **30**

The Son of God

Entitled "The Son of God," Ben Witherington III's[1] essay continues the discussion on another significant title of Jesus, which we will now consider.

Witherington offers a very tentative argument trying again to establish that Jesus believed that he was divine. He notes that the phrase the Son of God

> often connotes divinity in modern Christian discussions, but it seldom did so in Jewish antiquity. It is true that sometimes angels were called sons of God (see Gen. 6:2), but when Jews thought about a son of God they normally thought of a king anointed by God. For example, it is perfectly clear in Psalm 2 that the discussion is about the Davidic King who has been anointed by the high priest and thereby [crowned] as king.

He notes that Psalm 2 says "You are my son. Today I have become your father," while Mark 1:11 says "You are my beloved Son" in the baptism of Jesus. Witherington says that the omission of the second phrase is significant

> because Mark does not want to suggest that Jesus was merely adopted as God's Son at the point of baptism. Rather, the

---
[1]Ben Witherington III is a Bible scholar and Amos Professor of New Testament for Doctoral Studies at Asbury Theological Seminary and on the doctoral faculty at St. Andrews University in Scotland.

baptism is the juncture where the Father confirms to the Son the identity he has always had, and that will now be publicly revealed.

Witherington notes that there

> can be no doubt, however, that Jesus did not view his relationship to God as simply identical to the relationship King David had with God. For one thing, it tells us a lot about Jesus that he prayed to God as *Abba*, which is the Aramaic term of endearment, which means dearest Father.

He asks:

> What sort of person could Jesus be if he thought he could not only save people but give people alienated from God a relationship with God unlike any that human beings had had previously? This in itself implies a lot about Jesus's self-understanding.

He also considers Matthew 11:27, "No one knows the Son, except the Father; neither does anyone know the Father, except the Son, and he to whom the Son desires to reveal him." Witherington notes that Jesus:

> sees himself as knowing God in a way and to a degree that others do not, and furthermore, he sees himself as the conduit or unique mediator of that knowledge to other human beings. Not only so, but Jesus is said to get to choose whom he reveals this intimate knowledge to. While this does not in itself prove that Jesus thought of himself as divine, this saying puts Jesus in a unique and unprecedented position when it comes to the knowledge of God, and also in his role as the dispenser of the knowledge of God. It is not a surprise that Paul, some thirty-five or so years later, would stress, 'For there is one God and one mediator between God and men, the man Christ Jesus, who gave himself as a ransom for all' (1 Tim. 2:5–6 NIV). Later Christian theology was right to draw the inference that if Jesus was indeed the mediator of the saving knowledge and power and presence of God, and it was right to see him as a mediator, then he had to be able to represent God to humankind, and humans to God. In short, he had to partake of both the nature of God and the nature of human beings.

Witherington also offers us the parables as one of the "indirect ways that Jesus revealed his identity to his disciples and others." He considers the parable of the vineyard[2]. Here the vineyard, a symbol of the Jewish people, is tended by a sequence of people, interpreted as prophets, priests, and kings, and then by the owner's "beloved son," taken (according to Witherington) to mean "only begotten son." Witherington asks: "Did he [Jesus] understand that he had a unique relationship to the Father because of his distinctive origins (see Matthew 1 on the virginal conception)? This seems a plausible deduction."

Witherington finishes:

> The title Son of God, while more frequently conveying royalty than divinity in early Judaism, nonetheless had overtones of divinity for the very good reason that in the wider culture that surrounded Israel, kings were quite readily believed to be God's son in a divine sense. Certainly, when this title was used by someone like Paul to speak of Jesus to gentiles in the Greco-Roman world, the title must have sometimes carried this sort of significance. It is important to recognize then that it was Jesus's own use of the term Son of God that set this train of thought in motion, even though it was more fully amplified, explained, and expounded on after Jesus's death by Paul and various others.

Response

There is a chain of reasoning implied here: Did the biblical Jesus believe in his own divinity? If so, did the historical Jesus do so? If so, was he correct? In this chain, the only one with a supernatural element to it is the last. But Witherington is acknowledging that even the first of these is in serious doubt, with the result that the rest of it is moot.

Looking through his arguments, it should be apparent that the words ascribed to Jesus were not convincing divinity claims. That Witherington is defending a predefined outcome is very clear when we contrast the Son of Man with the Son of God statements.

In the former (met in the previous chapter), we are told that Jesus's usage is meant to make us look back at the verses in Daniel 7 ("there came with the clouds of the sky one like a son of man"), ignore the 'like', and concentrate on the hints of divinity that Jesus omitted in the New Testament account.

With the latter, we are told to look back on the verses in Psalm 2 ("You are my son; today I have become your father") and note that the omission of the phrase containing "today" at Jesus's baptism (Mark 1:9–13

---

[2]Mark 12:1–12

and parallels) is significant: Witherington says that it "is omitted because Mark does not want to suggest that Jesus was merely adopted as God's Son at the point of his baptism."

So for the Son of Man, we are to look at the unquoted context and assume it applies to Jesus, while for the Son of God we are to ignore the unquoted context and assume that it does not apply to Jesus. Why do we treat these verses so differently? A skeptical mind would say that it is done to support a presupposed position.

A plain reading is that the Jewish terms were not linked to divinity. Paul explicitly says "man" in 1 Timothy 2:5–6 which Witherington quotes on page 202 and it is not even clear that the historical Jesus said all the things that are ascribed to him in the Bible since it was written down later as the theology was evolving.

The idea that Jesus thought he was special because of the virgin birth is highly suspect since the historical Jesus presumably never heard his supposed origin story: the stories in the gospels are incompatible with each other, and are probably what they appear to be: two separate myths that grew up to reconcile Jesus of Nazareth with the authors' understanding of the Old Testament prophecies (see Chapter 27 on page 186).

Finally, Witherington states that surrounding cultures may have interpreted Son of God to mean divine and, rather than seeing this as syncretism, suggests that Jesus planned it as a stealthy way to reveal his divinity after he was gone. Objectively, the facts are that Jesus's Son of God statements were not divinity claims in Jesus's culture, and that the surrounding cultures re-interpreted them later. Once again we are asked to assume that God acted in a way that is indistinguishable from what would happen if He did not exist at all, since an evolving religion is the most natural way to understand these facts.

One also has to ask how Witherington can quote Genesis 6:2 to show "that sometimes angels were called sons of God" with no further comment. Genesis 6:1–2 says "When men began to multiply on the surface of the ground, and daughters were born to them, God's sons saw that men's daughters were beautiful, and they took any that they wanted for themselves as wives." This looks like the angels had the same weak concept of consent as the society that wrote the Bible. When you see a story with heavenly beings behaving with the same antiquated and immoral value system as the culture writing the story, it is convincing evidence that they invented the heavenly beings. The same applies to the ten commandments[3], or when

---

[3]I wrote an essay on the ten commandments called *What about the teachings?* It is available at glentonjelbert.com/what-about-the-teachings.

Jesus called the Canaanite women a dog[4].

So how can these stories be better understood? I think two other lenses cast more light than Witherington's approach. The first is to see it as a story evolving and developing over time. The second is to ask why this story grew to a position of such prominence.

Firstly, we can plainly see the growth of the stories of Jesus, in which biographical details were added over time. Following this same arc is the shift from rigid Jewish monotheism to the modern doctrine of the Trinity. Paul and the early gospels do not see Jesus as God, but by the time John is written Jesus's divinity is more accepted. It is only after the Bible is written that the doctrine of the Trinity is developed to reconcile Jesus's divinity to monotheism: in the immortal words of Alan Bennett, "Three in one, one in three, perfectly straightforward. Any doubts about that see your maths master."

Witherington's essay shows that Jesus did not teach the doctrine of the Trinity. Even John 10:30 ("I and the Father are one") merely indicates a special relationship, similar to Witherington's discussion of Matthew 11:27 (quoted on page 202).

The risen Jesus is reported to have commanded the disciples to baptize all the nations in the name of the Father, and of the Son, and of the Holy Spirit[5]. But even this cannot be seen as historical since in Acts baptism was done in the name of Jesus alone, and Peter was reluctant to spread the message beyond the Jews[6], not to all the nations. In other words, it is more likely that these words were attributed to Jesus during the later development of the Christian theology.

And what of the phrase "Son of God"? What did it mean to Jesus and his followers? It is explicitly linked to David being called God's Son in Psalm 2. The house of David was supposed to last forever[7], and when the Babylonians disproved this in the 6th century BCE, the idea of a Messiah arose, a human king who would re-establish the throne of David.

Christians may no longer see it this way, but that is how it was in Jesus's day. So when the Gospels say "Son of God," it is not a claim to divinity: it is a claim to be David's heir, the Messiah, the King of Israel, or the King

---

[4]Matthew 15:21–28

[5]Matthew 28:16–20

[6]Acts 10 describes Peter's vision in which he is allowed to eat unclean animals and how this is interpreted to mean that there should be a mission to the gentiles also. He was reluctant before receiving this vision to "make disciples of all nations," even though we are to suppose that he was present for Jesus's great commission in Matthew 28:16–20. The most straightforward way of understanding this is that these words were put into Jesus's mouth by Christians of Matthew's day.

[7]2 Samuel 7:16: "Your house and your kingdom will be made sure forever before you. Your throne will be established forever."

of the Jews. Jesus thought of himself this way and the Romans ultimately killed him for it (on the charge of being King of the Jews).

Many of the references to the Son of God in the Gospels are directly linked to the Messiah or Christ. For example, Mark begins "The beginning of the Good News of Jesus Christ, the Son of God." (Mark 1:1). It then leads straight into Jesus's baptism with a reference to Psalm 2 ("And a voice came from heaven: 'You are my Son,'" Mark 1:11). Mark 14:61 has Jesus before the Sanhedrin:

> Again the high priest asked him, "Are you the Christ, the Son of the Blessed?"

The same scene in Matthew 26:63 has the high priest say:

> "[T]ell us whether you are the Christ, the Son of God."

John 1:49 has Nathanael declaring:

> "Rabbi, you are the Son of God! You are King of Israel!"

Other references to the Son of God occur when Jesus does something powerful, such as casting out demons or walking on water, or when he is mocked for failing to do something powerful, such as the temptation in the wilderness or the criminals on the cross next to him. Either way, the Son of God is linked to acts of power, just like the Messiah. The demons recognize him, and Jesus tells them not to tell anyone, perhaps an acknowledgment of the danger of claiming to be the Messiah[8].

The first lens, then, suggests that we read the Biblical books in the order they were written, and track the arc of the developing religion. The second asks why this religion might have developed to its current level of dominance. It is clear that humanity has a propensity for religious thinking. The success of obvious scams like Mormonism or Scientology is an embarrassment to the claim of human rationality and demonstrates that reason is something that does not just happen: it requires effort. That effort, sadly, is all too easily redirected into the defense of an entrenched position.

If we consider the vast tapestry of religious claims and personalities competing for success in humanity's collective conscience, we can see it as something akin to evolution. Religions that appeal to some proportion of the population and have a tendency to spread dominate to a greater extent than those that do not. So the second lens suggests that rather than try

---

[8]Luke 4:41

to force Christianity into a truth claim and make it coherent (something plainly difficult to do), we consider what characteristics the religion has that caused it to be successful.

Christianity values faith and obedience over reason; it upholds church authorities and gives them appealing levels of control; it undermines self-worth, making us question our own senses and reasoning abilities; it promotes wishful thinking with ideas of eternal life and eventual justice; and it exhorts its practitioners to proselytize. It is not hard to imagine that a religion with these characteristics would be successful. Note, success here does not equate to good or true. It is simply a question of what works in the environment of the human mind. I will discuss this idea more in Chapter 51. I am not claiming that this speculation is necessarily accurate, but rather that this could be a useful way to understand the existence of religions and religious texts.

All of this discussion, though fascinating in its own way, does not elevate Witherington's essay to one that constitutes evidence for God. The unswerving defense of a position is, in fact, inimical to the search for truth. Note, that I am not here defending a belief, but rather presenting a response as to why I do not find the evidence for theism convincing. The burden of proof is on the one making a claim, in this case, the theist. If no theist proof is persuasive, the rational response is not to accept theism: this is the precise definition of atheism.

Witherington's essay does not even attempt to provide such evidence. He argues that the Biblical Jesus claimed he was divine, but does not establish that the Bible accurately relates what the historical Jesus said, or that there is such a thing as divinity, or that Jesus or his followers were accurate in their claims. In fact, when looked at closely, Witherington's argument supports the notion that Jesus claimed to be the Messiah, but not that he claimed to be God.

CHAPTER 31

Jesus as God

Next, Ben Witherington III continues from the previous chapter where he argued that Jesus saw himself as divine. As mentioned previously such an argument cannot be properly considered to be evidence for God. Firstly, there is the gap between what is attributed to Jesus and what Jesus actually did. Secondly, many people have claimed to be God, so such a claim does nothing for the cause. And thirdly, it is begging the question to discuss this when the existence of God has not been established.

Witherington begins by acknowledging some of the issues with this discussion:

> It is safe to say that no Jew before the time of Jesus viewed God as a Trinity ... The term god wherever it occurs in the Old Testament refers to Yahweh, or to some false pagan god. In the New Testament as well, the term *theos* refers almost always only to God the Father, though there are some seven places in the New Testament where this Greek term is used of Jesus.

Witherington then seeks to understand why Jesus did not plainly state his divinity:

> If we try to think as Jesus thought, in his own environment, it becomes clear why Jesus did not parade around Galilee saying, 'Hi, I'm God.' The reason is obvious—this would have been

understood to mean, 'I am Yahweh' or as Christians would put
it, 'I am the Heavenly Father' and would have led to his being
stoned on the spot.

He acknowledges that John 10:31 ("I and the Father are one") speaks
to a special relationship, rather than one being or divinity. He claims that
"Jesus chooses different ways, less prone to misunderstanding, to reveal his
special and divine identity."
He states that:

> One of these ways is clear enough in Mark 12:34–40. Jesus in
> this discussion suggests that [the] Messiah will be David's Lord.
> He, of course, chooses the method of indirection, so the audience
> will have to tease their minds into active thought to figure out
> what he means, but the implication is there nevertheless.

He also alludes to the references to the "Son of Man" and its link with
Daniel 7, saying that "the title with the most divine overtones is *Son of
Man* rather than *Son of God.*"
There are "other indirect ways" that Jesus reveals his divinity. Jesus
precedes his pronouncements with the term *amen*. He does not say "thus
sayeth the Lord." He speaks on his own authority with the phrase "you
have heard it said ... but I say to you" (Matthew 5:21), which "speaks
volumes in a culture where everybody cited earlier authorities to validate
their points." Jesus also "feels free" to make changes to the Mosaic law
in various ways. Some of Jesus's parables and actions also show what he
thought of himself.
He concludes that:

> Jesus, unique among his contemporaries, chose to reveal his
> divine nature in his own way, in his own words, and in his
> own good time, and for good measure he came back on Easter
> Sunday morning to reconfirm these truths to his frightened and
> flawed disciples.

Response

As discussed in the previous chapter, this is not evidence for the existence
of God. What Jesus thought or did not think of himself is irrelevant in the
absence of evidence for God. Plenty of people have made such claims, and
humanity routinely rejects all but their own religions, where their skepticism

suddenly falters. Jesus's claims only make sense in the light of the Old Testament claims, which are equally unsupported.

Witherington mentions the resurrection appearance at the end to "re-confirm these truths," but the resurrection does not 'confirm' anything, supported as it is by only weak and contradictory evidence, as we shall see in Chapter 35. Witherington begs the question by assuming the resurrection. I used to be a Christian based on what I was assured was the good evidence for the resurrection. A closer examination of that evidence caused me to reject Christianity and adopt my current position.

Later I came to realize the significance of the fact that the Old Testament does not predict the resurrection at all, so it does not confirm anything. It is not associated with the Son of God, the Son of Man, the Messiah, God or anything else. Therefore, even if it happened, it would not support any of Jesus's claims.

Witherington makes statements like "If we try to think as Jesus thought . . . it becomes clear" and "He, of course, chooses the method of indirection, so the audience will have to tease their minds into active thought to figure out what he means."

These are problematic for me. I think it is alway risky to suppose that you know someone else's motives. But, more germane to this discussion, Witherington is ascribing motives to Jesus that reconcile an issue that only exists if you believe that Jesus is God. In other words, Jesus appears to be reticent to state that he is God, and the natural conclusion is that he did not do so and therefore is not. But Witherington is creating a motive for Jesus that bridges the gap between the evidence and Witherington's own beliefs. This does not make for a valid or convincing argument.

In Chapter 29, I looked at the *Son of Man*. It is notable that Witherington admits that "the title with the most divine overtones is *Son of Man* rather than *Son of God*" because of the "allusions" to Daniel 7:13–14. In Daniel, it refers to one who is "*like* a son of man," or more accurately "like a human being." In other words, it affirms the notion that son of man refers to a human: Daniel is dreaming about a divine figure who is compared with a man; Jesus just calls himself a man. To infer divinity from Jesus's statement that he is a man, or perhaps "the man," is tenuous at best. As discussed in Chapter 29, it is likely that Jesus thought of the Son of Man as a divine figure who would descend in power from the clouds within the lives of his followers—many of the Gospel references make more sense if understood this way. His later followers came to identify Jesus with the Son of Man, and these verses also appear in the Gospels.

The seven "theos" statements are interesting, and much ink has been spilled over them. Daniel Wallace wrote a textual examination of it from a

Christian perspective[1]. But even this sympathetic treatment admits:

> No author of a synoptic gospel [Matthew, Mark, and Luke] explicitly ascribes the title θεός [theos] to Jesus. Jesus never uses the term θεός for himself. No sermon in the Book of Acts attributes the title θεός to Jesus. No extant Christian confession(s) of Jesus as θεός exists earlier than the late 50s ... And possibly the biggest problem for [New Testament] Christology regarding this topic is that textual variants exist in every potential passage where Jesus is explicitly referred to as θεός.

To say that this looks like an evolving understanding over the course of the time it took to write the New Testament is probably not even very controversial. But to claim that Jesus had knowledge of this and chose not to share it is a stretch, and cannot be called evidence.

Witherington also adduces Jesus's willingness to adjust the Mosaic Law as evidence that he believed in his own divinity. The example given is the law on the Sabbath. It certainly tells us he thinks he was special, but note his argument was more with the Pharisees' interpretation of how the law was to be applied. The Pharisees had developed complex rules to be sure that the law was kept, but most Jews of the time did not follow these additional rules, including Jesus[2]. In fact, Jesus explicitly affirms the immutability of the law[3], so it is not the case that he was unilaterally adjusting the Mosaic Law, but rather incorporating a different understanding of it.

But even if you grant Witherington his point that Jesus unilaterally adjusted the Mosaic Law, you are thrown into a quagmire of contradictions. In this case, for example, he says that Jesus overturned the teaching on the Sabbath. But we are at the same time asked to believe that the Sabbath teaching came directly from God in the ten commandments and that the ten commandments constitute divine wisdom apparently unfiltered by human prophets since it is the only part of the Bible written by God directly. So how are we supposed to understand this? Witherington did not give us his answer to this question, but again whatever answer is given, its purpose is to provide a motive for God to behave in a way that makes it look as though the Bible was a human construction.

---

[1] Daniel B. Wallace (who is also an author in *Evidence for God* of Chapter 43), *Jesus as Θεός (God): A Textual Examination.* Available at Bible.org/article/jesus-\%CE\%B8\%CE\%B5\%CF\%8C\%CF\%82-god-textual-examination.

[2] Bart Ehrman, *How Jesus Became God: The Exaltation of a Jewish Preacher from Galilee.*

[3] Matthew 5:18

Ultimately, it is clear that the *biblical* Jesus thought he was special. But the early biblical authors were unwilling to say that he was divine, and the obvious inference is that the people writing closest to when he lived did not believe it. Gradually, this changed, and the biblical authors began to believe in his divinity, though the paradox that this created was not resolved until the later church invented the trinity. The *historical* Jesus, on the other hand, probably did not say he was divine, but rather thought he was the King of the Jews for which treason he was ultimately crucified[4]. Pontius Pilate did not bother to differentiate between a theological King of the Jews and a political one. Fascinating though this historical study is, none of it can be taken as evidence for the existence of God.

---

[4]See Bart Ehrman, *Did Jesus Exist?: The Historical Argument for Jesus of Nazareth* for more on this.

CHAPTER **32**

Did Jesus Predict His Violent Death and Resurrection?

Craig A. Evans's[1] asks: "Did Jesus Predict His Violent Death and Resurrection?" It is to this discussion that we now turn.

Evans states that gospel critics have frequently asserted that Jesus's predictions of his death and resurrection "have long been recognized as secondary constructions of the church" (Evans quoting Rudolf Bultmann). The predictions are

> found in the Synoptic Gospels (see Mark 8:31; 9:31; 10:33–34; and parallels in Matthew and Luke). It must be admitted that these predictions have been edited in the light of the events that overtook Jesus. But there are very good reasons to believe that Jesus did, in fact, anticipate his violent death and his vindication by means of resurrection.

He goes on to list these reasons, and I will discuss them in my response below.

Response

Teasing apart events after the fact is difficult, and will require us to be ruthless in our application of logic and objectivity. This is particularly true

---

[1] Craig Evans is the John Bisagno Distinguished Professor of Christian Origins and Dean of the School of Christian Thought at Houston Baptist University in Texas.

when determining what predictions were made before certain events when
they were written about after them.

In Evans's discussion of the prediction of Jesus's death, he confuses
Jesus's ability to assess his risk of death with his ability to predict his death.
For example, after John F. Kennedy's assassination in 1963, Martin Luther
King Jr. told his wife, "This is what is going to happen to me also." This
is just a risk assessment, which happened to be accurate, not a prediction.
No-one ascribes supernatural powers to Martin Luther King Jr. as a result
of this successful prediction. As for the discussion of the resurrection, Evans
assumes (or is convinced) that it happened. Predictions of things that do
not happen are commonplace. Jesus may well have believed he was going
to rise again, but without convincing evidence of the resurrection, it just
marks him as deluded. I will address the evidence for the resurrection in
Chapter 35.

Evans first discusses Jesus's anticipation of his violent death. He says:

> [T]he fate of John the Baptist surely portended to Jesus his
> own fate. The close association of Jesus and John is highly
> probable, so it is reasonable to assume that in continuing John's
> proclamation of repentance and the appearance of the kingdom
> of God, Jesus surely recognized his danger.

Related to John, "Jesus tells the parable of the Wicked Tenants (see
Mark 12:1–12), implying that the 'son' of the vineyard owner (i.e., Jesus)
will be murdered."

In as much as these stories are true, they demonstrate Jesus's awareness
of the risks he faced at the hands of religious people who stood ready to
murder on behalf of their best understanding of the will of their God. He
was right to be fearful of religion: his was neither the first nor the last blood
spilled by religious people following their God with zeal. But fearing what
people could do is merely a sensible precaution, then as now. It does not
validate any claim Jesus may have made to divinity. Jesus's association with
John the Baptist also supports the view that Jesus was an apocalypticist[2],
which I will discuss in the next chapter.

Evans continues that:

> Perhaps the most compelling evidence that Jesus anticipated
> his death is seen in the garden prayer, on the eve of his arrest,
> in which Jesus exhibits his fear in view of impending events.
> Falling on his face, Jesus says: 'Abba! Father! All things are
> possible for You; remove this cup from Me; yet not what I will,
> but what You will' (Mark 14:36 NASB).

[2]Bart Ehrman, *Did Jesus Exist?: The Historical Argument for Jesus of Nazareth*

Evans believes that this must be authentic because early Christians would not "invent an utterance in which Jesus appears frightened and reluctant to go to his death." He says that he is invoking "the 'criterion of embarrassment,' whereby it is understood that it is improbable that the early church would have invented material that would become the source of its own embarrassment." He contrasts this with John, which portrays Jesus with more dignity. This, of course, undermines John as a valid historical source and reflects instead evidence for the evolving nature of the religion.

But is Evans' "criterion of embarrassment" really so convincing? Though a valid historical technique in general, one has to apply it carefully, or it will devolve into an argument from incredulity. Has Evans turned over every stone looking for other explanations? There are a number of issues.

Firstly, Jesus's anguish at the thought of his death supports the idea that Mark believed that Jesus was more man than God.

Secondly, the anguish, courage, and sacrifice are beautiful rather than embarrassing. This may be the most moving verse in all scripture.

Thirdly, any embarrassment is plausibly resolved by considering the possible evolution of the story. Isaiah 53[3] sets a psychological backdrop for the religion: someone would need to suffer for us to be saved. Of course, Jesus was not actually crushed but crucified, and a reading of Isaiah 53 suggests suffering and recovery rather than death and resurrection. In any event, in applying this symbol filled passage to Jesus, myriad problems arise, such as how does the resurrection work, did God plan it, and, of relevance here, how did Jesus feel about the prospect of death?

Paul (writing first) is very clear that this was all God's will, not even mentioning Judas for example, and can discuss the matter dispassionately. For example, Colossians 1:19–20:

> For all the fullness was pleased to dwell in him; and through him
> to reconcile all things to himself, by him, whether things on the
> earth, or things in the heavens, having made peace through the
> blood of his cross.

Paul does not include any mental anguish that Jesus might have had in this description.

But if Jesus was God and he was sent by God to suffer through God's will to save us from God's judgment, was Jesus really suffering? Here is a fine line to walk: God in Jesus has to suffer, or there will be no salvation; Jesus cannot suffer serendipitously or God is not sovereign, so God must have inflicted it on him; but God cannot victimize his son, so Jesus must

---

[3]Consider Isaiah 53:5: "But he was pierced for our transgressions. He was crushed for our iniquities"

suffer willingly. How can this be resolved? Jesus's anguish in Mark 14:36 ties this theology up rather neatly, even if it is inconsistent with John and the epistles.

So, far from being too embarrassing to be inauthentic, this may merely highlight a theological issue that arose and evolved very rapidly to reconcile the need for suffering with God's apparent cruelty. These kinds of wide discrepancies between the various accounts often occur when there is a theological issue driving a rapid change (we will see another example when considering Judas's culpability in Chapter 50).

Evans also notes that:

> Jesus told his disciples to take up the cross and come after him (see Mark 8:34) ... What is interesting here is that, in a sense, Jesus himself fails to do what he taught his disciples. When the time came to take up his cross, he could not do it; someone else carried his cross (see Mark 15:21). The tension between the saying and what later actually happens strongly argues for the authenticity of the saying, for post-Easter fiction would have Jesus say something fully consistent with the events of the passion.

Again, this is an argument from incredulity. And again there are other solutions. It is unlikely that the religion was manufactured maliciously or knowingly. The authors probably sincerely believed what they wrote and sought out stories from the community in good faith. The inconsistencies in the stories arose because different stories evolved in the community before they were written down. In a religiously-charged environment like this, stories could grow, and speculation could be retold as fact, and it all be done earnestly. This tension may indicate that the two stories evolved independently and the author of Mark wrote them both down faithfully. We can applaud him for not trying to smooth out this inconsistency, but this is an indication of his sincerity rather than the accuracy of the stories he was told.

So, while Jesus may well have understood the danger he was in, it is far from convincing that he predicted his violent death in the sense that Evans implies, with all the connotations of divinity.

Secondly, Evans asks: "Did Jesus anticipate his resurrection? It is probable that he did ... Had he not anticipated it, it would have been very strange, for pious Jews very much believed in the resurrection of the dead."

Here Evans is saying that belief in resurrection was common back then, so Jesus probably believed it of himself. It is a banal point. Indeed his disciples may have believed it of him too. Resurrections apparently happened all the time back then. Matthew 27:52–53 assures us that

> The tombs were opened, and many bodies of the saints who had
> fallen asleep were raised; and coming out of the tombs after his
> resurrection, they entered into the holy city and appeared to
> many.

This story in Matthew is not corroborated by anyone, not even the
rest of the Bible. On top of this, Jesus is said to have raised people from
the dead, but again this lacks corroboration outside of the scriptures. If
everyone back then was claiming resurrection, any statement that Jesus
may have made cannot be admitted as evidence that he was making a
prediction. If he said it, he was merely reflecting the *zeitgeist* of the time.

One of Jesus's predictions of his death leads to Matthew 16:28: "Most
certainly I tell you, there are some standing here who will in no way taste
of death, until they see the Son of Man coming in his Kingdom." This is a
prediction that is simply false, although theologians have spilled much ink
trying to explain the mystery.

Modern Christians would perhaps assert that "coming in his Kingdom"
refers to the resurrection of Jesus. But the Son of Man is an apocalyptic
figure, and the resurrection cannot be described as an apocalypse. For
example, the context of the previous verse (Matthew 16:27) states:

> For the Son of Man will come in the glory of his Father with
> his angels, and then he will render to everyone according to his
> deeds.

It requires significant interpretation to see the biblical resurrection story
in these words. The point is that if someone makes a number of "predictions," some true, some false, then they are just guessing. Even the Bible
warns us not to heed such people[4].

Also, note that this is one of the instances in which Jesus refers to the
Son of Man in the third person and that this is once again evidence that
Jesus was an apocalypticist (as discussed in Chapter 30).

For me, then, Evans's essay establishes nothing. Evans is implying that
Jesus made some divinely inspired predictions that came true and therefore
he must be God. Admittedly, he does not say this in as many words, so
I hope I am not overstating his case. But Jesus's "prediction" of death
turns out to be a risk assessment related to the danger associated with
apocalyptic teachings like those of John the Baptist. His "prediction" of

---

[4]Deuteronomy 18:22: "when a prophet speaks in the name of Yahweh, if the thing
doesn't follow, nor happen, that is the thing which Yahweh has not spoken: the prophet
has spoken it presumptuously, you shall not be afraid of him."
This verse also allows believers to re-interpret predictions after the fact in a way that
makes me scientifically uncomfortable.

his resurrection turns out to be a reflection of prevailing belief at the time. And his "prediction" that some of the people listening to him would not die until his (or the Son of Man's) second coming turns out to be untrue: even Christians must admit this (though they might re-interpret Jesus's statement). Evan's ignores straightforward explanations that explain the facts without resorting to the supernatural. Rationally, nothing he says requires the existence of God, and therefore, logically, one should not believe in God based on what he says. This means that his essay is not evidence for God in any meaningful sense, and it does not even establish that Jesus prophesied his death or his resurrection in a supernatural way.

CHAPTER 33

Can We Be Certain That Jesus Died on a Cross?

Evidence for Jesus's death on the cross will now be considered as we look at Michael R. Licona's[1] essay: "Can We Be Certain That Jesus Died on a Cross? A Look at the Ancient Practice of Crucifixion."

Licona responds to a well-known and long since abandoned line of skepticism: the "swoon" theory. If the Romans crucified someone, I would not bet my life against that person being successfully killed. This argument is often presented as an example of how desperate and foolish critics of the resurrection are. Wells[2] discusses:

> [T]he theory that Jesus did not die but merely 'swooned' on the cross, recovered consciousness in the cool tomb, crept out unnoticed when the earthquake rolled the stone away, and showed himself from time to time to his followers. Such nonsense is ... not the result of 'excessive criticism', but of yielding up only some of the traditional assumptions while clinging obstinately to others. In this example, belief in miracles has been surrendered, but the view that the gospels are based on eyewitness reports is retained, so that the miracle of resurrection is construed as a misunderstanding on the part of Jesus's entourage.

[1] Michael Licona has a Ph.D. in New Testament Studies (University of Pretoria). He serves as associate Professor in theology at Houston Baptist University.

[2] G. A. Wells, *Cutting Jesus Down to Size: What Higher Criticism Has Achieved and Where It Leaves Christianity.*

Wells goes on to note that "[i]t is equally unsatisfactory to trace the gospel resurrection narratives to deliberate lies by eyewitnesses of the crucifixion who concocted resurrection stories they knew to be false," a viewpoint I endorse: stories can grow by stages from speculation to fact in good faith. The recent examples of Mormonism or Scientology show similar growth, though in both those cases there is a prominent, central, delusional person.

To return to Licona's essay, he discusses four reasons why we should believe that Jesus died on a cross. Firstly, he mentions the Christian and non-Christian sources reporting Jesus's execution. Secondly, he states that "[o]nly one account exists of a person surviving crucifixion." Thirdly, he discusses crucifixion with two ER doctors, who support the notion of crucifixion generally being fatal. And lastly, he describes the swoon theory and asks "how likely is it that Jesus could have convinced his disciples in his wounded condition that he was the risen Lord of life in an immortal body." He concludes that "the historian must conclude that Jesus was crucified and that the process killed him."

Response

By itself, this chapter is not evidence for God. Licona is building towards Chapter 35 where the evidence for the resurrection will be considered. The challenge with the story is the resurrection, not the death. Although difficult to judge, it probably *is* more likely that someone "swooned" and somehow made a convincing reappearance than that Jesus was God somehow made into a man, while remaining fully God, so that he could be killed by men to save men from God/himself, but only if they believed that the above was factually accurate based on meager evidence. In other words, the alternative that Licona is offering us is so outrageous that almost anything else, however unlikely, becomes plausible. However, it is a false dichotomy, and there is a much simpler explanation available to us: the resurrection accounts are not accurate, which is more likely than either the swoon or the resurrection theories.

The preceding comments notwithstanding, we will accept that crucifixion was usually fatal, and that the swoon theory is far fetched. This is the thrust of Licona's second, third, and fourth points. These three points lead us to the conclusion that *if* Jesus was crucified, he died. Let us accept this as reasonable and move on. So Licona's second, third, and fourth arguments need not concern us anymore.

But what of his first? This is the point that Jesus's crucifixion is reported by many ancient sources, both Christian and non-Christian, and is the argument that attempts to establish that the crucifixion indeed occurred. This is Licona's first argument in full:

> Jesus's execution is reported in a number of ancient sources: Christian and non-Christian. In addition to the four Gospels and a number of letters contained in the New Testament, all of which were written in the first-century, Jesus's execution is even reported by a number of ancient non-Christian sources. Josephus (late first-century), Tacitus (early second-century), Lucian (early to mid second-century), and Mara bar Serapion (second to third centuries) all report the event. The fact that these non-Christians mentioned Jesus in their writings shows that Jesus's death was known outside of Christian circles and was not something the Christians invented.

To go through Licona's sources in reverse order: Mara bar Serapion, Lucian, and Tacitus are too late to be seen as confirmatory. Wells writes:

> Since the eighteenth century it has repeatedly been pointed out that, when Tacitus wrote that 'Christians derive their name and origin from Christ who was executed by sentence of the procurator Pontius Pilate in the reign of Tiberius' (*Annals*, 15:44), he was simply repeating uncritically what Christians of his day were saying. The Catholic scholar J.P. Meier allows that Tacitus, and Pliny too, both writing around A.D. 112, 'reflect what they heard Christians of their own day say' and are not 'independent extracanonical sources.'

Josephus wrote a paragraph about Jesus in *Antiquities of the Jews*, known as the *Testimonium Flavianum*[3]. This is the only extant extra-Biblical evidence to the historicity of Jesus, and is not considered original.

---

[3] In C.E. 93 Josephus published his history of the Jews. While discussing the period in which the Jews of Judea were governed by the Roman procurator Pontius Pilate, Josephus includes this passage, which has come to be called *The Testimonium Flavianum*:

> About this time there lived Jesus, a wise man, if indeed one ought to call him a man. For he was one who performed surprising deeds and was a teacher of such people as accept the truth gladly. He won over many Jews and many of the Greeks. He was the Messiah. And when, upon the accusation of the principal men among us, Pilate had condemned him to a cross, those who had first come to love him did not cease. He appeared to them spending a third day restored to life, for the prophets of God had foretold these things and a thousand other marvels about him. And the tribe of the Christians, so called after him, has still to this day not disappeared.

Even conservative Christians accept that at least some of the words were added by later, Christian scribes. For example, Paul L. Maier, who wrote Chapter 27, elsewhere argues that the passage cannot be entirely authentic because "no Jew could have claimed Jesus as the Messiah who rose from the dead without having converted to Christianity."[4]

So the sources supporting Jesus's execution all originate in Christianity. Wells regards the crucifixion of Jesus as legendary, stating that Paul created an ethereal Christ theology based on his visions of "the risen Lord," and that this merged with the story of Jesus of Nazareth. However, this view is not representative of the vast majority of scholarship, which accepts Jesus's crucifixion as historical[5]. The main reason to take the crucifixion of Jesus as historical is the criterion of embarrassment (which can properly be applied here): a community that believed the Messiah would be a military leader would not invent his ignominious death. With historical research, we cannot be certain of anything, but it seems that the Romans probably crucified Jesus of Nazareth and that this killed him.

How and why this happened is of interest to scholars, and Bart Ehrman describes a widely accepted scenario which I will outline here.

First, Ehrman notes that Jesus was almost certainly an apocalypticist, believing that the Son of Man was soon to descend in a cloud and put the Messiah back on the throne. Ehrman argues this convincingly and in detail, but the essential points are that Jesus starts and ends his ministry with apocalypticist views, and was therefore likely an apocalypticist the whole way through.

He starts with John the Baptist who was from the "repent for the end is nigh" mold. Luke 3:9 has him saying: "Even now the ax also lies at the root of the trees. Every tree therefore that doesn't produce good fruit is cut down, and thrown into the fire." The baptism is likely historical because early Christians would not have wanted a story suggesting that Jesus was inferior to John the Baptist.

The end of Jesus's ministry can be seen in the earliest Christian writings, in which Paul has a clear expectation that he would be alive when Jesus returned. For example, 1 Thessalonians 4:16–17 says:

> For the Lord himself will descend from heaven with a shout, with the voice of the archangel, and with God's trumpet. The dead in Christ will rise first, then *we who are alive*, who are left, will be caught up together with them in the clouds, to meet the Lord in the air. So we will be with the Lord forever.

[4]Paul L. Maier, *Eusebius: The Church History*.
[5]Bart Ehrman, *Did Jesus Exist?: The Historical Argument for Jesus of Nazareth*.

So the beginning and end are apocalyptic. Also, many sayings of Jesus are apocalyptic in nature. His first recorded words (Mark 1:15) are "The time is fulfilled, and God's Kingdom is at hand! Repent, and believe in the Good News." Mark 8:38–9:1 is even more explicit:

[Jesus said:] "For whoever will be ashamed of me and of my words in this adulterous and sinful generation, the Son of Man also will be ashamed of him, when he comes in his Father's glory, with the holy angels."

He said to them, "Most certainly I tell you, there are some standing here who will in no way taste death until they see God's Kingdom come with power."

This message evolves over the course of the time it takes to write the Bible since the apocalypse fails to come, but it seems to start that way. So Jesus was an apocalypticist who thought that heavenly beings were imminently going to arrive in power and glory.

Second, Jesus visited Jerusalem during the Passover, a time when Jews flooded Jerusalem and celebrated a previous occasion when God had freed them from their oppressors (there is no archæological evidence for the exodus from Egypt, but whether this was an historical event is not important here). Tensions and nationalistic fervor are high, particularly when the Jews are expecting a Messiah who will lead an armed revolution. Pilate is visiting Jerusalem from Caesarea to keep the peace. Jesus enters the temple complex, crowded with Jews from all over who are changing money (Roman coins, with the image of Caesar on them, would not be allowed into the temple) to buy animals for their sacrifices, and takes umbrage with what he sees as corruption. He makes a scene, throws over some tables and says that the temple is going to be destroyed.

Apparently, the imminent destruction of the temple was not an uncommon threat for apocalypticists in those days. Josephus records someone else doing so also, as some Jewish sects saw the temple as corrupt. In Mark 13:2 Jesus says "Do you see these great buildings? There will not be left here one stone on another, which will not be thrown down." This is not accurate as there are stones left on top of each other in the Western Wall to this day.

It also is unlikely that Jesus brought temple operations to a halt single-handedly[6]. The temple complex encompassed "an area roughly 500 yards by 325 yards", so it would require a small army to shut it down. Jesus also says that he will rebuild the temple in three days, which is taken as

---

[6]Mark 11:15–16

a prediction of his resurrection but reduces the impact of the prediction of the real temple's eventual destruction.

The chief priests and Sadducees do not take the disturbance well and report him to Pilate. But on what charge? Interestingly, he was crucified for being "King of the Jews," which ties in with the Romans wanting to quell any nationalistic fervor. The Romans decide who the king is, and if Jesus wanted to put himself in that role, they would not hesitate to make an example of him. In Chapter 30, I argued that Son of God was understood this way, and John 19:7,12 has the Jewish leaders make this conflict explicit: "...he ought to die, because he made himself the Son of God ... Everyone who makes himself a king speaks against Caesar!" In this scenario, the body would likely not be handed over for burial as it would be left for the animals as part of the punishment and as a deterrent to others.

Of course, Jesus never used the words "the King of the Jews"; but Ehrman presents the theory that he said this privately to his disciples. Matthew 19:28:

> Jesus said to them, "Most certainly I tell you that you who have
> followed me, in the regeneration when the Son of Man will sit
> on the throne of his glory, you also will sit on twelve thrones,
> judging the twelve tribes of Israel."

If the Son of Man has brought in the new age and the twelve disciples (including Judas—an embarrassment which speaks to the authenticity of this saying) are each ruling a tribe, then it is plausible that Jesus was ruling them as the King of Israel. This would then be Judas's betrayal: not where he was or who he was (both easily discovered without Judas) but what he was saying about himself.

In any event, what seems clear is that Jesus was taken before Pilate, found guilty of calling himself the Messiah, the King of the Jews and was immediately flogged and crucified. He was dead within six hours. So on this point, we will accept Licona's thesis. Of course, the crucifixion itself is not evidence for God. But the context of the crucifixion supports the position that Jesus was an apocalypticist, a deluded one since the apocalypse did not come. This delusion undermines the claims of his divinity.

CHAPTER 34

The Empty Tomb of Jesus

Your attention is now drawn to Gary Habermas's essay which presents evidence to support "the view that Jesus was buried in a tomb that was subsequently found to be empty." He discusses seven of "the more than twenty arguments that have been cited in favor of the empty tomb." As mentioned in the previous chapter, Jesus's body was probably left to rot on the cross, so we will need to examine these lines of evidence closely.

The first argument, which Habermas regards as "perhaps the most powerful" is the tomb's location in Jerusalem. Habermas states that:

> [I]t is precisely since Jesus's grave was located nearby that we have a serious problem if it were anything but empty. Unless Jesus's tomb was unoccupied, the early Christian preaching would have been disproved on the spot. How could it be preached that Jesus had been raised from the dead if that message were starkly confronted by a rotting body?

Secondly, we have the

> unanimous agreement that women were the first witnesses to the empty tomb ... But why should these writers highlight female testimony unless the women really were the first to discover this fact? To do so would be to weaken their case considerably in the eyes of most listeners.

227

Third, while the empty tomb accounts in the Gospels are later than Paul's writings, it is crucially important that the empty tomb accounts are witnessed by many. In other words, whichever major view of Gospel origins one takes, the empty tomb narratives arose from more than one independent source.

Fourth, most recent scholars seem to agree that, while Paul does not explicitly mention the empty tomb, the early tradition that this apostle reported to others in 1 Corinthians 15:3–4 implies an empty tomb.

Habermas acknowledges that this point is not as strong as it could be since "Paul does not specifically mention the empty tomb."

Fifth, Habermas adduces the sermon found in Acts 13, which is attributed to Paul and "clearly teaches that Jesus's body was placed in a tomb. Then he was raised and appeared to his followers without undergoing any bodily decomposition." Habermas argues that if this sermon is indeed Paul, then he is tacitly acknowledging an empty tomb.

Sixth, according to reports found in Matthew 28:11–15, Justin Martyr, and Tertullian, for almost two centuries or more, the Jewish leaders tried to explain that the tomb was empty because Jesus's disciples stole his body. This means that the Jewish hierarchy even acknowledged the fact that Jesus's body was no longer there!

Habermas believes this supports the existence of the empty tomb, but that we cannot accept the Jewish leaders' explanation since the disciples were willing to die for their beliefs.

Lastly, Habermas mentions the work of N. T. Wright and others.

In the ancient world—whether pagan, Jewish, or Christian—writings up until the second-century AD were in complete agreement that the very definition of resurrection was clearly a bodily notion ... This would indicate that Jesus's resurrection was conceived in a bodily manner, necessitating that the tomb was empty.

Habermas concludes:

In light of arguments such as those we have produced here, this conclusion seems to be very difficult to avoid. The normal application of historical rules to the various data indicates that, just shortly after his death, Jesus's tomb was indeed found empty.

Response

I do not find his seven arguments convincing, as I will demonstrate below when I go through them. We should also not miss that all the arguments Habermas presents stem from Christian sources, and even these are diluted by internal disagreements and contradictions as we will see.

Firstly, Habermas discusses the location of the alleged tomb, stating that since the Gospels are unanimous that it was in Jerusalem, Christianity could easily have been exposed. This presupposes that someone wanted to do so at the time. But if this tradition only evolved later, then no-one at the time would have known to check. Note that Acts 1:15 places the Christian community back then at one hundred and twenty (in a city of 25–30,000) hardly enough to have their claims checked by the authorities.

There are also reasons to believe that Paul imagined that Jesus was taken up to heaven immediately on his death; his appearances are a spiritual body visiting from heaven. This certainly was Paul's experience on the Damascus road, and so early Christians would not even have considered Jesus's dead body as relevant. As mentioned in the previous chapter, it is probable that Pilate would not have released the body for burial anyway, so the tomb would not have entered into it.

Habermas does not address this objection, instead countering straw man arguments:

> A creative response might be to assert that perhaps the body was indeed in the tomb, but that, very soon afterward, the body would have been unrecognizable, due to its decomposition. Or perhaps the tomb was still simply closed without being opened for inspection. But these questions entirely miss the point of the Christian preaching that the tomb was empty. Therefore, if any body was found in Jesus's tomb, whether Jesus's or even someone else's, or if it were still closed, this would have contradicted the teaching that it was *empty*. In Jerusalem, the mistake would have been exposed in no time.

Habermas is assuming that there was a tomb for inspection, but this is unlikely. Even on the point of it being open or closed the narrative is disjointed: Matthew has the women arriving at a closed tomb, which is then opened by an angel. But Jesus had already gone, so why bother opening it? And why is the tomb open in the other accounts if Jesus can escape with it closed?

Habermas's argument makes two assumptions: firstly, that the gospels are reliable, which is what he is trying to establish; and secondly that anyone of significance would care about Christianity enough to set about disproving it *at the time.*

The gospels are clearly not disinterested here and contradict each other, and the rest of the New Testament, on this very issue (How many women visit the tomb? Are there guards there or not? Is the tomb open or closed when Jesus leaves? How many angels are there? When do they appear? These questions are answered differently in the different Gospel accounts).

The disciples are represented as dispirited after Jesus's death (which is plausible), either hiding in Jerusalem or fishing in Galilee depending on which story you follow, so no-one would have cared enough to check.

But couldn't people have gone to check the tomb years later after Christianity gained momentum? Again, it is hard to know what happened, but there is no record of anyone having done so. Christian teachings explicitly encouraged belief without sight, so perhaps then, as now, it was considered too skeptical to check the claims.

To explore the Christian context of belief without sight, consider John 20:29 where Jesus says to Doubting Thomas: "Blessed are those who have not seen, and have believed." Or Paul in 1 Corinthians 1:19: "I will destroy the wisdom of the wise, I will bring the discernment of the discerning to nothing." Or Hebrews 11:1: "Now faith is assurance of things hoped for, proof of things not seen." Modern Christians will sometimes repudiate this with 1 Thessalonians 5:21 ("Test all things, and hold firmly that which is good"), but contextually this is actually exhorting *more* acceptance of prophecy, not less, and is suggesting goodness as a test of truth, counter to scientific practice and common sense.

As for non-Christians, there is no record of anyone checking one way or the other. Even if someone had checked, their first assumption on finding an empty tomb would not be that the occupant had risen from the dead, so it is not clear that it is a claim worth checking.

Secondly, Habermas notes that it is impressive that all four gospels mention the women who visit the tomb, despite it being apparently unsupportive of their case. I would agree that this is impressive. But this argues against the malicious or deceitful creation of the story by the authors of the gospel, rather than for the veracity of the stories themselves. This might seem a subtle distinction, but it is important if the origin of the Bible is to be understood. The gospel authors almost certainly sought to understand and relay what they believed happened (albeit with a theological overlay in some cases). But if the gospel writers wrote that women discovered the tomb, it is probable that they believed it.

However, again, the origin of these stories can be explained, and in fact explained better, in terms of very human behavior. Note that Paul knows nothing about these women and does not even mention the tomb (a point we will return to below). Mark has the women visiting the tomb, but not telling anyone[1]; the women in the later gospels are not so shy. This discrepancy might naturally come about if the story were not widely known when Mark wrote, and so this fact needed explanation. When the later gospels were written, the story was common knowledge, and so the women's reticence was not necessary and could be dropped with some amount of sincerity.

In Mark the women go to anoint the body with spices. Luke also has the women taking spices, expecting to be able to enter the tomb. But in Matthew, the women are planning simply to look at the tomb[2]. This discrepancy arises because Matthew introduces the guards, who are not mentioned anywhere else in the canonical Bible. He adds the guards for the specific apologetic purpose of defending the notion that the body was stolen[3], but it causes the various stories of the women visiting the tomb to be incompatible.

This is not separate witnesses looking at the same event from different angles, as is sometimes claimed. Matthew had a copy of Mark and changed it, so the differences do not suggest a lack of collusion: the collusion happened. It shows that Matthew was not convinced that Mark was a reliable source and that Matthew was willing to introduce narrative to defend his position.

Also, the women's visit to the tomb would have originated with the women themselves. Mark has Mary Magdalene, Mary the mother of James, and Salome visiting the tomb. Matthew drops Salome. Luke has Mary Magdalene, Joanna, Mary the mother of James, and "the others with them." John has just Mary Magdalene. So Mary Magdalene is common, but who else? The only four sources we have of this event supposedly originate with the women themselves: Mark has three women; Matthew two; Luke has at least five; John just has one.

What they see varies across the accounts also. Mark has the stone already rolled back and "a young man dressed in a white robe sitting on the right side" as they enter the tomb; Matthew has an angel descend from heaven and roll back the stone in front of them (even though Jesus has already somehow left the closed tomb); Luke has them enter the empty tomb, and two men suddenly appear standing next to them; John has two angels sitting in the tomb already when Mary looks in.

---

[1] Mark 16:8: "They went out, and fled from the tomb, for trembling and astonishment had come on them. *They said nothing to anyone*; for they were afraid."

Compare this with Luke 24:9: "[They] returned from the tomb, and *told all these things to the eleven, and to all the rest.*"

[2] Compare Mark 16:1 and Luke 24:1 with Matthew 28:1.

[3] Matthew 28:11–15

All this suggests that the gospel writers did not interview the women directly themselves and that this story evolved over time in the community. Certainly, it is not very convincing evidence that there was an underlying event involving an empty tomb. Again, I do not dispute that the gospel authors believed it. I suppose that they interviewed people in the community in good faith and related a version of what they heard. But the credibility of the gospels is severely undermined, and the growth of the story suggests that we are seeing the evolution of a legend.

Third, Habermas states that there are several independent narratives because there are several different witnesses to the empty tomb. Habermas states that "scholars think that there could be as many as three or four independent traditions in the Gospels, which very strongly increases the likelihood that the reports are both early and historical."

This claim, however, is undermined by several inconvenient facts.

Paul (writing first) does not mention the tomb at all.

The tomb is consciously introduced by Mark to fit in with Isaiah 53:9[4]. As discussed above, Mark feels compelled to explain that the women "said nothing to anyone" (Mark 16:8), while Luke 24:9 says they "told all these things to the eleven, and to all the rest." The most natural explanation for this is if Mark introduced the story but needed to explain why it was not common knowledge, while Luke 'corrects' this misunderstanding since by then it was widely known. Luke also adds that Peter runs to the tomb to check. It is easy to see how something like this would evolve to bolster confidence in the story, which also explains why it did not exist in earlier writings.

Fourth, Habermas considers 1 Corinthians 15:3–4, where Paul is trying to convince the Corinthians of the death, burial, and resurrection of Jesus, something that he "received" (15:3). Habermas states that this implies an empty tomb, but this is not so.

Burial does not necessarily imply a tomb at all.

If there were a known empty tomb, Paul might well be expected to use its existence to persuade the Corinthians.

The dead, buried, risen narrative ties in theologically with baptism, and that is the way Paul discusses it.

Paul's "witness" of the resurrection (15:7), offered as proof to the Corinthians, does not involve a body but rather a vision (or perhaps a spiritual body visiting from heaven), so again does not imply an empty tomb[5].

---

[4] Isaiah 53:9: "They made his grave with the wicked, and with a rich man in his death; ..."

[5] Acts 9:1-9 relates the account of Paul's (then known as Saul) witness of the resurrected Jesus. Paul sees this as evidence of the resurrection (as related by him in 1 Corinthians 15:7), but it is clear that this is not evidence of the resurrection as under-

When Paul says "last of all he appeared to me" (1 Corinthians 15:8) it implies that he has presented an exhaustive list, but he has not mentioned the women who found the tomb.

For all these reasons, 1 Corinthians 15:3–4 does not imply an empty tomb at all.

Fifth, Habermas discusses a sermon written by the author of Luke and attributed to Paul[6]. Luke already wrote about the empty tomb, so naturally, would understand and interpret any story he heard in that light, so this cannot be seen as independent evidence, even if Luke personally listened to a similar sermon by Paul and was trying to relate it faithfully. Any paraphrasing would be in terms of how Luke understood the message. It is doubtful that Luke heard Paul preach this sermon anyway, as it was a common historiographic practice of the time for authors to put their narrative into the mouths of other people. It would seem odd that Peter (an uneducated, Aramaic fisherman) and Paul (a highly educated Jew) use indistinguishable language in Acts. So this sermon cannot be taken as indicative of Paul's view.

Sixth, Habermas claims that "the Jewish leaders tried to explain that the tomb was empty because Jesus's disciples stole his body" which is tacit acknowledgment that the tomb was empty. Habermas cites Matthew 28:11–15, Justin Martyr, and Tertullian to back this up. Justin Martyr and Tertullian cannot be primary sources for this claim, as they were both second-century Christian apologists. Matthew 28:11–15 is tied up with the improbable story of the guards, a story incompatible with the other gospels and so evidence against an empty tomb in the sense that it undermines the credibility of the only sources for it. It is apparent that Matthew introduces the soldiers to assure us that the body was not stolen.

To look at this more carefully, consider Matthew's narrative: The chief priests and Pharisees go on the Sabbath to request a guard for the tomb from Pilate who gives them one. The angels knock the soldiers out when opening the tomb door with an earthquake. They recover and head back to the chief priests, who bribe them to say "His disciples came during the night and stole him away while we were asleep." The chief priests confidently assert that they will keep the guards out of trouble from the governor.

Not one of these sentences is plausible, and no other extant writing including the other gospels corroborates any of them.

Could the chief priests and Pharisees have convinced Pilate to give them a Roman guard? The chief priests went after the body was already unattended for a night? They went on the Sabbath? Could any amount of

---

stood by modern Christians.

[6]Acts 13:29: "...and laid him in a tomb."

money have convinced the guards to stay silent if they saw this? The chief priests could placate the Roman governor? Could Matthew realistically have had knowledge of all this, including verbatim reporting? Surely Habermas does not expect us to take this story as evidence when Matthew's motive for writing it is so clear.

Seventh, Habermas argues that resurrection almost always was thought of as bodily back then, so the tomb would have to be empty. Again, this is a stretch. A body raised from a mass grave would not leave an empty tomb for instance, so this is not evidence for his claim at all.

Paul is quite clear that it is not the same body that is raised as died. Firstly, note, that his witness of the risen Lord is ephemeral, invisible to his companions. Secondly, later in the very same chapter that Habermas quoted is Paul's discussion about the resurrection body (1 Corinthians 15:35–56). It is some of his clearer writing and says:

> That which you sow, you don't sow the body that will be, but a bare grain, maybe of wheat, or of some other kind. But God gives it a body even as it pleased him, and to each seed a body of its own ... [The body] is sown a natural body; it is raised a spiritual body ... As we have borne the image of those made of dust, let's also bear the image of the heavenly. Now I say this, brothers, that flesh and blood can't inherit God's Kingdom; neither does the perishable inherit imperishable.

This is the early Christian conception of the resurrection appearances and is unconcerned by the natural body which has been sown into the ground. Paul even uses the word "buried" which in the context of sowing a seed implies a grave rather than a tomb. However, the theology evolved, and so the gospel accounts gradually get more and more physical, with sudden appearances and disappearances and a lack of physical contact gradually replaced by someone who ate meals and invited touch. Luke essentially contradicts Paul by explicitly saying that Jesus is "flesh and bones" (Luke 24:39) while Paul says that "flesh and blood can't inherit God's Kingdom." Again, the evolution over time is evident.

Habermas makes a brave attempt to establish that there really was an empty tomb. An empty tomb would not prove that there is a God, of course, or even a resurrection, but it at least has the possibility of supernatural overtures. However, even this claim is not sufficiently supported by the evidence. To the contrary, examining the issue closely highlights myriad problems with the biblical stories and supports the view that the empty tomb and the surrounding stories evolved and grew over time. Most damning is that Pilate would simply not have released the body, and the

Sanhedrin would not have asked for it, so it is doubtful that there was a tomb at all.

CHAPTER 35

The Resurrection Appearances of Jesus

On to the question of "The Resurrection Appearances of Jesus" also by Gary Habermas. The previous two chapters made the case that Jesus died on the cross (a point I conceded in Chapter 33) and that there was an empty tomb (this is unconvincing, as discussed in Chapter 34). Habermas now presents the case for the resurrection appearances of Jesus. It is on this precise issue that I lost my faith.

I will note that, though Habermas and Paul[1] both say that the resurrection is the *sine qua non* of Christianity, it is not so for everyone. Christians have myriad beliefs that allow them to remove this from the narrative while maintaining their Christianity. Such approaches might have some merit if you already accepted Christian claims for some reason but were not persuaded by the evidence for the resurrection, or if you wanted to be a Christian for cultural reasons. However, here I am looking for that "some reason" that causes belief in the first place. Habermas is offering us the resurrection, and so I am considering it. If there is some other reason to believe, we will have to consider that separately. But I take 1 Corinthians 15:17–19 at face value: "If Christ has not been raised ... we are of all men most pitiable."

Habermas presents ten reasons to accept the resurrection. The first four are from Paul's epistles. Habermas comments that "[s]cholars uniformly regard Paul as the earliest and best witness to the resurrection appearances."

---

[1] 1 Corinthians 15:12–19

The remaining six are "taken from other New Testament sources."

The crux of Habermas's argument is that *"the early disciples' experiences plus the failure of naturalistic theories equals the resurrection appearances of Jesus"* (emphasis in the original).

Response

Habermas's statement that naturalistic theories cannot explain the evidence and therefore Jesus must have appeared after he died is an argument from ignorance, a known logical fallacy. Even if someone known to you made a claim that they had seen someone believed by you to be dead, you would assume that there was a misunderstanding somewhere. It would take an awful lot to shift you from that position.

In this case, the witness is someone unknown to you, who was not an eyewitness, from thousands of years ago, in a time when miracles were commonly accepted, transmitted through a document that has been edited by people with a motive to persuade, and was only written down after the stories percolated through the community orally. A very rudimentary understanding of human nature and our penchant for the supernatural would seem to provide all the naturalistic explanation that is needed. In many cases, the antiquity and partiality of the evidence mean that we will need to accept that we may never know what happened in detail. This ignorance does not require us to accept the narrative as factual.

I was surprised that Habermas did not use the resurrection accounts from the gospels (apart from revisiting the empty tomb discussion from the previous chapter). These narratives are irreconcilable, something that scholars have known for generations, so perhaps Habermas is tacitly acknowledging this. However, his presumed audience, the laity, may not be aware of this (I certainly was not), so it is a shame that he did not discuss the issue. But it is worth noting that *all* of the evidence Habermas presents is from the Bible.

Without further ado, I will now discuss Habermas's ten arguments.

First, Habermas assures us that "Jesus's appearance to Paul certainly qualified him, being a scholar on both Judaism and Christianity, as an exceptionally strong witness to the resurrected Jesus." Paul converted from a high rank in Judaism and a persecutor of "the assembly of God" (Galatians 1:13) to Christianity as a result of this, so it must have been something impressive to him.

However, we cannot accept this as evidence of the resurrection in the way that modern Christians understand it. Paul saw it as such because he saw the resurrection as spiritual (see 1 Corinthians 15:44 "it is sown a natural body; it is raised a spiritual body" and the surrounding passage). The accounts in Acts 9 and Acts 22 of the Damascus road experience cannot be taken as evidence of a resurrected physical body since the people with Paul saw nothing, so Luke is describing nothing more than a vision.

Note that 1 Corinthians 9:1 ("Am I not an apostle? Haven't I seen Jesus Christ, our Lord?") implies that the qualification for being an apostle is to be a witness of the resurrection (only later did Luke use the word to mean the twelve disciples). In other words, there was an incentive to be counted among those who witnessed the resurrection. With this motive, it is not hard to imagine Paul being susceptible to such a vision. Whether or not he believed he had the vision is moot. The only question is whether this counts as evidence of the resurrection, that is, of Jesus's physical body reanimated after death, and it does not.

Second, Habermas states: "Few conclusions in current study are more widely held by scholars than that, in 1 Corinthians 15:3, Paul recorded a very ancient tradition that actually predates his book." Habermas believes that Paul is claiming to have "received" these words from others. These are both reasonable claims.

However, there is no reason to think that Paul believed his experience was different from that of the other people listed in 1 Corinthians 15, that is, a vision (or a visit from a spiritual body) rather than a physical appearance. Further evidence of this claim abounds.

1 Corinthians 15:35–58 discusses the resurrection body in this context, linking Jesus's resurrection to that of believers. He explicitly denies that the resurrection is flesh and blood (1 Corinthians 15:50 "...flesh and blood can't inherit God's Kingdom;"). Paul does not ever mention the tomb, empty or otherwise because the question of the physical body never enters the equation.

Philippians 2:8–9 has Jesus dying on the cross and then being exalted "to the highest place" (NIV) with no intervening steps; there is no suggestion of his body coming back to life in between. So for Paul and the early Christians Jesus's appearances were directly from heaven.

Luke 23:43 has Jesus saying to the second criminal "today you will be with me in Paradise," perhaps a reference to this theology which was still evolving towards a later physical resurrection.

Paul, aligned with Jewish thought of the time, believed that martyrdom was propitiating, so one could easily imagine this idea transforming over time to give the martyr some post-death compensation. In fact, this idea remains with Islamic martyrs. Even Isaiah 53's suffering servant has suffering and death as salvific, not resurrection.

Paul refers to "Scriptures" (1 Corinthians 15:3), but no scripture is ever produced to support the idea of resurrection. Jonah is later used in the gospels, but this is a stretch, and Jonah does not die anyway. Many Christians do not appreciate how fundamental this point is. It means that there is no Old Testament basis for the resurrection to mean that Jesus is God, or the Messiah, or the Son of God, or anything else. It means that even the resurrection could be granted without conceding that Jesus is God or even the Messiah.

Related to this is another early creed quoted by Paul in Romans 1:4, which says Jesus Christ "who *was declared* to be the Son of God with power, according to the Spirit of holiness, *by the resurrection* from the dead." This is very striking, in that it indicates the early Christian theology in which Jesus Christ, a man (or perhaps a lesser divinity), becomes the Son of God *at the resurrection.*

All the above makes Paul an extremely weak witness of the resurrection. Habermas assures us that "[s]cholars uniformly regard Paul as the earliest and best witness to the resurrection appearances." Paul himself, however, believes the message to be "foolish"[2], which means the objective evidence is unconvincing even to him. Paul himself was persuaded by his vision.

Third, Habermas notes that "Paul was so careful to assure the truth of the gospel message that he returned to Jerusalem fourteen years after this initial visit (see Gal. 2:1–10)." Paul says that Cephas, James, and John assured him that he was on track.

But this actually does not support Habermas's case: it means that Paul was in doubt. We only have Paul's testimony that they agreed with his message.

We also have a serious question as to whether verses 7b-8 were in the original (this argument comes from Wells[3], paraphrasing Barnikol). Tertullian (a second-century Christian apologist) wrote five books arguing that Paul was not the only genuine apostle (responding to the Marcion heresy of the second century). He quotes Galatians 2:1–5 and 2:9, but not 2:7b-8 ("to the uncircumcision, ...to the Gentiles"). This beggars belief if he had it available to him, as it plainly makes his exact point. Excising these verses means that Paul never refers to Peter, only Cephas, which is more consistent. Leaving them in means that Paul bizarrely refers to Peter in verses 7 and 8, and Cephas in 9, and undermines his earlier emphasis of there only being one gospel[4].

Either way, Paul's evidence for the resurrection appearances is not improved by this passage. It indicates a conformance to an early orthodoxy

---

[2] 1 Corinthians 1:18

[3] G. A. Wells, *Cutting Jesus Down to Size: What Higher Criticism Has Achieved and Where It Leaves Christianity.*

[4] Galatians 1:6–10

that does not necessarily involve a physical resurrection of Jesus of Nazareth but rather one like Paul's Damascus road experience.

Fourth, Habermas tells us that "Paul asserts that he also knew what the others were preaching" based on 1 Corinthians 15:11, and only briefly mentions that "Paul had just recorded separate appearances to two of them: Peter (see 1 Cor. 15:5) and James (see 1 Cor. 15:7)."

This does not constitute meaningful evidence. It is curious that Habermas does not go through the details of the appearances as recorded in Paul's quote of the creed[5], though if the only thing they saw was a vision, it hardly matters. The appearances described there do not specify time or place, and the creed asserts that "the twelve" saw this vision, which is often associated with Jesus's disciples in the Gospels. However, this makes no sense, since a creedal statement would not be careless about the number, and the Gospels are clear that only eleven disciples witnessed the resurrection[6]. Matthias only joined after the ascension. Even if he were a witness of the resurrection, he was not part of the twelve at the time. The women are also not mentioned here even though Paul implies it is an exhaustive list of witnesses with the phrase "and last of all he appeared to me."

Fifth, Habermas states that the book of Acts (and "many other New Testament books") also contain creed like summaries of early preaching and that these affirm the death and resurrection of Jesus Christ. This, too, can be explained by the evolution of the belief, and the merger of different traditions. We can accept that "the resurrection" is central to Christianity, but if that originally meant a vision appearing to Cephas and later meant a physical resurrection of Jesus of Nazareth, then these similarities cannot be seen as impressive.

Some of these early creeds are worth a closer look: Acts 2:36 states: "God has *made* him [Jesus] both Lord and Christ." And also Acts 5:31: "God *exalted* him with his right hand to be a Prince and a Savior..." Like Romans 1:4 quoted above, these indicate a theology in which Jesus is exalted to divinity by God at the resurrection. Again the evolution of belief stands out: the earliest Christians believed that God exalted Jesus at his death; Mark believed that it happened at his baptism; Matthew and Luke believed it happened at his birth; John believed that Jesus was God from the beginning of time[7]. Now Christians believe that Jesus is eternal, pre-dating the creation of time.

Sixth, Habermas notes that the disciples

---

[5] 1 Corinthians 15:3–8

[6] Matthew 28:16

[7] For more on this point, see Bart Ehrman, *How Jesus Became God: The Exaltation of a Jewish Preacher from Galilee.*

were willing to die *specifically for their resurrection belief.* Down through the centuries, many have been willing to give their lives for political or religious causes. But the crucial difference here is that while many have died for their *convictions*, Jesus's disciples were in the right place to know the truth or falsity of the event for which they were willing to die.

This willingness to die is very impressive, and this held my personal faith together for a while. It almost certainly means that they died for something that they believed. However, Habermas is right to note that this is no new phenomenon, as it testifies to the strength of their beliefs rather than the accuracy. Our position is simply to weigh the evidence. The direct evidence of the resurrection is contradictory and poor.

The martyrs in the Bible are as follows: John the Baptist, who died before the resurrection[8]; Stephen, who was stoned for preaching the gospel[9], but was not a witness of the resurrection (although he claims to see a vision in Acts 7:55 and this act is said to inspire Saul/Paul); and James the brother of John is killed by King Herod[10] who is a witness recorded in the gospels. Interestingly, the canonical Bible does not record the deaths of Paul or Peter, so the only witness who is martyred in the Bible is James, though there are later traditions of Paul and Peter also being martyred. Paul is not a witness of the physical resurrection anyway.

So, if we accept James's martyrdom, we have to ask whether James was a witness of the resurrection. Paul's creed (1 Corinthians 15:7) is very scant on details: we do not know which James is meant, where or when it happened, whether it was more than a vision (though the implication is that it was not), or why the list is in such stark disagreement with the gospel accounts (the women are not mentioned, he says twelve instead of eleven, Cephas may or may not be Peter, the five hundred are mentioned nowhere else, and the other people mentioned in the gospel are not mentioned here). The gospels accounts are completely at odds with one another. In fact, even Habermas does not discuss the gospel appearances in his essay.

Furthermore, the epistle of James is striking for not making any reference to the death, resurrection or divinity of Jesus. Traditionally, James was written by James the brother of Jesus, though this is disputed. But the omission of a description of the resurrection here leaves Habermas's claim unsupported.

Similarly, Peter does not describe his experience in 1 Peter or 2 Peter. 1 Peter is more widely believed to have been written by Peter than 2 Peter,

---

[8]Matthew 14:1–12
[9]Acts 7:54–60
[10]Acts 12:2

though again the authorship of both is disputed.

Luke 24:34 has the disciples saying: "The Lord is risen indeed, and has *appeared* to Simon [Peter]!" The word "appeared" implies a vision or heavenly visitation, and certainly that is how it is used in other instances in the Bible[11]. Luke 24:34 may therefore reference a vision that Peter had. If so, it may be the genesis of all Christianity.

Furthermore, Acts 10:9–16 describes Peter having a vision and hearing a voice that he attributes to the Lord (that is, the risen Jesus). This vision, just reported by him, is sufficient authority to change a significant teaching. There is no evidence that the initial resurrection appearance referred to in Luke 24:34 was of a different sort.

Again, it is far easier to see these claims as evidence of a theological evolution than of a resurrection. It seems that after Jesus had died, several people including Peter and Paul had a vision of him. The early gospels have Jesus not being recognized, appearing and disappearing suddenly, and entering locked rooms. By the time John 21 is appended (I say appended because of how final John 20:30–31 is, and how John 21 looks to be an attempt to patch the discrepancy between the gospels regarding the location), Jesus is cooking them a meal on the beach since they have apparently given up and gone fishing in Galilee even though Jesus just appeared to them in a locked room in Jerusalem. It is very hard to take this as evidence when the theological evolution is so clear.

Seventh, Habermas points to the evolution of James the brother of Jesus from skeptic to church leader and attributes it to a resurrection appearance. I will quote his point in full:

> Seventh, it is almost always acknowledged that during Jesus's ministry, his brother James was a skeptic (see John 7:5). He was probably one of the family members in Mark 3:21–35 who thought that Jesus was insane! But how do we account for the surprising reports that James later led the Jerusalem church (Gal. 1:18–2:10; Acts 15:13–21)? According to the creedal comment in 1 Corinthians 15:7, Jesus appeared to James, yet another pointer to a resurrection appearance.

The Gospels of Mark and Matthew mention a James as Jesus's brother, Matthew copying Mark. John does not mention anyone called James at all but does mention a skeptical, unnamed brother. Mark discusses family (which could be translated as associates) who think he is insane. However, the gospels do not have a resurrection appearance to James the brother of Jesus. Is this the same James who comes to lead the church and who

---

[11] For example, Luke 1:11, 9:30.

features in the creedal statement? There is no evidence of it, though the inference has been made. The creedal statement of Paul is referring to a vision, so it would not really qualify as evidence for the resurrection, and the statement does not specify which James has this vision.

Briefly going through the relevant verses, Luke writes in Acts 15:13 of James, but does not specify which one he is. From the context it is clear that this is the one Paul is referring to in Galatians 1:19, but not necessarily the actual brother from Mark 6:3. I say this because the term brother is used loosely: in Acts 15, both Peter and James refer to the group that James is leading as "brothers" (Acts 15:7,13); Paul refers to a group called "the Lord's brothers" in 1 Corinthians 9:5. It is in this context that Paul refers to "James, the Lord's brother" in Galatians 1:19, never referring to him as Jesus's brother.

For Paul, the Lord referred to the risen Lord, not to the historical Jesus (see Romans 10:9), and when Paul quotes a saying, it is always a saying of the Lord, never a saying of Jesus. He also often seems to contradict Jesus[12].

Putting this all together, James the brother of Jesus of Nazareth was not necessarily the same person as James the leader of the Lord's brothers in Jerusalem. And, relevant to this discussion, neither James is a witness of the resurrection: the former because there is no record of it, and the latter because only a vision is recorded to a James that may or may not be him. So if we accept that the James in the creed is the actual brother of Jesus, then we will be accepting that he too had a vision of the resurrection, which is not a significant concession. This makes Habermas's argument moot.

Eighth, Habermas brings up the supposedly empty tomb again, which he admits "does not prove the resurrection appearances." This was discussed in detail in the previous chapter, with the conclusion that there is insufficient evidence to conclude that there even was a tomb, let alone an empty one.

Ninth, Habermas states that Jesus's resurrection was the center of early Christian faith because unbelievers "could not disprove the rock on which it was founded: Jesus's appearances."

But the burden of proof is not on the unbeliever, and, in any event, it is impossible to disprove a vision, such as the one Paul had. One merely remains skeptical, which is the atheist position. Besides, early Christian teaching immunized Christians ever since against any form of proof. Jesus invites Thomas to touch his hands and side (the wound to the side is only reported in John) and then says "Blessed are those who have not seen, and have believed" (John 20:29), a very thinly veiled admonition to future believers. Note that Thomas here was skeptical of the other disciples' claims

---

[12]We will return to this point in Chapter 41.

despite knowing them well; our position is hardly stronger than his. Paul also tells Christians to expect to be called fools. So evidence and proof are not relevant to Christians, as is still often the case today.

Lastly, Habermas states that "two thousand years of attempts by non-believers to explain what happened to Jesus in natural terms have failed."

This assumes that a natural explanation is required to reject an extraordinary claim that is not supported by the evidence: it is not.

It assumes that natural explanations do not exist: they do, though some of it is lost in the mist of time; a lack of certainty is all the more reason to reject a supernatural claim.

It assumes that non-believers had the freedom to present their case over the last two thousand years: they did not; Christians have systematically persecuted those who threaten them, and controlled people through well-understood mechanisms such as fear and the idea of blasphemy.

It assumes that Christianity has remained roughly constant throughout this period: it has not; modern Christians have largely rejected creationism and hell, for example, and the church is continuing to evolve its beliefs on women, homosexuality, the reason for the cross, reformed theology, and many other things; the range of opinion on this within Christianity shows that it is not a monolithic structure with a clear explanation of its own, but rather an evolving tree of disparate beliefs.

In any event, Habermas's final statement, suitably tweaked, could be used to support virtually any religious belief.

Habermas states that the "early disciples' experiences plus the failure of naturalistic theories equals the resurrection appearances of Jesus."

But the early disciples' experiences are at best vague since the evidence is contradictory and contained only in the Bible. Detailed naturalistic theories are not required, but an understanding of human nature and an appreciation of the evolution of Christianity over time would appear to suffice.

Habermas's essay, the apex of the book, does not persuade me of the resurrection. On the contrary, it exposes lines of evidence that point to the human origins of the narrative. It was an exploration of these issues that caused me to lose my faith in the first place. The story of sacrifice, the promise of eternal life, and the idea of divine justice are evocative and appealing. The history of what caused the Bible to be written and Christianity to emerge is fascinating. But without evidence, I can only appreciate them on a human level. The arguments Habermas gave do not persuade me that the resurrection happened or that there is a God.

CHAPTER 36

Were the Resurrection Appearances of Jesus Hallucinations?

Up next, Michael Licona receives the baton from Habermas and continues the argument from what they have supposedly established, which is that the disciples believed that they were witnesses of the resurrection. My previous chapter demonstrates that what the early Christians believed they saw was no more than a vision (what Paul calls a spiritual body). But Licona takes it as given that the later understanding of the resurrection was what they believed they saw, and then seeks in this essay to eliminate a possible naturalistic explanation for the appearances, namely mass hallucinations. It seems that Licona expects us to accept that mass hallucinations are unlikely and therefore the physical appearances must be real.

Licona says: "Another specialist, Dale Allison, refers to the topic of the historicity of Jesus's resurrection as the 'prize puzzle' of New Testament research." This simple sentence succinctly concedes atheism (at least as it pertains to Christianity) and demonstrates the presuppositional nature of his research. Atheists claim nothing more than to be unconvinced by the evidence that theists present, and this quote shows that even conservative scholars agree that more is needed. That Allison calls it a "prize" shows that this research intends to show a pre-specified result rather than just search for the truth.

The conclusion of Licona's essay is:

[T]he proposal that hallucinations can account for the post-resurrection appearances of Jesus fails on several accounts. Although at least a few if not all of Jesus's disciples may have been in an emotional state that rendered them candidates for a hallucination, the nature of some of the experiences of the risen Jesus, specifically those that occurred in group settings and to Jesus's enemy Paul, and the empty tomb strongly suggest that these experiences were not hallucinations.

Response

I want briefly to address the logic of this straw man fallacy before returning to the details of Licona's essay. Suppose we roughly categorized possible explanations for the resurrection stories in the Bible as follows:

1. Jesus is God, and the resurrection is real. Any inconsistencies, immoralities, or incomprehensibility in the stories themselves or the Bible generally must be explained by our lack of understanding, or through the introduction of new facts that are not in the Bible, or left as a mystery.

2. Everything in the Bible is historically accurate, but it all has naturalistic explanations. The Christian God may or may not exist in this scenario.

3. Nothing in the Bible is accurate. The whole thing is a malicious fraud invented from scratch. The Christian God is a fraud, though there may or may not be some other God.

4. The Bible results from a complicated evolution over time through human processes, mostly or all done in good faith based on deeply held religious beliefs such as a resurrection appearance. The evidence for the Christian God is insufficient to accept it. This is roughly equivalent to saying that there is (or at least may be) a naturalistic explanation for the existence of the Bible including the inconsistencies, inaccuracies, immoralities, and incomprehensibilities.

I am not claiming that this categorization is complete or rigorous, but it suffices to demonstrate why I believe an essay like Licona's is logically flawed. I would regard the above categories to be ordered (roughly) from least likely to most likely, with the first three all being incredibly unlikely and the last one being likely. I will not quibble on the order of the first three since they are all approximately zero. The reason for this is that the first three are all highly specific and require enormous certainty. The last expresses a general skepticism and a broad acceptance of uncertainty. It is not saying that in principle mystical, religious or divine explanations are impossible: just that the evidence presented is not sufficient to support such conclusions.

In the context of this essay, Licona is considering a particular case in category two (another example is the swoon theory discussed in Chapter 33). He is then asking us to believe that, since he has eliminated that case (and elsewhere eliminates other cases in categories two and three[1]), we must logically accept case one. But this elimination, and the uncertainty inherent in his discussion, simply adds more weight to category four and does nothing to address the issues with category one.

I say that he has eliminated the hallucination theory, but in reality, he has not, and, even though I regard the mass hallucination theory as unlikely, it remains more likely than the explanation that Licona is defending.

Licona discusses the craziness of the hallucination theory during an appearance to the disciples:

> Perhaps one [of the disciples] would have said, 'I see Jesus over by the door,' while another said, 'No. I see him floating by the ceiling,' while still another said, 'No. I only hear him speaking to me,' while still another said, 'I only sense that he's in the room with us.' Instead, what we have are the reports that the disciples *saw* Jesus.

Here Licona is being irrationally rational. Or, to put it another way, to ascribe to people experiencing an irrational hallucination the level of rationality that he himself has. It is not a stretch to imagine how, in such conditions, peer pressure, excitability, and hysteria would cause the stories to conflate. "I see Jesus over by the door," is far more likely to be met with "me too!" than anything else.

Licona quotes Gary A. Sibcy as saying:

> I have surveyed the professional literature (peer-reviewed journal articles and books) written by psychologists, psychiatrists, and other relevant healthcare professionals during the past two decades and have yet to find a single documented case of a group hallucination, that is, an event for which more than one person purportedly shared in a visual or other sensory perception where there was clearly no external referent.

---

[1]Michael Licona has a page on his website called *Top 10 Myths About Jesus' Resurrection*. It is a set of 10 videos and is available at
www.risenjesus.com/top-10-myths-about-jesus-resurrection.

This is a very carefully worded statement. But the numerous apparitions of Mary over the course of time, including the somewhat famous example of an appearance to six children in 1981 in Medjugorje surely suggest that people are susceptible to such visions. Perhaps Sibcy is asking us to delay judgment as to whether there was indeed an "external referent" in these cases, but this unfairly shifts the burden of proof away from those making the assertion. I will merely comment that it is interesting that Mary only seems to appear to those who are immersed in a culture that reveres her and know a great deal about what she ought to say.

So if mass hallucinations are not outside the realm of potential human experience, we are still left to consider the evidence of the Bible. Licona makes a great deal of the notion that Paul was an enemy when he saw the resurrected Jesus. But we must remember that the Bible never claims any experience for Paul that was distinguishable from an hallucination (read the Damascus road experience in Acts 9 and Acts 22), and in any event it occurred after the ascension, so not during the period of time when modern Christians believe Jesus of Nazareth to have been physically on Earth.

Furthermore, Paul (as Saul) is said to have watched Stephen saying: "Behold, I see the heavens opened, and the Son of Man standing at the right hand of God!" (Acts 7:54–60) while being stoned to death. It is not hard to imagine such an emotional and traumatic experience impressing even an "enemy."

As for the group experiences, the confusion of these stories in the Bible makes it unconvincing that they ever occurred, which makes the discussion of mass hallucination moot. In the previous chapter, Habermas did not even use the group experiences to try to persuade us of the resurrection. Of course, anything is possible. But we should remain skeptical until convinced. The different accounts in the Bible are wholly irreconcilable, and there is no other evidence.

The earliest manuscripts of Mark have no resurrection appearance, but there is a later addition with Jesus appearing to two unspecified people, and then at a table, presumably in Galilee before ascending[2].

Matthew has the eleven on an unspecified mountain in Galilee, with no ascension[3].

Luke has him appearing to the two near Jerusalem (and vanishing) and then appearing through a locked door to the eleven in Jerusalem. Jesus ascends apparently on the day of his resurrection[4].

Acts (by the same author) has the ascension 40 days later, but also in

---

[2]Mark 16:9–20
[3]Matthew 28:16–20
[4]See footnote 8 on page 252 for a discussion on this point.

Jerusalem. Jesus gives strict instructions not to leave Jerusalem, eliminating the possibility of a reconciliation between the accounts[5].

John has them in Jerusalem twice (8 days apart) and then in a boat in Galilee[6], plainly the same story as Luke 5:1–10, but moved from the beginning of the ministry to the end.

These are all supposed to be based on eyewitness accounts, from the same group of witnesses who experienced the same thing at the same time. One does not need to postulate mass hallucinations to reject these accounts as unhistorical.

Ehrman points out the significance of the doubt traditions[7]. He says:

> Jesus does not appear to anyone in Mark's Gospel, but he does in Matthew, Luke, John, and the book of Acts. Most readers have never noticed this, but in every one of these accounts, we have rather direct statements that the disciples doubted that Jesus was raised. In Matthew 28:17 we are told that Jesus appeared to the eleven, but 'some doubted.' Why would they doubt if Jesus was right there, in front of them? ... Then, even when Jesus appears to [the disciples in Luke], he has to 'prove' that he is not a spirit by having them handle him. And even that is not enough: he needs to eat a piece of broiled fish in order finally to convince them (24:37–43) ... In Acts 1:3 we are told that after his resurrection Jesus spent forty days with the disciples—forty days!—showing them that he was alive by 'many proofs.' How many proofs were needed exactly? And it took forty days to convince them?

The more likely alternative is that these stories evolved. I should reiterate that it is possible for such stories to develop in good faith, so to speak.

For example, consider Luke 23:43, where Jesus says to the penitent criminal "Assuredly I tell you, today you will be with me in Paradise." The versions in Mark and Matthew have two rebels who both just insult Jesus, while John simply has two others crucified with Jesus but playing no part in the drama. The story in Luke has a fable quality to it, and it is easy to imagine a story like this emerging over time. But Luke 23:43 is an apparent contradiction since we know that Jesus died, only rising again

---

[5]Acts 1:3–4

[6]John 20:19-21:12

[7]Bart Ehrman, *How Jesus Became God: The Exaltation of a Jewish Preacher from Galilee.*

three days later, and only ascending on that third day[8], or perhaps forty days after that (Acts 1:3).

Category four explains this contradiction very naturally: the early idea that Jesus was glorified by his death straight to heaven (as implied in Philippians 2:8–9, and the resurrection discussion of 1 Corinthians 15) survived in this story and the later idea that he rose physically survived in other parts of the gospel. Luke faithfully records all the traditions ignoring the contradiction that the shifted theology has caused.

Theologians, however, have proven very adept at defending orthodoxy, and so, instead of accepting this conclusion, devise all manner of explanations. Perhaps the comma is in the wrong place, and the vast majority of translators are wrong: Jesus actually said, "Truly I tell you today, you will be with me in paradise." Others argue that paradise means an interim state before heaven. Others argue that time has no meaning to God. Others argue that the language is picturesque[9]. All of them claim or imply that the other interpretations are incorrect.

For the purpose of illustration, I want to consider an article that argues that the comma was in the wrong position[10]. It is done with sincerity but has a definite purpose, which is to *add* an explanation that clears up the contradiction while maintaining the presupposed orthodoxy. It has these words:

> By placing a comma before 'today' ... rather than after it, they
> [the Bible translators] have Jesus saying something He never
> intended. We know this *because the Bible clearly says Jesus*

---

[8] Luke 24 begins with the women going to the tomb and finding the stone rolled away. They tell Peter who runs to the tomb. Verse 13 says "that very day" and has the appearance on the road to Emmaus.

After this interaction, verse 33 states "They rose up that very hour, returned to Jerusalem, and found the eleven gathered together..."

Verse 36 says "As they said these things, Jesus himself stood among them..."

He speaks with them and eats, and then verse 50 says "He led them out as far as Bethany..." without any indication of time passing and Jesus has his ascension. So it seems that Luke has Jesus ascending on the day that he was risen. By the time he writes Acts, he has heard a different version which he adopts readily (see the next footnote).

The appearance on the road to Emmaus has the classic fable element of the two people not recognizing Jesus and telling him the story of himself. Eventually, he breaks bread, they recognize him and he disappears. This is suggestive of an earlier narrative where Jesus's resurrection is not quite physical in the normal sense. The next passage has him appearing suddenly and eating fish, but still ascending. The evolution of increasing physicality is clear.

[9] Grace Communion International, 1989, *The Comma of Luke 23:43*. Available at www.gci.org/Bible/luke/comma.

[10] Beyond Today, United Church of God, 2009, *Did the thief go to Heaven?* Available at www.ucg.org/Bible-study-tools/Bible-questions-and-answers/i-am-not-clear-about-luke-23-43-where-jesus-told-one.

Himself did not go to paradise or heaven on the day He died! (emphasis mine)

This is precisely how stories evolve with sincerity: something that someone thinks they know causes them to reinterpret, add to or adjust a plain statement. A small tweak here and a small tweak there, all done to help. Add to this that Christians believe that God speaks to them in a still, small voice[11] so that any thought could be God's revelation to them, and you have a powerful evolutionary mechanism.

The above is a modern example of what you might call microevolution: it is a tiny, almost unnoticeable change in the story. Our situation is that the stories have been written down, which makes significant changes much harder (though not impossible judging by the diversity of Christian sects).

But in the early days of the church, where everything was transmitted orally, and where the early Christian tradition of a vision of the risen Lord was evolving into the story of the reanimation of Jesus of Nazareth's body, far bigger shifts could easily occur. A shifting environment is a powerful mechanism in natural evolution, and that seems to be the case here, possibly because the effort to fix contradictions would tend to generate many new "facts," similar to the above modern example.

In summary, I agree with Licona that the argument for mass hallucinations is weak, but it would only ever be needed if you accepted the biblical account as historical but rejected divinity on principle. Most atheists do neither. The historicity of the biblical account is undermined by the palpable inconsistencies, the lack of objectivity of the authors, and the lack of external, corroborating evidence. The existence of God is not rejected on principle, but on the basis that the evidence is not strong enough to require it, so we should remain uncertain and skeptical. On the other hand, even now we have clear examples of Biblical stories evolving with the telling, and there is no reason to believe that the early Christian community was exempt from this universal human tendency.

---

[11] 1 Kings 19:12: "After the earthquake a fire passed; but Yahweh was not in the fire. After the fire, there was a still small voice."

As with many verses that are in the collective consciousness it comes from the King James Version, which is the basis of the World English Bible. The NIV has "a gentle whisper," which means much the same thing as "still small voice" but somehow does not sound as *right*.

CHAPTER 37

The Trinity

Switching gears, Bill Gordon[1] writes an essay on the Trinity[2]. It is curious to find this essay in a book called *Evidence for God*. It assumes that God exists and then tries to shore up some of the problems that this assumption creates, in this case for Christianity specifically rather than god or gods in general.

Gordon says:

> The doctrine of the Trinity is one of the most important beliefs of Christianity. It is central to the Christian understanding of God and is accepted by all Christian groups ... While the word *Trinity* is not found in the Bible, its truth is expressed in many biblical passages. The Bible recognizes the Father as God, the Son as God, and the Holy Spirit as God.

Gordon goes on to demonstrate this with numerous verses from the Bible and a few other ancient sources.

He ends:

> The only conclusion is that the Christian doctrine of the Trinity accurately describes the biblical testimony about God. Finite

---

[1] Bill Gordon is a research consultant for the People Group/Interfaith Evangelism Team of the North American Mission Board.

[2] His essay, *The Trinity*, is also available at www.namb.net/apologetics/the-trinity.

humans cannot rationally explain the doctrine of the Trinity. This should not surprise us since there are many things the Bible teaches about God that we cannot fully understand. For example, the Bible affirms the existence of God, the creation of the universe, atonement from sin, and the resurrection of the dead, despite the fact that none of those truths can be totally understood by finite minds. As with the doctrine of the Trinity, Christians do not accept these teachings because they can rationally explain them, but because the Bible teaches them.

Response

There is no argument for God here. Gordon seems to assume that the Bible arrived as a monolithic and consistent structure, with each part having equal weight. The consistency assumption means that new facts can be inferred and introduced to patch up any apparent inconsistency, and the doctrine of the Trinity is an example of this. It asserts that three is one and proclaims this to be a mystery. His concluding paragraph where he exhorts us to accept some things "because the Bible teaches them" is the precise opposite of providing evidence for God: it is an argument from authority. But, a rational and reasonable question is: on what does this authority rest? Lacking evidence for God, the rest of the discussion is moot.

To be clear, I am fine with accepting that if there were a god he or she would be beyond my comprehension and do things that seemed surprising to me. What I am looking for is a reason to accept god in the first place. The contradictions in the Bible make it look like a human construction. If that is not so then we will be forced into the kind of mental contortions that the doctrine of the Trinity represents. But what reason is there to believe that it is other than it appears to be? Nothing has convinced me so far.

An attack on reason is often tied into theistic justifications. The logic presented in this article, which tells us to believe despite not understanding and because the Bible says so, is a typical example. As mentioned previously, Jesus supposedly tells doubting Thomas, who displayed what today would be called healthy skepticism, that those who believe without evidence are blessed (John 20:24–29), a sentiment endorsed to this day.

Gordon also asserts that the Trinity "is accepted by all Christian groups," which is easily recognized as the no true Scotsman fallacy[3]. In point of fact,

---

[3]We met this in the footnote on page 28. The conversation would go like this: "All Christian groups accept the Trinity." To which someone may respond "I am a Christian,

CHAPTER 37. THE TRINITY

it took hundreds of years for the doctrine of the Trinity to evolve.

The mixed views on the Trinity expressed in the Bible verses quoted by Gordon make much more sense when seen in the context of an evolving religion. Earlier books are more equivocal, while later ones gradually become clearer.

A simple analysis of Gordon's essay shows this with remarkable clarity:

- Mark, the earliest of the gospels, does not support the divinity of Jesus, and Gordon does not quote Mark even once.

- Matthew is quoted nine times: four of those are Matthew 28:18–19, the great commission, which almost certainly reflects doctrine from Matthew's day rather than words spoken by Jesus (see the next paragraph); Matthew 12:31 ("but the blasphemy against the Spirit will not be forgiven men.") is used by Gordon to show that the spirit is separate, but introduces myriad other theological and moral problems associated with unforgivable sins; only Matthew 1:23 and Matthew 9:6 attempt to show the divinity of Jesus from Matthew, though they require interpretation. Note that 1:23 says they will call him Immanuel, but no-one calls Jesus this in the whole Bible. The Son of Man was discussed in Chapter 29.

- Luke is quoted twice by Gordon: Luke 1:35 and Luke 12:12 are used to show that the Holy Spirit is separate from God.

- But Gordon quotes John, by my count, forty-four times, four times as many as the other three gospels combined. Gordon was probably unaware of this bias, but looked at this way the evolution of belief over time is clear.

Matthew 28:18–19 is the great commission where Jesus says to go to all the nations and baptize in the name of the Father, the Son, and the Holy Spirit. This verse is unconvincing since Peter resists the notion of a mission to the Gentiles and no-one quotes these words to persuade him. Furthermore in Acts, the Trinitarian formula is never used for baptism (see Acts 2:38 where baptism is done in the name of Jesus Christ). The conclusion (argued by Wells[4] and references therein) is that Matthew makes Jesus "cite the trinitarian formula used by Christians in his [Matthew's] own day." Just the possibility that Matthew would do this is deeply unsettling and casts more doubt on the credibility of the Bible.

---

but I do not accept the Trinity!" This receives the clarification: "All *real* Christians accept the Trinity."

[4]G. A. Wells, *Cutting Jesus Down to Size: What Higher Criticism Has Achieved and Where It Leaves Christianity*

Matthew 28:17 is part of the remarkable doubt theme uniformly associated with Jesus's resurrection: "When they saw him, they worshiped him; but some doubted." I discussed this in the previous chapter.

So this chapter does not provide evidence for god. Instead, we get an argument from authority and a fiat assertion that three can equal one by declaring it a mystery. This constitutes an attack on rationality. Closer examination of Gordon's argument supports the notion that the Trinity is a belief that evolved over time, which is what it appears, and which is well-known in scholarly circles[5]. But whatever the details of the doctrine of the Trinity, this cannot be seen as evidence for god. It is most likely what it appears to be: an attempt to paper over theological issues that emerged as the religion evolved.

---

[5]Bart Ehrman, *How Jesus Became God: The Exaltation of a Jewish Preacher from Galilee.*

CHAPTER **38**

Is Jesus Superior to All Other Religious Leaders?

Having looked at the core Christian claims in the last few chapters, the book now gives Tal Davis[1] an opportunity to defend Christianity over other faiths[2]. He concludes that "all religions [are] not equal and that Jesus Christ was and is superior to the founders of the other major religions of the world." This conclusion is "based on five lines of truth." Jesus Christ is the only major world religion founder who:

1. had no beginning in time or space,

2. came into the world as he did,

3. lived a perfect and sinless life,

4. died as a sacrificial atonement for the sins of humanity, and

5. rose from the dead to demonstrate his power and authority.

He supports these "truths" with Bible verses. He ends his essay:

> Christianity does not stand or fall on its moral principles or depth of mystical experience. If that were true, then it would

---

[1] Tal Davis is the Executive Vice President of MarketFaith Ministries.
[2] The essay is: Tal Davis, 2012, *Is Jesus Superior to All Other Religious Leaders?* Available at
www.marketfaith.org/is-jesus-superior-to-all-other-religious-leaders.

259

be no better than any other religion in the world, and Jesus Christ would be only another great religious or moral teacher. No, Christianity stands or falls entirely on the person and word of one man: Jesus Christ. Either he was who he claimed to be, the Lord of the universe, who came to earth as man, lived a sinless life, died on the cross as an atonement for our sins, and rose again from the dead, or the entire Christian faith is a gigantic lie.

Response

This is not direct evidence for God, but rather a set of claims about Jesus that are exceptional. Davis's points can be categorized as follows:

1. "no beginning in time and space" and 4. "died as a sacrificial atonement" are not provable claims and cannot be admitted as evidence. I can appreciate the idea of sacrifice as something beautiful, but the notion of atonement is problematic as I will discuss;

2. "came into the world" (that is, the virgin birth) and 5. "rose from the dead" are historical claims that are insufficiently attested by the evidence, as discussed in Chapters 27 and 35 respectively;

3. "lived a perfect and sinless life" is a moral and historical claim, though not a particularly exceptional one relative to other religious figures.

I want to discuss the third claim a little more, that is the claim that Jesus lived a perfect and sinless life. Davis quotes biblical verses that assert that Jesus was sinless. He also quotes Pontius Pilate as saying "I find no basis for a charge against him," which could be said of any non-criminal[3]. This, according to Davis, qualifies Jesus "to do what was necessary to make salvation available to humanity." Of course, the notion of atonement was admitted by Gordon in the previous chapter to be beyond the understanding of finite minds, and this leads us into another moral quagmire, which I will discuss below.

Apart from the biblical assertions that Jesus is sinless, what evidence is there? For many Christians asking this question is seen as blasphemous.

---

[3]It is also not true: as far as we can tell, Pilate found him guilty of the treasonous charge of calling himself the King of the Jews. This story evolved to exonerate Pilate because there was an anti-semitic desire in the early church to lay the blame squarely with the Jewish authorities. In fact, later tradition has Pilate becoming a Christian, which is unlikely and also not a good advertisement for Christianity.

For many, his sinlessness is a question of definition: Jesus defines perfection, so any action he takes must be perfect. This is sometimes used to justify God's commands to commit genocide in the Old Testament: it would be bad for a person to do it, but if God does it, it is good by definition. This makes moral discussions challenging, as we are exhorted to do as we are told. In fact, we are told that the only item of importance is whether you believe a set of claims[4]. This undercuts the discussion because we are asked on what basis we are judging this. It seems a bit arrogant to judge God. It also brings us to the concept of revealed truth, which requires us to suppress our intelligence, rationality, and moral compass.

But our position is to judge the morality of someone who claims to be (or at least whose followers claim is) God. As such, we need to use rational processes to judge moral ones. This is harder than being handed a set of rules, and at the margins, these discussions are very complex and important. Often, Christians involved in such discourses quote verses from the Bible and an interpretation of them to the situation under review. At its best, this is a way of using rational processes to make moral judgments; at its worst it abrogates responsibility for the decision and undermines rational debate. For the purpose of this essay, however, I will discuss things that are somewhat clear cut.

Consider the notion of atonement. Why does God need to kill himself/Jesus because of our sins? What is the mechanism by which this works? If Jesus and God are one how did Jesus die and God not? What does death even mean when applied to an infinite being? Why would God be satisfied by this? None of these questions have any meaningful answers and the doctrines that have been introduced simply assert that no contradiction exists. Christopher Hitchens and Thomas Paine have pointed out that it is morally repugnant for someone else to take the guilt for our actions:

> [Y]ou may if you wish take on another man's debt, or even to take his place in prison. That would be self-sacrificing. But you may not assume his actual crimes as if they were your own; for one thing you did not commit them and might have died rather than do so; for another this impossible action would rob him of individual responsibility[5].

---

[4]John 8:23–24: "He [Jesus] said to them, 'You are from beneath. I am from above. You are of this world. I am not of this world. I said therefore to you that you will die in your sins; for unless you believe that I am he, you will die in your sins.'"

It is also noteworthy that the Bible is not consistent on this: in Matthew 25:31–46 Jesus discusses separating the sheep from goats and says that heaven will be for those who fed, clothed, and housed the needy, while hell is for those who did not.

[5]Christopher Hitchens, 2001, *Letters to a Young Contrarian*. Quoted from en.wikiquote.org/wiki/Christopher_Hitchens.

Bertrand Russell discusses the issue of the superiority of Jesus[6]. The following paragraphs will loosely paraphrase some of his points. In this discussion, I am simply taking the sayings attributed to the Jesus described in the Bible. These may not accurately reflect the historical Jesus, with later authors attributing to Jesus sayings that he may not have said. But the Jesus of the gospels is what Christians believe in, so we will look at this.

First, Russell acknowledges some of Christ's wisdom, saying that he, in fact, accepted it to a larger degree than do most Christians. For example, Matthew 5:39 says "don't resist him who is evil; but whoever strikes you on your right cheek, turn to him the other also." Russell says of this that it "is not a new precept or a new principle. It was used by Lao-tse and Buddha some 500 or 600 years before Christ." Another excellent principle is found in Matthew 7:1: "Don't judge, so that you won't be judged." And Matthew 5:42: "Give to him who asks you, and don't turn away him who desires to borrow from you." And Matthew 19:21: "If you want to be perfect, go, sell what you have, and give to the poor." All these verses reveal great wisdom, though there is no convincing evidence of which I am aware that Christians follow this advice more or less than non-Christians.

Second, Russell points out some areas where Jesus may not have been very wise. "He certainly thought that His second coming would occur in clouds of glory before the death of all the people who were living at that time." For example, Matthew 16:28 has Jesus saying "Most certainly I tell you, there are some standing here who will in no way taste of death, until they see the Son of Man coming in his Kingdom." As discussed in Chapter 29, it is likely that Jesus was saying that a heavenly being known as the Son of Man would soon arrive, but this does not change Russell's essential point that Jesus was an apocalypticist. This led to some unwise advice from Jesus, such as Matthew 6:34 "Therefore don't be anxious for tomorrow, for tomorrow will be anxious for itself. Each day's own evil is sufficient." This is another saying that Christians interpret heavily so that they can get on with their lives.

Third, Russell takes issue with some of the moral teachings of Jesus. The most serious of these is the belief in hell, a concept from which many modern Christians have backpedaled, but which the Jesus of the Bible took very seriously[7]. The very notion of eternal punishment is immoral and inhumane. But more than this, it is dished out in an immoral way (not that any use of such cruel and unusual punishment could ever be warranted): live your life as best you can, honest and hard-working, but

[6]Bertrand Russell, *Why I Am Not a Christian*, (based on a 1927 lecture).
[7]Matthew 25:31–46, Mark 9:43, Luke 16:23–24

unpersuaded by the evidence for Christ and you get eternal damnation; live a life of cheating, theft, rape, and murder but repent before the end: you get heaven. It is very difficult to see this at just, but as Christians we are often told to trust that God will set everything right in the end. This should not be enough to make us put our morality on hold.

Other moral issues are perhaps less significant, but if perfection is the standard, then a few should be mentioned. Calling the Canaanite woman a dog (Matthew 15:26), is sometimes excused by claiming "that Jesus had a wry smile" when he said it[8], but I do not find it very funny especially in the context of gender and race issues within the church[9].

Slaughtering the herd of pigs[10] is needlessly cruel both to the pigs and the owners who remained uncompensated.

Cursing the fig tree though it was out of season[11] also seems harsh. Matthew (who has a copy of Mark's gospel when he writes his) removes the reference to it being out of season (perhaps he too felt it unjust?). He also evolves the story to have the tree wither immediately, rather than gradually, showing a nice example of Jesus's miraculous abilities increasing with the telling.

Davis tries to show that Christianity differs from other religions, and does so by showing that some of the claims it makes for itself are more spectacular than those of other religious leaders. But spectacular claims are harder to believe. Merely asserting them is insufficient. More and better evidence should be produced. However, some of the claims are so otherworldly as to defy comprehension, let alone proof. Others are simply poorly supported, by contradictory evidence from biased sources that lack credibility. And, if we can step back objectively, there are areas where Jesus's morality is questionable. Acceptance of this dramatically diminishes Davis's point and means that Christianity is not only not superior, but is inferior to many other methods of thought.

---

[8]For example, nagasawafamily.org/matthew_dev_15_21-28.htm.

[9]There is a guest post on my blog entitled *Women in religion*, available at glentonjelbert.com/guest-post-women-in-religion that discusses this issue.

[10]Matthew 8:32, Luke 8:33

[11]Mark 11:12–25, Matthew 21:18–22

CHAPTER 39

Is Jesus the Only Way?

On to Michael Licona's next essay which considers whether Jesus is the Only Way? This appears to assume that there is a way to begin with, and therefore is not evidence for God. Licona assumes God and defends the (dominant) Christian position that Jesus is the only way. In fairness, he refers to the historical case for the resurrection, which I discussed in Chapter 35 and found unconvincing, and his and Gary Habermas's book[1] but admits "[s]pace does not permit me to provide a historical case for Jesus's resurrection."

In this essay, Licona asks us to "assume for the moment that Jesus was truly who he claimed to be" and sets about trying to deal with the uneasiness brought about by some of Jesus's sayings, such as "I am the way, the truth, and the life. No one comes to the Father, except through me." (John 14:6).

Licona first argues that there "is widespread evidence that Jesus claimed to be the only way to God." I discussed this in Chapter 31 and was unpersuaded. He then states that his claim was verified by his resurrection and attempts to reconcile the apparent unfairness of the exclusiveness with the supposed character of Jesus by examining three questions: What is truth? What is ethical? And what is required? He does not expound on why exactly it is unfair referring instead to an "uneasiness it brings."

---

[1]Gary R. Habermas and Michael Licona, 2004, *The Case for the Resurrection of Jesus.*

The first of these questions (what is truth?) is to exhort us to deal with the objective truth regardless of "our politically correct culture." If Jesus is who he said he is, then we, mere mortals, will simply have to learn to deal with our injured sense of justice because it must reflect a deficiency on our behalf.

The second of these questions (what is ethical?) tells us that truth triumphs over hurt feelings, so we should not water down the truth for the sake of political correctness. He also says that:

> [W]hen someone claims that my belief that Jesus is the only way is intolerant and offensive, they ignore the fact that their pluralist approach is likewise intolerant and offensive. They are being intolerant of exclusivist views and offensive to those who hold them.

The third question (what is required?) gives Licona a chance to affirm his interpretation of biblical salvation. He ends with a rhetorical question and answer:

> How can I share the gospel with others, given their aversion to the exclusive claims of Jesus? I'd like to suggest three actions. First, understand the answers to the three rudimentary questions we have discussed: What is truth? What is ethical? What is required? Second, clothe Jesus's message with love. Be winsome and humble. People don't care how much you know until they know how much you care. Third, recognize that timing is important. Some may think you're being narrow-minded now. However, if a time comes when their life is falling apart, or they have just learned that they have cancer, they may want you to give them the answer and will respect you for holding true to your faith.

Response

The first and most important response for the purpose of this work is that this is not evidence for God. The whole thing hinges on the historicity of the resurrection, which is poorly attested and was never predicted. Licona himself in Chapter 36 called the historicity of the resurrection "the prize puzzle," implying that it is not yet established. Under this condition, the only logical course of action is to remain unpersuaded, at which point Licona's essay and key aspects of versions of his religion collapse. I nonetheless want to examine some other issues with his piece.

Though Licona says he is uneasy with Jesus's exclusivist claim, he does not say why. Half of it is the question of people who have never heard the gospel, which Licona discusses in the next chapter, so I will not discuss it here. The second half of it, unacknowledged in his essay, but possibly more important is tied into the obvious follow-on question to Jesus's claim: *from whom are you saving us?* It turns out it is from himself. If an earthly father said to his child that he was going to lock her in a cupboard unless she admitted that she was no better than Hitler, we would not regard that as a generous offer of salvation. If the father went on and said that the child needed punishment for all her many wrong-doings, but that the father was instead going to smash his own hand with a hammer, we would be horrified. The exclusivist claim incorporates hell, heaven, vicarious redemption, and the equivalence of all human sin, all of which are deeply unjust, so Licona's feeling of unease is understandable.

As I wrestled with the arguments in *Evidence for God,* I found I was sometimes torn in two directions. Apologists tell us that we have a conscience that guides us and that this is evidence of God (discussed in Chapter 2). Now, our conscience is pricked by something Jesus says that is unfair. But this, we are told, is because we are fallen people who cannot judge God and must accept his divine wisdom. So we are told that our conscience is evidence of God and that we should suppress it when looking at something that Jesus said. Surely, this is a double standard?

Licona says that the resurrection verifies the truth of Jesus's unjust claim, so we must accept it. But he could, perhaps with more logic, have said that the contradiction of God making an unjust claim indicates that the resurrection did not happen. This is a proof by contradiction, where you make an assumption (in Licona's words: "assume ... that Jesus was truly who he claimed to be"), infer a contradiction (we must accept unjust claims from a perfect God who gave us a conscience) and deduce that the original assumption was wrong (in other words, Jesus was not who he claimed to be). In my experience, when I bring this up with apologists, I find that the first step in their response is to undermine my ability to judge this situation as unjust.

The second response on ethics correctly asserts that if you believe in something as vicious as hell you must try to convert people. He says that people are free to say "thank you, but no thanks." This ignores the countless episodes in history where such freedoms were not granted and where consent was not required. It ignores the peer pressure applied to children growing up in Christian homes and Christian societies. It ignores the very vocal Christians in politics who are trying to push a Christian agenda into public policy, for example, trying to usurp science education[2]. It ignores Deuteronomy 13:6–15 where God commands that people trying to convert the Israelites must be killed.

The trouble is that religious beliefs are built on a foundation, and from that foundation, inferences are made and acted on. In Licona's case, the foundation is the resurrection, and the inference is that "Jesus is the only way." But the strength of the actions Licona wants to take far exceeds the strength of the foundation.

In this question, Licona also argues that

> when someone claims that my belief that Jesus is the only way is intolerant and offensive, they ignore the fact that their pluralist approach is likewise intolerant and offensive. They are being intolerant of exclusivist views and offensive to those who hold them.

This is incorrect. Your beliefs can be intolerant, while you are still tolerated. Licona makes the mistake of identifying himself with his beliefs and therefore taking offense at an attack on his beliefs. The biggest issue with his beliefs is that they are not supported by the evidence, and saying so is not intolerance. Political correctness barely registers as an issue. His right to hold his beliefs is fought for, while the beliefs themselves are fought against as unjust. As Ayaan Hirsi Ali[3] says: "Tolerance of intolerance is cowardice," so inasmuch as Licona's beliefs cause intolerant actions they are not tolerated. But Licona himself is. He can choose to take offense at this skepticism, but as he himself says "there are times when truth should not be sacrificed for the sake of avoiding offense."

His third question invites us to dismiss a more liberal and inclusive salvation; to dismiss the many Christians who interpret the Bible and Jesus's teachings this way; to dismiss any doubt that the whole structure lacks evidence; to dismiss any unease you may feel at the injustices of the doctrine and to hold fast to the assertion that Jesus is the only way. But this fiat assertion that his interpretation is correct, in fact, an unwillingness to admit that he is interpreting at all, is again the opposite of evidence and the opposite of rationality. It requires the conditional: if it is true. What it shows is that we need to re-examine his claims.

Finally, Licona offers some pastoral advice to Christians to encourage them to continue to evangelize. Following years of preaching tradition, he has three points. The first is to study the words that he, Licona, has

---

[2] An example of this is found in Chapter 12: *What Every Student Should Know about Science.*

[3] Ayaan Hirsi Ali is a Somali-born, Dutch-American activist and author.

written: I tried to engage with them in the above paragraphs and found I came away unsatisfied. The second is that we are to be humble and winsome. I do not disagree with this, but neither am I willing to suppress my conscience. Third, Licona tells us to find people who seek solace when they are at their weakest. He did not phrase it like that, but that is the idea[4].

I will follow his lead and make three points of my own.

Firstly, we agree that the Christian community can be a wonderful support, though that is not to say that other communities are not, because they are, and human goodness is not a measure of objective truth.

Secondly, the Christian philosophies are not, in general, much comfort in times of real pain. To reconcile God's goodness, omnipotence, and his divine plan with true suffering is an exercise in futility that leads only to cognitive dissonance. Stephen Fry comments that he would find it easier to believe in a capricious Greek god based on the world we see.

And thirdly, Christians should reflect on this need for deathbed conversions. For example, Darwin's supposed deathbed conversion was faked[5], but the tendency is understandable, even inevitable, if you believe in hell and have an ounce of humanity in you. The thought of anyone you know suffering in hell for eternity is too awful to contemplate. Hell has also been a tool for frightening people into belief.

I remember the moment when I realized that I was no longer convinced that there was a God. The very next thought I had was: "What if I am wrong and I am going to hell?" It is fascinating to me how closely linked my belief in God and a fear of hell were, especially since hell was not a big part of my theology. The very next moment I thought: "There is no point pretending to believe. If there is a God and He wants me to believe, He is going to have to persuade me."

Licona's tendency in this direction is evident in his essay: he holds his orthodox line firmly, yet seeks to evangelize those on death's door because the idea of hell is so repugnant. However, the other way to look at this is that the difficulty of uniting unfairness with perfection is evidence that Licona's version of Christianity is wrong. Either way, this essay does not provide evidence for God.

---

[4]He phrased it like this: "Third, recognize that timing is important. Some may think you're being narrow-minded now. However, if a time comes when their life is falling apart, or they have just learned that they have cancer, they may want you to give them the answer and will respect you for holding true to your faith."

[5]Even Answers in Genesis has an article proclaiming the deathbed conversion as fake. Tommy Mitchell, 2009, *Darwin's Deathbed Conversion—a Legend?* Available at answersingenesis.org/creationism/arguments-to-avoid/darwins-deathbed-conversion-a-legend.

CHAPTER 40

What About Those Who Have Never Heard the Gospel?

Understanding Jesus's exclusivist claims more fully requires us to consider Licona's second essay on the subject, which addresses another area of apparent injustice: "What About Those Who Have Never Heard the Gospel?" As discussed in the previous chapter, this is not necessarily the biggest issue (which is that a God of justice is imposing infinite punishment for finite infractions), but it is a problem, and it is the one that Licona looks at more closely in this chapter.

He considers the fate of babies and the mentally disabled and those who have never heard about Christ and asks whether they will receive eternal punishment (he uses the more in vogue phrase "eternal separation").

> These are difficult questions deserving thoughtful replies. Since the Bible does not address these issues directly, we will have to engage in speculation. In the end, we can provide plausible solutions to these questions by recognizing two divine principles.

The divine principles Licona recognizes are that "God will judge us according to our response to the knowledge we received," and "God does not hold accountable those who lack the mental capacity to choose between good and evil." Licona uses analogs in the Bible to support these views.

He mentions that:

[O]ther reasonable answers have been proposed. Some hold that
God knew before he even created the world who would respond
to the gospel and caused them to be born in a location where
they would one day hear it. Still others hold that God is able to
communicate the gospel to those truly seeking truth by sending
missionaries and by communicating the gospel through dreams
and visions.

Licona does not hold these views currently, though he regards them as
plausible.

He ends by saying:

The other side of this answer, however, is that God does hold
us accountable for what we have received and understand. In
most cases, this is a full knowledge of the gospel of Jesus Christ.
So the remaining issue is not the other person, but you. What
are you going to do about Jesus?

Response

Licona accepts the teaching that Jesus is the only way, but has subtly
stepped away from the teaching that hell is eternal punishment (see Matthew
25:46[1]) by using the phrase "eternal separation." At the least, this demonstrates that his view is an interpretation of the Bible. This ability to interpret is part of what has made Christianity so resilient, as it allows people
to shift it to something that suits them, most often subconsciously rather
than maliciously.

Licona, in the previous chapter, is dismissive of pluralists who soften
Jesus's exclusiveness claim, saying that he responds: "On what foundation
is such a belief based? It's not from the Bible, The Qur'an, or any other
holy book. Why should I believe it? Have you heard personally from God?"
But, here, Licona is doing the exact same thing.

In this essay, Licona says: "Since the Bible does not address these issues
directly, we will have to engage in speculation. In the end, we can provide
plausible solutions..." Juxtapose this with the quote at the end of the
previous paragraph. This seems to be inconsistent. When he does it, we are
expected to accept something that he finds plausible even without evidence.
But when others do the same thing and come to different conclusions, he
is incredulous that they would expect him to engage with them.

---

[1]Matthew 25:46: "'These will go away into eternal punishment, but the righteous
into eternal life.'"

Licona establishes two divine principles: "God will judge us according to our response to the knowledge we received," and "God does not hold accountable those who lack the mental capacity to choose between good and evil."

Jesus's cursing of the fig (Mark 11:13–14) would seem to go against both. So would God's command to wipe out the Amalekites (1 Samuel 15:3) where children, infants, and animals are included among God's victims. So would Noah's flood. Or Hosea 9:16, where God says he will slay Ephraim's children. Or 2 Samuel 12:14 where the Lord punishes David by killing his newborn baby. Or 2 Kings 17:26 where God sends lions to kill people because they "don't know the law of the god of the land." In other words, Licona's divine principles are a matter of interpretation, and we would do well to ask Licona his own question: "Why should I believe it?"

Licona mentions "other reasonable answers." These answers, apart from being uncaring, demonstrate another attack on reason. Licona shows us that an approach where we try to bridge the gap between unfairness and perfection leads to multiple possible answers. The issue is a failure to engage with what is demonstrably true. Humans are incredibly good at inventing narratives to make incoherent facts fit together: just ask a child (or an adult) who is caught red handed to explain and you will see how easily they can do it. Licona's interpretation and speculation (a word he himself uses) avoid the underlying problem of a lack of evidence. We are not looking for fabrications meant to hold it all together. We are looking for the truth. Licona's guesses, at odds with the guesswork of other people who use the same methodology and at odds with our own conscience, will not do.

Finally, Licona exhorts us not to be concerned about other people. We should not worry that the Bible did not attempt to resolve this injustice, or even to care about it. Licona has a "plausible" answer to some of the inequity, which should suffice. He asks: "What are you going to do about Jesus?" This is the ultimate affront to rationality: we are asked to believe out of fear and in spite of the injustice. The evidence may be unconvincing, but you could end up in hell, so suppress your conscience and confess that you believe in him. But in the absence of evidence for hell, judgment, God, and the resurrection, the answer to Licona's question is: nothing.

CHAPTER 41

Did Paul Invent Christianity?

Looking now at Paul, Ben Witherington III starts his essay[1] as follows:

> The question, Did Paul invent Christianity? has frequently been
> asked. In fact, some have been so sure that Paul was the origina-
> tor of this religion that they called him the first great corrupter
> of the simple religion of Jesus. We still hear today the cry 'back
> to Jesus,' which has as its flip side, 'and away with Paul.' You
> hear this for example from various members of the Jesus Sem-
> inar. Like so many caricatures, this one deserves to be put in
> its place.

Witherington notes that the

> earliest followers of Jesus did not see themselves as creating a
> new religion. They were sectarian Jewish followers of Jesus.
> However, through a process that involved a variety of factors
> (growth, evangelization, and conversion of many gentiles; chris-
> tocentric rather than Torah-centric focus; expulsion from var-
> ious synagogues in the empire) the Jesus movement *de facto*
> became a separate entity from early Judaism, and in fact it
> appears that this was already the case during the lifetime and

---

[1]Ben Witherington III, *Did Paul Invent Christianity?* Available at
www.namb.net/apologetics/did-paul-invent-christianity.

ministry of Paul ... Paul was not the inventor of Christianity, but in some sense its midwife, being most responsible for there being a large number of gentiles entering this sectarian group, and not on the basis of becoming Jews first.

Witherington argues from various texts that Paul saw himself as having moved away from Judaism. Witherington also sees Paul as a "trailblazer" advancing Christianity, for example, through "his insistence that salvation or the new birth must be by grace through faith in Jesus" with an abandonment of "religious living" and "the Mosaic law." Witherington states "it is indeed right to see Paul as the midwife who helped give birth to a new form of religion centered on the worship of Jesus Christ" but notes that "[t]his does not mean that Paul invented the idea that Jesus was divine" or various other Christian doctrines.

Witherington concludes:

[O]ne can say that Paul was a shepherd leading God's people in new directions and through uncharted waters to a new promised land where Jew and gentile would be united in Christ on the very same basis and with the very same discipleship requirements. Though Paul did not call this end result Christianity, he more than any other of the original apostles was responsible for the birthing of the form of community that was to become the early church.

Response

This is not a direct attempt to provide evidence for God. Witherington insists that the answer to the titular question is "no," but allows that "the answer to this question depends on what one means by *invent* and also what one means by *Christianity*." He shows that Paul influenced the shift from a Jewish sect to a separate religion, and he does not at all discuss the reasons why some people believe Jesus and Paul should be separated, dismissing the idea as a "caricature." Witherington can do this because he believes that "though [Paul] did not invent [Christianity's] doctrines or even its ethics, he most consistently applied its truths until a community that comported with these truths emerged." In other words, Witherington already believes in the "truths" of Christianity and is interpreting everything through that lens.

I only recently happened upon this idea that Paul corrupted the religion of Jesus[2]. One example, of relevance to Witherington's discussion, is that Jesus says in the Sermon on the Mount (Matthew 5:17–19):

> "Don't think that I came to destroy the law or the prophets. I didn't come to destroy, but to fulfill. For most certainly, I tell you, until heaven and earth pass away, not even one smallest letter or one tiny pen stroke shall in any way pass away from the law, until all things are accomplished. Whoever, therefore, shall break one of these least commandments, and teach others to do so, shall be called least in the Kingdom of Heaven; but whoever shall do and teach them shall be called great in the Kingdom of Heaven."

Contrast this with these words from Witherington's essay: "in 2 Corinthians 3:7–18 [Paul] speaks of the Mosaic law, and even the Ten Commandments, as a glorious anachronism, something that was glorious in its day but which is rapidly becoming obsolete." The extent of this contradiction is extraordinary, and Witherington's failure to discuss it is baffling.

A second example can be seen in Paul's "insistence that salvation or the new birth must be by grace through faith in Jesus" (as Witherington puts it). Contrast this with Jesus's parable of the sheep and goats (Matthew 25:31–46). In this Jesus says "whatever you did for one of the least of these brothers and sisters of mine, you did for me," and rewards them with eternal life.

Now, from my perspective, this all demonstrates a clear evolution of the religion. Witherington acknowledges this, saying "[i]n any religious movement that endures for any length of time there are always pioneers or trailblazers who see the way forward more clearly than others, and certainly, Paul was one of these." This statement at a stroke admits that religions evolve, that Paul was instrumental in some of Christianity's key evolutionary steps, and that Christianity is not significantly different from other religions in this regard. If you changed the phrase "see the way forward more clearly than others" to "influence people to adopt the religion" you would not modify the meaning other than to remove the qualitative and unsupported judgment that Paul improved matters. The phrase could then be applied to any religion that survived through mechanisms analogous to biological evolution[3].

---

[2]Edgar Jones, *Paul vs. Jesus: A List of Contradictory and Incompatible Statements.* Available at www.voiceofjesus.org/paulvsjesus. This link contains a list of apparent contradictions between Paul and Jesus, with which Witherington does not engage. I am not endorsing this list nor trying to arbitrate between their two positions. I merely show it because Witherington does not.

[3]This will be discussed more in Chapter 51: Why is Christianity So Big?

Can we know what Paul's views were? Ehrman offers some fascinating insights, relevant because Paul is the earliest Christian writer, and so gives us insight into some of the earliest Christian beliefs[4]. I will discuss some of his points here. Ehrman distinguishes between two theological understandings of the divinity of Christ: adoptionist and incarnation. In the former, Jesus, a man, became God because God raised him up at some point, while in the latter Jesus, a divine being, became a man. The latter became the orthodox view, but early Christians primarily believed variations of the former. It is not as clean as that since Paul may have believed that Jesus was an angel who was incarnated and then exalted later to a higher level of divinity. Though these views may seem shocking and heretical to modern Christians, they are barely disputed among scholars.

Here are some of the biblical verses and arguments discussed in Ehrman's book to support this. In Galatians 4:14, Paul writes "but you received me as an angel of God, even as Christ Jesus." Generally, we read that as two different alternatives, but scholars argue that the Greek construction "but as ... as ... " represents an equivalence. For example, 1 Corinthians 3:1: "Brothers, I couldn't speak to you as to spiritual, *but as* to fleshly, *as* to babies in Christ." Here Paul is equating "fleshly" with "babes in Christ" using the "but as ... as ... " construction. The implication is that Galatians 4:14 demonstrates that Paul believes that Jesus Christ is an angel.

Philippians 2:5–11 implies this blended theology that Jesus started as a lower divinity and was exalted by God: Jesus "didn't consider equality with God a thing to be grasped" (v 6); and Jesus's death on the cross meant that "God also highly exalted him" (v 9).

That God exalted Jesus was discussed briefly in Chapter 35, but it is worth going through in more detail here.

Paul quotes another early creed in Romans 1:4, which says Jesus Christ "who *was declared* to be the Son of God with power, according to the Spirit of holiness, *by the resurrection* from the dead, Jesus Christ our Lord" This is a very striking verse because it states that Jesus becomes the Son of God *at the resurrection*.

Acts 2:36 states: "God *has made* him both Lord and Christ, this Jesus whom you crucified." Or consider Acts 5:31: "God *exalted him* with his right hand to be a Prince and a Savior... " Or Acts 13:32–33 where Paul is made by Luke to quote Psalm 2, "You are my Son. *Today* I have become your father" as the result of God raising Jesus. All of these verses indicate Jesus became God at the resurrection. As we have seen (Chapter 31), Jesus did not claim to be divine in the earliest texts we have of him, though

---

[4]This is discussed in much more detail in Bart Ehrman, *How Jesus Became God: The Exaltation of a Jewish Preacher from Galilee.*

this belief evolved rapidly. So Paul believed that Jesus was exalted at his resurrection.

Again the evolution of belief is clear: The earliest Christians, including Paul, believed that God exalted Jesus at his resurrection.

Mark presumably believes that it happened at his baptism, which is where he starts his book. Consider Mark 1:10–11:

> Just as Jesus was coming up out of the water, he saw heaven being torn open and the Spirit descending on him like a dove. And a voice came from heaven: 'You are my Son, whom I love; with you I am well pleased.'

The implication is that the author of Mark reflects a view that Jesus became divine earlier than his resurrection: it happened at his baptism.

Matthew and Luke believe it happened at his birth and so begin their narratives there, unconvincingly placing the birth in Bethlehem, as discussed in Chapter 27.

John believes that Jesus was God from the beginning of time and so starts "In the beginning was the Word, and the Word was with God, and the Word was God. The same was in the beginning with God." (John 1:1–2).

This evolution continued after the Bible was written, with arguments about whether or not Jesus was inferior to God, and whether Jesus was created by God before creation or was eternal, and whether Jesus's kingdom would come to an end when the world ended among others. Every line in the Nicene Creed is there to settle a dispute of this nature.

So, to summarize, Witherington's essay does not provide any evidence for God, does not address the contradictions between Paul and Jesus, and acknowledges that Paul made a significant shift from a Jewish sect to modern Christianity by rejecting the Mosaic law. Whether this contribution could accurately be called 'inventing Christianity' is a semantic quibble. The real point is that Christianity evolved both before and after Paul, with significant steps influenced by Paul, in a similar way to other religions. This supports the atheist view of the human origins of religion and does nothing to gainsay that view.

Part IV

The Question of the Bible

CHAPTER 42

Is the Bible Today What Was Originally Written?

Discussion now turns to the question of the Bible, and we start with an essay by Andreas J. Köstenberger[1]. Köstenberger considers an issue that should be of some concern to Christians: "Is the Bible today what was originally written?" He breaks this into two questions:

> (1) Are the available manuscripts ... of the Bible accurate representations of the original [manuscripts] of the respective books of the Bible (the autographs of Scripture)? This is an issue of textual *transmission*. (2) Are the available translations faithful renderings of the Bible in the original languages? This is an issue of *translation*.

In other words, do we have the original text, and have we translated that text accurately?

The first question arises because "no original autographs exist of any biblical text; only copies are available." The second "involves a plethora of issues related to the nature of language and communication."

Köstenberger gets into a number of interesting details about the extant manuscripts and textual critics who

---

[1] Andreas J. Köstenberger is Professor of New Testament and biblical theology at Southeastern Baptist Theological Seminary, and the founder of Biblical Foundations.

adjudicate between readings through exacting criteria such as
dating, text type, attested readings (i.e., how many [manuscripts]
have a certain reading), and possible reasons for variants (e.g.,
smoothing out a theologically difficult reading).

He then tells us that:

Although textual criticism is a very complex and at times controversial science, it has provided us with at least two assured
results. First, none of the variant readings (including omissions)
affect the central message or theological content of the Scriptures. Second, it can confidently be asserted that the text of
the Bible today is an accurate and faithful representation of the
original autographs.

Köstenberger discusses different philosophies of translation, considering a word-for-word approach versus a phrase-for-phrase approach. Either
way, he is satisfied that "[t]he history of the English Bible satisfactorily
demonstrates that the Bible of today does indeed faithfully represent the
Scriptures in their original languages."

He concludes that:

[W]hen someone opens any English Bible (New King James Version, New American Standard Bible, New International Version,
English Standard Version, Today's New International Version,
Holman Christian Standard Bible), he or she may know that
generations of faithful scholarship have managed to preserve
and protect that Bible as it was originally given.

Response

I have had conversations with Christians who will listen to my points and
conclude that I am challenging the authority of scripture because of some
abstruse technical detail. They nod sagely and say something like: "You are
concerned about the dating. It is not very simple to do the dating, and you
might be basing your conclusions on the wrong dating." Or similar with
the manuscript or translation. "Did you read this in the original Greek?"
they may ask.

The biggest issue with this is that it is the words that are problematic;
the evidence that it presents; the contradictions and immoralities of even
uncontested readings. Having an earlier dating or a faithful transmission
or an accurate translation makes it worse: it means that the words we have

are those that were intended by the original author, with all the lack of credibility and morality that that implies.

So far in my responses to *Evidence for God*, I have accepted the translations and assumed that they were accurately transmitted. Köstenberger is correct to be concerned about these things, in the sense that they form another layer of the foundation upon which his religion rests. But in this situation, the solidity of this layer is irrelevant because layer above it is crumbling. The evidence provided by the Bible and other sources is not sufficient to conclude that the religion is true, even if the Bible as we have it exactly matches the original (non-extant) autographs.

Köstenberger does hit upon a few issues though:

> The sheer multiplicity of [manuscripts] does not, however, result in absolute uniformity of the texts. Thousands of variant readings (most of them minor) exist between the [manuscripts] ... Scribal errors can take on the form of unintentional and intentional errors ... Intentional errors resulted when scribes attempted to correct a perceived error in the text or altered the text in the interest of doctrine and harmonization. These errors often became standardized through subsequent copies made from the defective copy.

The attribute that Köstenberger attributes to the ancient scribes of correcting a perceived error continues to this day[2]. Since the source documents are somewhat locked down now, the major way this is done is through *interpretation*. The principle of explosion tells us that "from contradiction, anything follows," so interpretation has a broad scope. In other words, theologians have been able to justify both sides of so many issues over the centuries that the most logical conclusion is that the Bible is inherently flawed.

Köstenberger also tells us that:

> For centuries the only Bible available to Western people was the Latin Vulgate, prepared by Jerome, who was commissioned by Pope Damasus toward the end of the fourth century AD. The Vulgate served as the official version of the Bible throughout Medieval Europe and was restricted to the clergy, monastic orders, and scholars.

That Christianity and the Bible were used for so long to control people, and that this tendency continues to this day (see Chapter 5), is a strong

---

[2]See my previous discussion of this phenomena in Chapter 36 on page 252 in reference to the comma of John.

indication of the human origins of the religion. This issue is not addressed by Köstenberger but underlies the restriction of the Bible to the clergy that he mentions.

Lastly, Köstenberger assures us that "none of the variant readings (including omissions) affect the central message or theological content of the Scriptures."

However, Mark 16:9–20[3] is not in the oldest manuscripts. Without this section, Mark does not have any of Jesus's resurrection appearances. In other words, it looks as though someone has tampered with the earliest Gospel's evidence for the resurrection appearances. We met another example in Chapter 31, where a Christian apologist admitted that "textual variants exist in every potential passage where Jesus is explicitly referred to as 'theos.'" These examples seem to contradict Köstenberger's claim and undermine his assurances.

Of course, none of Köstenberger's discussion is evidence for God. The evidence is inadequate, and that should be an end to it. However, closer examination of the issues Köstenberger brings up undermine the evidence further and support the idea that the Bible had human origins.

---

[3] The NIV translators insert a comment after verse 8 that says "The earliest manuscripts and some other ancient witnesses do not have verses 9–20." This means that the women go to the tomb, find an angel and flee. "They said nothing to anyone, because they were afraid." There are, then, no direct appearances of the resurrected Jesus in this the earliest of the Gospel accounts.

This view is not universal. The WEB comments: "NU includes the text of verses 9–20, but mentions in a footnote that a few manuscripts omitted it. The translators of the World English Bible regard Mark 16:9–20 as reliable based on an overwhelming majority of textual evidence, including not only the authoritative Greek Majority Text New Testament, but also the TR and many of the manuscripts cited in the NU text."

CHAPTER 43

Inerrancy and the Text of the New Testament

Biblical inerrancy is the next topic. Daniel B. Wallace[1] defends against an argument against the inerrancy of the Bible. He is at pains to say that he is not arguing for inerrancy but rather knocking down one particular argument against it. He says:

> This chapter addresses a popular argument that is used against those who hold to an inerrant Bible. Essentially, the argument is posed as a question: How can you claim to have an inerrant original text when we don't even have the original text? On its face, this argument has seemed so compelling that some people never get beyond it. This chapter will show the underlying assumptions behind this question and why they are fallacious.

I will go through some of his arguments below. He concludes:

> In sum, there is an assumption made by non-evangelicals when they pose the question of inerrancy and the autographs. It is that the wording of the autographs is, in places, completely unrecoverable—that is, unknown and unknowable. But this assumption implies that the wording of the original in some places

---

[1] Daniel Wallace is Professor of New Testament Studies at Dallas Theological Seminary, and executive director of the Center for the Study of New Testament Manuscripts. He also wrote an article that I referenced in the footnote on page 212.

cannot be found in the manuscripts. That is manifestly not true. Pragmatically the wording of the original is to be found either in the text *or the apparatus* of the Nestle-Aland Greek New Testament. We have the original in front of us; we're just not sure at all times whether it is above the line or below it.

Response

Wallace's argument here is that we have the original text of the Bible somewhere, we just do not know what it is, but I do not see how this invalidates the argument against inerrancy. The original argument survives perhaps with a small tweak. He is urging agnostics to retire this argument and essentially says that the reason to retire it is that there are stronger arguments out there.

For example, he says:

> Which evangelical would not like a clean harmony between the two records of Judas's demise, uniform parallel account of Peter's threefold denial of Jesus, or an outright excision of the census by Quirinius? ...These are significantly larger problems for inerrancy than the few, isolated textual problems.

But these too are by far not the biggest issues. The biggest issue is that inerrancy is an extraordinary claim and the onus is on its proponents to support it, rather than on its opponents to dispute it. Simply put, inerrancy is predicated on the existence of God. Thus, inerrancy cannot be put forward as evidence for God.

Wallace believes that:

> [N]o cardinal doctrine is jeopardized by any viable variant ... By *cardinal* [he] mean[s] any doctrine essential for salvation; by *viable* [he] mean[s] any variant that has a legitimate chance of representing the wording of the autographs.

But this means that his view is based on a reading of the Bible that includes salvation, which means it includes God and the theology that Wallace himself holds. This circular reasoning means that the Bible is based on his faith rather than the other way around.

In summary, Wallace believes that a common argument against inerrancy (that the autographs do not exist) is "vacuous" and that there are stronger arguments out there (for example, contradictions in uncontested readings). We can fix the argument by saying that the autographs are unknown, but I would agree that this is still a somewhat obscure, technical point. The primary issue is that there is no evidence for inerrancy. Wallace therefore does not make an argument for faith or provide evidence for God.

CHAPTER 44

Why All the Translations?

Entitled "Why All the Translations", the forty-fourth chapter by Denny Burk[1] is next.

Burk's essay states that:

> [T]he sheer number of versions available can be quite overwhelming, and yet many Christians have no criteria by which to evaluate which translation is the best. This essay proposes to set forth some of the historical reasons for new translations and to explain some of the different translation philosophies that drive the production of so many different versions in our own day.

His essays lays out some of the issues and does not go beyond that. This is not an attempt to provide evidence for God, and so I find I have nothing to subject to consideration. The issue with the Bible is not in the technical details of translation and transmission but in the credibility of the central story.

---

[1] Denny Burk is a Professor of Biblical Studies at Boyce College (the undergraduate school of the Southern Baptist Theological Seminary, in Louisville, Kentucky).

CHAPTER 45

Archæology and the Bible: How Archæological Findings Have Enhanced the Credibility of the Bible

---

Archæological support for the Bible is next. John McRay's[1] essay takes us through some of the highlights, and we will consider it in detail. McRay states that:

> Archæological discoveries relating to these settings and periods have enlightened the cultural context in which many of the recorded events occurred and have enhanced the credibility of the biblical record of both the Old and New Testament periods. For example, many events recorded in the last one hundred years of this period of biblical history, during which the New Testament documents were written, have been illuminated through significant archæological discoveries. Following are some of these impressive finds.

He then writes eight sections in which archæological discoveries seem to corroborate Biblical stories. I will discuss these below.

---

[1] John McRay is Professor Emeritus of New Testament and Archæology at Wheaton College, Illinois. He worked on archæological excavations at Sepphoris and Herodium in Israel and supervised excavating teams for several years in Caesarea Maritima, Israel.

Response

It is a little ironic to have this chapter juxtaposed with the recent chapter (Chapter 43) on inerrancy. In that chapter, Wallace made the statement that "no cardinal doctrine is jeopardized by any viable variant," meaning that the inconsistencies are only to do with irrelevancies on the fringe and therefore can be safely ignored.

In stark contrast, McRay presents archæological evidence that is meant to bolster our confidence in the credibility of the Bible, but does so using stories that are even further removed from "cardinal doctrine." So in the case of archæological findings, the irrelevancies on the fringe are of central importance in establishing biblical credibility. We see then a splitting of the evidence into two: extraneous parts of the Bible which are true are regarded as important confirmation, and those that are false, contradictory, or wrong are considered to be irrelevant.

Of course, the problem with McRay's argument is that no-one is arguing that there was no historical context in which the Bible was written. We are arguing rather that the stories evolved, from speculation into fact and from historical characters into supernatural characters. Confirming some of the context is in no way sufficient to persuade us to accept the miraculous and divine claims.

For example, when Matthew 27:52–53 tells us "The tombs were opened, and many bodies of the saints who had fallen asleep were raised; and coming out of the tombs after his resurrection, they entered into the holy city and appeared to many." With such a dramatic event, we naturally look for corroborating evidence. It turns out that there is none anywhere, not even in the rest of the Bible, and so most people start to talk of Matthew speaking symbolically in this passage.

But whether symbolic or not, the fact is that there is insufficient evidence to accept this event as historical, and so Matthew's credibility as an historical source is undermined since he presented it as part of the narrative. Credibility, however, is a one-way street: once undermined, it is difficult to accept anything else that Matthew says. That does not mean that every single thing Matthew says is a lie (or symbolic); it means that we cannot accept his statements without further corroboration. In other words, you do not get credit for the occasional truth.

In this sense, McRay has set upon a hopeless task. The lack of credibility of the Bible does not come from the setting, and that is the biggest part of what archæology can verify. In principle, hundreds of people could (and perhaps would have been expected to) corroborate the idea of dead people walking around Jerusalem, and some record of this could have been found. But no such evidence has ever been found for this or anything else miraculous. My view is that it will never be found because the palpable inconsistencies in the Bible demonstrate that some of the key events simply did not happen as recorded. But, at the least, there is no good evidence for any "cardinal doctrine" or any miraculous event, and so we should be skeptical.

However, I do not want to be dismissed for being too dismissive, so let us consider the archæological findings that McRay has presented. I will first acknowledge that McRay is an archæologist and I am not, so I am not aiming to denigrate the findings he presents. On the contrary, it must be an incredible thrill to find an archæological site corresponding to an ancient text, so on that level, I am enthralled by the work he and others have done. McRay has chosen eight of the most impressive sites, and it is indeed amazing to read about them. However, it should be clear as we go through them that they are not evidence for anything miraculous, and nor are they evidence for God. As a Christian, it should give you pause that this is the archæological basis for your faith.

First, McRay discusses the Pool of Siloam, where Jesus sent a blind man to have him wash his eyes (John 9:7). The site of the pool was excavated in Silwan (modern spelling of Siloam), and "was probably a major facility for ritual purification before entering the temple. This may be the reason Jesus chose this pool for the miracle." Or it may be the reason that the story about this miracle evolved in the first place. The point is that the existence of the pool does not at all corroborate the miracle.

Second, McRay notes that "[m]any tombs from the time of Christ have been discovered in Jerusalem, and some of them still have these rolling stones by their entrance." This supposedly corroborates Matthew 28:2, where an angel rolled back the stone and sat on it. I can honestly say that the existence of a rolling stone door is not on the list of things that make me skeptical when I read the fantastical narrative of Matthew. But note that Matthew is again the only place where an angel rolls back the stone (though it is pointless to do so since Jesus has already gone). In the other three Gospels, the stone is already rolled back, so even on this bland point, we find the Gospels contradicting each other. It is also doubtful that Jesus was buried in a tomb at all[2].

Third, McRay mentions the Tomb of Caiaphas, a burial cave discovered in 1990

> that contains an ossuary with the name of Caiaphas carved into it ... The high priest before whom Jesus appeared just before his death was named Caiaphas (see Matt. 26:3, 57; Luke 3:2;

---

[2]See Chapter 34.

John 11:49; 18:13, 14, 24, 28). Later both Simon Peter and
John appeared before him in Jerusalem (Acts 4:6).

Some scholars disagree that the ossuary belonged to a high priest, for
various reasons, but again, no one is disputing that early Christians were
butting heads with the authorities, or that those authorities existed. The
existence of a high priest named Caiaphas does not conclusively demonstrate even that the trial took place.

Fourth, McRay considers Capernaum, where Jesus

taught in the synagogue (see Mark 1:21; 3:1; John 6:59). Archæological excavations conducted in Capernaum have discovered
the synagogue under the fourth-fifth century limestone structure still standing there.

My expectation, perhaps naïve, is that there were synagogues throughout the region during that period. In any event, the existence of a synagogue there is not a huge surprise to me. Jesus is known to have come from
Nazareth, the disparate attempts by Matthew and Luke to have him born
in Bethlehem notwithstanding[3].

Fifth, McRay considers Acts 17:6, where the Greek term "politarchs"
is used for city rulers in Thessalonica. McRay says that:

It has been adamantly asserted that no such office existed at
that time. However, an inscription containing this term has
been found in that city and is now displayed in the British Mu-
seum ... Thirty-five inscriptions have now been discovered that
contain this term; nineteen of them come from Thessalonica,
and at least three date to the first century AD. These inscriptions prove that the office of politarchs existed in Thessalonica
in the time of the New Testament and that the Bible is accurate
in its use of the term.

McRay seems to be making the argument that skepticism in the Bible
was unwarranted in this case, and therefore it is unwarranted in all cases.
But this is not true: skepticism is always warranted. The validation of the
term is achieved through the weight of evidence. If anyone "adamantly
asserted that no such office existed" they were obviously proved wrong:
a more accurate claim would be that there was no evidence that such an
office existed (apart from the Bible). But the name of the city rulers of
Thessalonica is clearly not as important as the claim to have seen Jesus

---

[3]See Chapter 27 on page 186.

resurrected. Thus we should be, if anything, more skeptical of the latter claim and require more corroborating evidence before accepting it.

Sixth, McRay considers Erastus in Corinth, who is referenced in Romans 16:23 as the director of public works. Excavations in Corinth have "revealed part of a Latin inscription carved into [a paved area], which reads: 'Erastus in return for his aedileship laid [the pavement] at his own expense.'" McRay argues that they are referring to the same person, specifically equating the Greek word 'oikonomos' with the Latin word 'aedile.' A scholar by the name of Gill wrote a more equivocal article[4], which contains the words:

> Are we to identify the Erastus inscription with the Erastus of Romans? It needs to be pointed out that the evidence will not allow a certain identification or a certain rejection.

In the end, we may never know. But does Paul's acquaintance with a public works' director validate, for example, his claims about seeing a vision? Clearly not.

Seventh, McRay relates that he "uncovered a large [fifth century] mosaic inscription of the Greek text of Romans 13:3." It turns out to be identical to the Greek New Testament and "as old as some of our oldest manuscript of the New Testament." While very impressive, it is not clear how it enhances the credibility of the Bible. At best it supports that Romans 13:3 is correctly transmitted from the autograph.

Romans 13:3 states:

> For rulers are not a terror to the good work, but to the evil. Do you desire to have no fear of the authority? Do that which is good, and you will have praise from the same.

One can imagine why some authority would want to enshrine this verse into a mosaic. This ideology is, in fact, an awful travesty. Once you have the idea that "there is no authority except from God, and those who exist are ordained by God" (Romans 13:1), you open yourself to all kinds of abuse. If you look back through the history of evil tyrants, both in government and inside the church, and try to square this with these verses, you are left with the very epitome of abuse: victim blaming.

The notion of a good and powerful God cannot coexist with these verses, so inasmuch as McRay is correct in establishing these as part of Paul's writings, he undermines the very idea of Paul's God.

---

[4]David W. J. Gill, Tyndale Bulletin, 1989, *Erastus the Aedile.* Available at www.tyndalehouse.com/tynbul/library/TynBull_1989B_40_08_Gill_ErastusTheAedile.pdf.

A Christian might respond that God's ways are mysterious or ask who am I to judge God. But we are here trying to establish that God exists, and failure to see in these verses the potential for abuse is a failure to care sufficiently about the plight of others. Certainly, a verse like this undermines the credibility of a Christian God, which is the exact opposite of what McRay is trying to achieve. Perhaps this issue can be fixed with some sophisticated interpretation, but then we are still left searching for the original reason for belief.

Finally, McRay discusses Paul being brought before Gallio at the Tribunal in Corinth (Acts 18). McRay presents archæological evidence that Gallio was proconsul of Achaia from "May or June of AD 51." McRay notes that this coincides well with Luke's statement in Acts 18:2 that Aquila and Priscilla had arrived from Rome because Claudius had ordered all Jews to leave:

> This expulsion is also referred to in other ancient sources and can be dated to AD 49. Suetonius, chief secretary to the emperor Hadrian (AD 117–38), wrote a biographical account of the Roman emperors titled *The Twelve Caesars*, in which he says, 'Because the Jews at Rome caused continuous disturbances at the instigation of Christ, he expelled them from the City.' Thus the accuracy of Luke's account in Acts is confirmed and illustrated.

Again, the archæological evidence is supporting background details. Ironically, that early Christians were butting heads with the authorities is in direct violation of Romans 13, discussed in the previous paragraph.

McRay presents archæological evidence which supports some of the background in which the New Testament is written. No miracles can be confirmed here, and even in the list that McRay gives us, there is much to dispute. To be clear, I could grant every one of McRay's list of archæological discoveries in every detail and accept every Biblical reference supported by them and remain skeptical of the miraculous stories and the modern theology. None of it is evidence for God. McRay focuses on the New Testament, but it is also noteworthy that there is not one piece of archæological evidence for the Old Testament story of the Exodus[5].

---

[5]A recent apologetic movie called *Patterns of Evidence* explored this issue. It attempted to piece together evidence for the Exodus, but an objective viewing of it shows that even a very sympathetic treatment cannot find any evidence for the Exodus, focusing instead on circumstantial parts of the story, and needs to discard a great deal of scholarship to make its case.

CHAPTER 46

The Historical Reliability of the Gospels

Next, we consider Craig L. Blomberg's essay that aims to support the historical reliability of the gospels. His essay

> briefly surveys the lines of evidence that, cumulatively, support the historical reliability of the Gospels, particularly the Synoptics (Matthew, Mark, and Luke). None of these arguments presupposes Christian faith; all proceed following standard historical approaches of evaluating the credibility of a wide variety of ancient documents.

He builds his argument step by step. He starts by arguing that "we can have enormous confidence in reconstructing what the original texts of the Gospels most likely said." He then claims that "[t]he authors were in a position to write accurate history if they so chose" since the authors "are at most two removes away from eyewitness information." He also notes how early the Gospels were written, comparing that with someone like Alexander the Great where the gap between the person and the writing is larger.

He responds to the arguments that the authors may not have been interested in preserving historical information since they believed that the world was about to end, and they had an ideological bias. He provides the example of the Jewish people ancient and modern who, he claims, preserved accurate history despite being in similar situations.

Next, Blomberg responds to the question of whether they could remember historical events accurately, even if they wanted to do so. To this, he responds that "first-century Judaism was an oral culture, steeped in the educational practice of memorization."

Blomberg is not concerned about the differences between the gospels:

> There is a whole host of reasons for these differences. Many have to do with what each author selected to include or leave out from a much larger body of information of which he was aware (John 21:25). Distinctive theological emphases, unique geographical outlines, and larger questions of literary subgenre account for many of these selections and omissions. But even where the Gospels include versions of the same event, verbatim parallelism usually remains interspersed with considerable freedom to paraphrase, abridge, expand, explain, and stylize other portions of the accounts. All this was considered perfectly acceptable by the historiographical standards of the day and would not have been viewed in any [way] as errant.

Were the gospels even trying to write a history or biography? Blomberg believes so because of Luke's prolog, and the fact that "the Gospel writers felt considerable constraint on what they could or could not include." For example, Jesus's command to hate father and mother in contradiction to the Mosaic law to honor them could easily have been omitted. On the other side, Jesus is not made to address issues of the time such as whether gentile adult males needed to be circumcised when such words could have been included had the writers felt free to do so.

Blomberg states that a

> dozen or so non-Christian writers or texts confirm a remarkable number of details in the Gospels about Jesus's life ... it is remarkable that Jesus gets mentioned at all by first-through-third-century non-Christian writers.

He also mentions the archæological confirmations of certain Biblical details.

He concludes:

> Finally, other Christian testimony confirms a whole host of details in the Gospels. Second-century Christian writers refer back to and even quote a considerable portion of the Gospel accounts with approval. More significantly, the letters of James, Peter,

and Paul, all concurrent with but primarily prior to the written form of the Gospels, contains numerous allusions to and occasional quotations of Jesus's sayings, which show that they must have been circulating by word of mouth in carefully preserved form. Perhaps most telling of all, testimony to Christ's bodily resurrection was phrased in catechetical language as that which would have been received and passed on by oral tradition and thus probably formed part of what Paul was taught at his conversion, a scant two years after the death of Jesus (1 Cor. 15:1–3). These are no late Hellenistic legends that evolved long after the life of Jesus, the simple Jewish rabbi. These were the revolutionary claims being made by his followers from the very beginning!

Response

There are two overarching challenges to Blomberg's argument. The first is that it is a chain, and is therefore only as strong as its weakest link. The second is that it deals monolithically with "history" as though we should accept all or none of it. Together these mean that we can accept much of Blomberg's argument without being convinced that there is a deity underlying it, or that the important parts are historically accurate.

Blomberg has a view that Christianity is based on an historical event and sets about trying to convince us that a set of facts about the Bible is consistent with such a view. However, one needs to ask whether the consistency exists when examined carefully and whether other theories are also consistent with the same set of facts.

First, we have the question of whether we have the original texts of the Gospels. I discussed this briefly in Chapter 43, but we can grant that we have something close. Some key passages are in dispute, but they need not concern us here.

Second, Blomberg says the authors of the Gospels were "at most two removes away from eyewitness information." This is a very significant issue. For some of the historical details it may not matter, but for others it is nowhere near adequate, especially considering that the authors had an agenda when writing and that we do not know exactly who the authors are. When considering the palpable inconsistencies of something like the resurrection appearances, the issue becomes irresolvable. Better evidence is needed to accept this aspect of history. I discussed the resurrection appearances in Chapter 35. The same applies to other key elements such as the birth narrative, discussed in Chapter 27. This is especially so when a story is consciously introduced to fulfill prophecy. For example, the birth in Bethlehem and the burial in the tomb.

Third, he discusses the dating of the Gospels compared with historians writing about Alexander the Great. But, again, if the historians of Alexander the Great made extraordinary claims about him, they too would be questioned. Or consider the burial chambers of ancient Egyptian Pharaohs, which were written within years of the death of the Pharaoh and claimed divinity for the Pharaoh. We do not accept these claims even though the writing is so soon after their death. So the dating is not a reason for blind acceptance.

Fourth, Blomberg asks if the early Christians were interested in preserving historical information? He says that:

> Because Christian faith depended on Jesus having lived, died, and been resurrected according to biblical claims (1 Corinthians 15), the Gospels' authors would have good reason to tell the story straight.

Funnily enough, I would be tempted to draw the exact opposite conclusion.

Fifth is the question of whether the memories would be reliable. This presupposes that there was an event to remember, rather than a reconstruction that grew within the Christian community. The tendency to add or subtract from an account to fill the gap between what is remembered and what is believed exists to this day. The evolution of these stories is more dramatic before the stories have been set down, though after they are set down the tendency continues through interpretation, which often involves adding details that the words do not contain. We will cover a couple of examples of this in the next few paragraphs. The notion that cultures with an oral tradition preserve their stories accurately is a modern myth: anthropologists have shown the opposite is true[1].

Sixth, Blomberg addresses the question of why the Gospels are not verbatim copies, even when they have a common source. He dismisses this

---

[1] See Bart Ehrman, *How Jesus Became God: The Exaltation of a Jewish Preacher from Galilee*, and references therein. He says:

> Anthropologists who have studied oral cultures show that just the opposite is the case. Only literary cultures have a concern for exact replication of the facts 'as they really are.' And this is because in literary cultures, it is possible to check the sources to see whether someone has changed a story. In oral cultures, it is widely expected that stories will indeed change— they change anytime a storyteller is telling a story in a new context. New contexts require new ways of telling stories. Thus, oral cultures historically have seen no problem with altering accounts as they were told and retold.

issue with a handful of possible reasons that plausibly account for some of the differences. However, the issue is not the occasions when reconciliation is possible: it is the examples where it is not. A single example of theological tampering should cause us grave concern over the credibility of the Gospel, even if a thousand other discrepancies can be explained.

An example of such tampering is when Luke alters Mark's angel's words to completely and deliberately change the meaning. Mark's angel clearly says that Jesus is going to see the disciples in Galilee (Mark 16:7). Matthew repeats this (Matthew 28:7). Luke changes that to a statement about remembering what Jesus said when he was in Galilee (Luke 24:6). This is not mere muddle. For Luke, Jerusalem is of great theological significance, and so he "corrects" Mark in a couple of places so that Jesus's resurrection appearances can occur in Jerusalem rather than in Galilee. In fact, Luke writes that Jesus explicitly commanded the disciples "Don't depart from Jerusalem" (Acts 1:4), effectively eliminating the possibility of reconciliation between the accounts.

Seventh, Blomberg asks whether the Gospel writers were trying to write a history. Blomberg points out the criterion of embarrassment: the Gospel writers must have felt compelled to include items that they could have removed, which indicates that they were trying to write an accurate, historical account. However, this would also be true if the Gospel writers were faithfully recording stories from within the community, at least for the most part.

The example in the sixth point above shows, perhaps, that the resurrection account was not yet as well established as some of the other sayings, such as Blomberg's example of "Jesus's command to hate father and mother" (Luke 14:26). It also helps us understand these "embarrassments": a person could well be expected to make contradictory and confusing statements, and filtering through the collective, spiritually-active memories of the early Christian community would only exacerbate that tendency. It is easier to believe this than to believe that Jesus Christ was a perfect and unchanging God whose statements only appear to contradict his earlier edicts. The "embarrassments" may mean that the saying was an authentic one of Jesus of Nazareth, but they also undermine the claim that he was divine.

Eighth, Blomberg states that a "dozen or so non-Christian writers or texts confirm a remarkable number of details in the Gospels about Jesus's life." He claims that it is remarkable that Jesus is mentioned at all. This contradicts the statement made in the previous chapter where Suetonius says that "Because the Jews at Rome caused continuous disturbances at the instigation of Christ, he [Claudius] expelled them from the City [Rome]." This expulsion is dated to 49 CE and is used in the previous chapter to support the accuracy of Acts 18:2. Now Blomberg claims the opposite to support his case, that is that it is remarkable that Jesus is mentioned at all. You cannot have it both ways.

Blomberg does not tell us who these non-Christian writers are, but in Chapters 28 and 33 we discussed the most commonly referenced examples (Josephus, Tacitus, Lucian, and Mara bar Serapion) and saw that even the best of these is admitted even by conservative Christian scholars to have a Christian source behind them, rather than being a truly independent corroboration of the history.

Ninth, Blomberg discusses the archæological support. I covered this in the previous chapter, and Blomberg does not add anything of significance here. Suffice it to say that a validation of the setting is not a validation of the story.

Finally, Blomberg considers other Christian testimony (I quoted his entire paragraph above). He says that "the letters of James, Peter, and Paul ... contain numerous allusions to and occasional quotations of Jesus's sayings." However, when Paul quotes Jesus, he is generally quoting the Risen Lord who he sees in a vision; he explicitly does not receive these words from man (Galatians 1:11–12). I also looked at every quote in James, 1 Peter and 2 Peter: only once is there any reference to a Gospel, which is 2 Peter 1:17, but this is quoting God speaking from heaven, rather than a saying of Jesus, and scholars do not generally believe that 2 Peter was written by Peter. But again, we can accept that Jesus of Nazareth existed and said certain things, without accepting all of it.

Blomberg notes that "Christ's bodily resurrection was phrased in catechetical language ... a scant two years after the death of Jesus (1 Cor. 15:1–3)." This dating makes the lack of any historical setting or detail in 1 Corinthians 15 very strange. The reference to "the Twelve" is also unintelligible in a catechism since the Gospels always refer to eleven (Judas having left), and Matthias not joining until after the ascension. Paul's discussion of the resurrection body in that same chapter (v35–58) makes the word "bodily" seem suspect at least in the way that modern Christians understand the resurrection.

This supports the idea that the Christianity of Paul was based on a "spiritual body" that he and two or three others saw in separate visions. In this scenario, the stories in the Gospels would arise through the telling and re-telling of various accounts, especially stories that would fulfill prophecies from Scripture. This scenario requires no supernatural events, explains the discrepancies between the accounts, and shows how the Gospel authors might feel constrained to record "embarrassments" accurately even though the stories are not all historical.

In other words, historians can use the gospels to deduce that Jesus probably said to hate father and mother; that he was an apocalypticist who said that the son of man was coming soon; that John baptized him; and that Pontius Pilate crucified him. But they can also use the same techniques to doubt that he was born in Bethlehem, or claimed to be God, or was buried in a tomb. Despite this, the Gospels may still have been written in good faith.

Thus Blomberg's chain of reasoning is broken. We can accept some of the Bible as historical, but there is insufficient evidence to accept it all. The "embarrassments" and other discrepancies can be explained far better with naturalistic ideas than with any appeal to the miraculous or the divine. On this view, we do not see the embarrassments as a signature of authenticity, but as a signature that the gospel writers were sincerely trying to capture the various stories that existed at the time. But we are also not left bewildered by these embarrassments, floundering for excuses or interpretations to explain them away; on the contrary, we would expect them as a natural result of the human origins of the document.

CHAPTER **47**

The New Testament Canon

Another essay by Blomberg attempts to defend the New Testament canon by looking at the history of how it arose including speculation on the origin of the order of the books. He concludes:

> For sixteen centuries there has been no significant controversy within Christianity regarding the extent of the New Testament canon. Christians are on solid ground in affirming that these twenty-seven books belong in the New Testament and that other ancient writings were excluded for good reason.

How were the books selected? According to Blomberg:

> [T]hree criteria prevailed for sifting the canonical from the non-canonical. First and foremost was *apostolicity*—authorship by an apostle or a close associate of an apostle—which thus, for all practical purposes, limited the works to the first hundred years or so of Christian history. Second was *orthodoxy* or noncontradiction with previously revealed Scripture, beginning with the Hebrew Scriptures that Christians came to call the Old Testament. Finally, the early church used the criterion of *catholicity*—universal (or at least extremely widespread) usage and relevance throughout the church. This excluded, for example, the Gnostic writings, which were accepted only in the sects from which they emanated.

307

Response

Once again, Blomberg is not presenting any evidence for God: you would already need to believe that there was a God for the idea of a canon to have any meaning. His assurances that the New Testament is legitimate sound a little hollow in the face of the somewhat haphazard history that he presents. There are some contradictions between his selection criteria and the statements he made in the previous chapter on the historical reliability of the gospels, which I will examine now.

His first criterion is *apostolicity*, meaning that the author must be "an apostle or a close associate of an apostle." But in his previous essay, he admitted that we do not even know who the Gospel authors are and that they could be "two removes away from eyewitness information." He even admits, in this essay, that "[t]he authorship of Hebrews has been uncertain from its initial publication." Neither of these is compatible with his definition of apostolicity.

Even worse than this, his second criterion is *orthodoxy*, meaning that it does not contradict "previously revealed Scripture." But in the previous essay, he referred to the criterion of embarrassment, where "it would have been far easier for Luke simply to omit [Jesus's command to hate father and mother] altogether and avoid the apparent contradiction with the Mosaic command to honor one's parents."

So the canon is selected because it does not contradict the Hebrew scriptures, and contradictions in the canon mean that the writers did not feel free to embellish. It is hard to imagine a view more impervious to evidence and analysis since both of the two conflicting views gets interpreted in a way that is benign to his religion. Blomberg himself is probably unaware that he is doing this, in which case it provides an example of an author attempting to reveal the truth in good faith but unaware of his own bias. In other words, Blomberg's own writing provides an example of how the Bible could have been written with sincerity while containing contradictions.

Regarding the *catholicity*, that is the widespread acceptance, one also has to ask when it was widespread. For example, it is clear that the doctrine of the trinity evolved over hundreds of years. Ehrman goes through this evolution[1] as applied to various understandings, and it is fascinating to note that orthodox beliefs in the early Christian community came to be considered heretical in later centuries.

For example, Justin Martyr, writing around 140 CE, believed that Jesus was "first begotten of God," that is brought into existence before the cre-

---

[1] This discussion draws from Bart Ehrman, *How Jesus Became God: The Exaltation of a Jewish Preacher from Galilee*, which goes into the evolution of various Christian beliefs in far more detail.

ation of the world. Colossians 1:15: "[The Son] is the image of the invisible God, the *firstborn of all creation*" would most naturally be understood this way too. He saw Jesus as the "preincarnate Angel of the Lord," associated with several appearances of the "Angel of the Lord" in the Old Testament, such as the burning bush. He has not quite embraced the doctrine of the Trinity, but says that "God is worshiped first, the Son second, and the prophetic Spirit third (*1 Apology* 1.13)" and that "the Son is subordinate to the Father." These views would later be considered heretical, though they were orthodox at the time.

In other words, this criterion for the selection of the canon was based on the dominant view at a point in time, and despite the fact that earlier orthodoxy had interpreted the very same scriptures to mean something later considered heretical.

In the end, however, the biggest issue is that a canon is only meaningful if there is an underlying truth, in other words, if there is a God directing the assembly of the canon. This means that Blomberg is assuming what he is trying to prove. He gives this away in his essay when he says: "It is true that God's law and God's word last forever." If that is true, then we must already know that God exists and is inspiring the scripture, but he has established neither of these assertions. People invented the criteria that Blomberg references (a point not in dispute), and closer examination reveals a very human application of them, consistent with the human creation of the canon and associated doctrines. So *Evidence for God* fails to deliver on its titular promise.

CHAPTER 48

The Coptic Gospel of Thomas?

The last of Blomberg's contribution to the collection is an essay on the Coptic Gospel of Thomas, a list of 114 sayings attributed to Jesus. Blomberg tells us:

> Gnosticism is a hybrid religion of philosophy that began with Plato's radical dualism, sharply differentiating between the material and immaterial worlds and finding only the latter redeemable. It mixed in a few Jewish concepts, quite a few Christian ones, and a pinch of additional Greek philosophy.

Blomberg tells us that the Gospel of Thomas is generally excluded from the New Testament canon, probably because of its Gnostic ideas, but it is considered worthy of study by many.

The dating of Thomas is probably the second-century, though some of the oral traditions may be older. As Blomberg notes "almost half of his sayings find at least a partial parallel somewhere in Matthew, Mark, Luke, or John." Although Blomberg does not mention it, it has been postulated that the Gospel of Thomas and Q have a common source for this reason[1].

Blomberg notes that "[a]lmost a third of *Thomas*'s sayings are fairly

---

[1]You will recall that Q is a non-extant, sayings gospel that is theorized to be a common source for Matthew and Luke. Matthew and Luke are also thought to have been based on Mark, but written independently of each other.

clearly Gnostic in origin." He refers to saying 3b and 29[2] as examples. He says that "[t]he rest of Thomas's teachings are neither demonstrably orthodox nor necessarily Gnostic. Most are ambiguous enough that they could be taken in a variety of ways." He refers to saying 42: "Become passers-by," the shortest of the sayings, and speculates on different interpretations. Blomberg finds this category intriguing since they might "reflect genuine sayings of Jesus not preserved elsewhere." He gives saying 98 as an example, which says:

> The Kingdom of the Father is like a certain man who wanted to kill a powerful man. In his own house he drew his sword and stuck it into the wall in order to find out whether his hand could carry through. Then he slew the powerful man.

His conclusion is:

> *Thomas*, or Gnosticism more generally, can at first glance appear more 'enlightened' from a modern (or postmodern) perspective than parts of the New Testament. But if one is going to accept a Gnostic worldview, one has to take all of it. And the final saying of this enigmatic Gospel has Peter telling Jesus and the other disciples, 'Let Mary leave us, for women are not worthy of life.' Jesus replies, 'I myself shall lead her in order to make her male, so that she too may become a living spirit resembling you males. For every woman who will make herself male will enter the Kingdom of Heaven.' Modern appropriations of *Thomas* seldom incorporate this perspective! Indeed, *Thomas* can appear superior to the canonical Gospels only by highly selective usage of its teachings. Despite what some may claim, it does not open any significant window into first-century Christian history and origins, only into its later corruption.

Response

Blomberg is dismissing the teachings of the Gospel of Thomas based on a single saying that he finds morally repugnant. If that were basis enough, Christianity would not fare well. I discussed many of the morally dubious sayings of Jesus in Chapter 38. If Blomberg finds saying 114 to be too much, one wonders how he deals with Matthew 15:21–28, in which Jesus

---

[2]For the Gospel of Thomas quotes, I will use Lambdin's translation, which can be found at gnosis.org/naghamm/gthlamb.html.

calls a Canaanite woman a dog before healing her daughter. These seem to be morally on a par with each other. However, Christian theologians can justify the Matthew verse in a plethora of creative ways, and I feel confident that similar creativity could rescue the Thomas saying to which Blomberg refers, were he so inclined.

Blomberg dismisses Gnosticism implicitly through a second argument also. In the previous chapter, he stated that Gnostic writings were excluded because they "were accepted only in the sects from which they emanated." However, in this one, he says that "in her bestseller *Beyond Belief*, Elaine Pagels rejects orthodox Christianity in favor of the more attractive religion she thinks she finds in [the Gospel of Thomas]." So he rejects it because it is not widely accepted, and laments how popular this "bestseller" is. Which is it? Perhaps it is to do with the lack of acceptance early on? But then Christianity should also be rejected on this basis as early on only there were only one hundred twenty Christians (Acts 1:15). He is splitting hairs here: the differences are not so marked.

Blomberg refers to Thomas as a "corruption" of previous teaching, but he could also have used the word "evolution." Possibly the clearest and most famous example of this evolution that includes the Gospel of Thomas is related to the end of days teachings.

If Jesus believed that the world was going to end, then he died "a deluded fanatic." Christian apologists either "regard the relevant gospel pronouncements as not spoken by Jesus, but as ascribed to him by the early church, or as not meaning what they say, but something innocuous."[3] Verses that need such explanation include Mark 9:1:

> He said to them, "Most certainly I tell you, there are some standing here who will in no way taste death until they see God's Kingdom come with power."

Or Mark 13:24–30, where Jesus is speaking:

> But in those days, after that oppression, the sun will be darkened, the moon will not give its light, the stars will be falling from the sky, and the powers that are in the heavens will be shaken. Then they will see the Son of Man coming in clouds with great power and glory. Then he will send out his angels, and will gather together his chosen ones from the four winds, from the ends of the earth to the ends of the sky ... Most certainly I say to you, this generation will not pass away until all these things happen.

---

[3]Quoted from G. A. Wells, *Cutting Jesus Down to Size: What Higher Criticism Has Achieved and Where It Leaves Christianity.*

Wells, quoting Allison, asks:

> Do we really have suitable reasons, other than saving our the-
> ology, for holding that, when the Jesus tradition speaks about
> the Son of Man coming on the clouds of heaven, this was not
> meant literally?

Paul also believes that this is imminent and that he expects still to be
alive when it happens. He writes in 1 Thessalonians 4:15–17:

> For this we tell you by the word of the Lord, that *we who are
> alive, who are left to the coming of the Lord*, will in no way
> precede those who have fallen asleep. For the Lord himself
> will descend from heaven with a shout, with the voice of the
> archangel, and with God's trumpet. The dead in Christ will
> rise first, then *we who are alive, who are left, will be caught up
> together with them in the clouds*, to meet the Lord in the air.
> So we will be with the Lord forever.

The sections I have italicized are hard to interpret in any other way.
Similarly, we see 1 Corinthians 7:29–31: "But I say this, brothers: the time
is short . . . For the mode of this world passes away."

When the expectation of the second coming is not met, the references
to it are toned down. Compare the earlier writing of Mark with the later
writing of Luke. In Mark 14:62, Jesus addresses the Sanhedrin and says:

> "You will see the Son of Man sitting at the right hand of Power,
> and coming with the clouds of the sky."

Luke 22:69 changes this to

> "From now on, the Son of Man will be seated at the right hand
> of the power of God."

In other words, an evolution from the specific, imminent, and impressive
to the general, on-going, and invisible.

Or compare Mark 9:1, where Jesus says that "there are some standing
here who will in no way taste death until they see God's Kingdom come
with power," with Luke 9:27 where Luke quietly drops the words "with
power."

By the time 2 Peter is written (the last of the New Testament books to
be written), the author includes this exhortation (2 Peter 3:3–4):

in the last days mockers will come, walking after their own lusts, and saying, "Where is the promise of his coming? For, from the day that the fathers fell asleep, all things continue as they were from the beginning of the creation."

The author is still holding on to the belief that he is in "the last days," but the hope is dwindling, and new theological arguments to deal with the disappointment of the world not ending must be invented.

Which brings us back to the Gospel of Thomas, in which Jesus is now made to mock the disciples when they ask how their end will be. Jesus responds to them (Thomas 18): "Have you discovered, then, the beginning, that you look for the end?" When the disciples ask him when the kingdom will come, Thomas 113 has Jesus answering: "It will not come by waiting for it. It will not be a matter of saying 'here it is' or 'there it is.' Rather, the kingdom of the father is spread out upon the earth, and men do not see it." In other words, the theology continued to evolve to deal with reality from the early biblical references where the second, glorious coming was imminent to the later ones where the theology was on the defensive, to the Gospel of Thomas, which is disparaging of an eschatological understanding of Jesus.

Wells puts it like this:

> To summarize the development, the apocalyptic message begins to be muted by the end of the century, and in the fourth gospel it has virtually disappeared. Then it begins to be explicitly rejected [in the Gospel of Thomas]. Christians, says Ehrman, had to take stock of the fact that Jesus was wrong in saying that the end would come, and 'changed his message accordingly. You can hardly blame them'.

From Blomberg's perspective, all this is "corruption" of the New Testament canon. But the evidence demonstrates a perfectly natural evolution through the canon and beyond, and is suggestive of the human origins of the stories. He rejects the Gospel of Thomas on the basis of one of its teachings and for its lack of early acceptance. But these arguments are not convincing as they could easily be applied to the canonical Bible too. In any event, the fine distinctions that Blomberg uses to undermine the Gospel of Thomas were invented *ex nihilo* by Christian apologists who were attempting to defend their position, so they cannot be taken as objective truth. He misses that banal, human, religious tendencies provide superior explanatory power for the origin of the Bible than does anything supernatural.

Of course, Blomberg in this chapter is not attempting to provide evidence for his version of the Christian God, or indeed any version of God:

he is on the defensive. He is like a man with a sword shouting that he will not let you into his castle when anyone can plainly see that behind him the castle is simply not there. We need to be convinced of the existence of the castle before we can take his defenses seriously.

CHAPTER 49

The Gospel of Peter?

Here we respond to Charles L. Quarles's[1] essay on the Gospel of Peter. He begins with the contention that:

> Skeptics frequently allege that the true story of the real Jesus appears not in the four New Testament Gospels but in other 'lost Gospels,' which were suppressed by the early church. One of these allegedly superior sources is the Gospel of Peter. This article will summarize the contents of the Gospel of Peter, discuss the implications of affirming the reliability of the document, and present compelling evidence that the Gospel of Peter is later and less reliable than the four New Testament Gospels.

The Gospel of Peter[2] was referred to by several early sources but remained a mystery until a fragment was discovered in Akhmim, Egypt in 1886–87. "Because the final verse of the fragment identifies Simon Peter as the author, most scholars have concluded that this fragment is a portion of the long lost Gospel of Peter." Quarles also notes that:

> Scholars are not sure of the length of the original document. The fragment begins with an allusion to Pilate's handwashing

---

[1]Charles Quarles is Professor of New Testament and Biblical Theology at Southeastern Baptist Theological Seminary.
[2]I will use the M. R. James Translation available at
gnosis.org/library/gospete.htm

at the end of Jesus's trial and breaks off at the beginning of
a description of an appearance of the resurrected Jesus to his
disciples. This portion of the document was apparently all that
was available to the scribe responsible for copying it since orna-
ments at the beginning and end of his manuscript indicate that
the manuscript is complete.

After examining various challenges with some of the stories in the Gospel
of Peter, and dating it to the mid-second-century, Quarles concludes as
follows:

This evidence confirms the traditional Christian claim that the
four New Testament Gospels are the most reliable accounts of
Jesus's trial, death, burial, and resurrection. The accounts of
crucifixion and resurrection in the four Gospels are based on
eyewitness testimony rather than naive dependence on an un-
reliable source like the alleged Cross Gospel. The Gospel of
Peter (and the so-called Cross Gospel) is clearly later than the
New Testament Gospels and is sprinkled throughout with imaginative elements and traces of legend. Although the Gospel of
Peter is helpful for understanding the thought of some sectors
of the church in the mid-second-century, it is of little value for
understanding the details of Jesus's final days on earth.

Response

Quarles's statement that "[s]keptics frequently allege that the true story of
the real Jesus appears not in the four New Testament Gospels but in other
'lost Gospels,' which were suppressed by the early church" seems odd to
me. I can honestly say that I have never heard that argument made by
someone who calls themself a skeptic. Skeptics are not trying to present
increasingly fantastical narratives as historical. Quite the reverse: skeptics
do not even accept the New Testament canon as credible, and are certainly
not trying to replace it with even wilder claims.

Quarles argues that the Gospel of Peter is dependent on Matthew. This
dependence, however, provides more support for the notion that there is
a clear evolution over time. Paul, the first to write, gives a simple list of
people who had a vision of the risen Lord. Such experiences are shared
across many religions.

The next stage was to give actual descriptions (not mere list-
ings) of the appearances, as in the canonical gospels. Finally, in

the apocryphal Gospel of Peter, there is a description of the resurrection itself: Jesus is actually seen emerging from the tomb[3].

Matthew writes that an angel rolls the stone away when the women
arrive, but when they look in Jesus is already gone. It is apparently early
enough in the evolution of the story that Jesus can pass through solid rock.
That Jesus is already missing makes the opening of the tomb unnecessary,
of course, other than for the women to look inside and confirm that he is
gone.

The other gospels have the women simply arriving at an open, empty
tomb (there are no soldiers in the other three gospels), with the implication
that it was opened for Jesus to exit.

By the time the Gospel of Peter gets written, the soldiers are there
with the centurion and the elders and witness two angels coming down, the
stone door rolling aside by itself, the angels entering and bringing Jesus out
followed by a floating, talking cross. The angels' heads reach the heavens,
and Jesus's head is even higher.

This is too much for Quarles who tells us that the Gospel of Peter "is
sprinkled throughout with imaginative elements and traces of legend." But
it is a difference only of degree from the resurrection stories in the four New
Testament Gospels. Skeptics are calibrating themselves only very slightly
differently from Quarles when they dismiss the canonical gospels for their
"imaginative elements and traces of legend," in the same way as Quarles
does for the Gospel of Peter.

We also find another double standard, this time in the question of the
dating. In Chapter 46 on the historical reliability of the gospels, Blomberg
tells us that the "life of Alexander the Great ... depends on Arrian and
Plutarch's late first- and early second-century biographies of a man who
died in 323 BC" and that this gap of more than a two centuries still allows
for "a fair amount of accuracy." But here Quarles dismisses the Gospel of
Peter for being a second-century work, "clearly later than the New Testament Gospels."

To me, the dating is a secondary issue, but it is interesting to see the
double standard at work, interpreting all data in a way that supports his
basic presupposition. We were told that since we accept the historicity of
Alexander the Great, we must accept the canonical gospels because there
is a smaller time gap; now we are told that we need not accept the Gospel
of Peter because it is later than the canonical gospels even though the gap
is smaller than it is for Alexander.

---

[3]G. A. Wells, *Cutting Jesus Down to Size: What Higher Criticism Has Achieved and
Where It Leaves Christianity.*

This is not evidence in support of God, or even in support of the Bible. It is a reason to dismiss an inconvenient, ancient work that is more similar to the gospels in form and content than Quarles might like to admit. He is not defending against a common skeptical argument, as skeptics are as happy to leave the Gospel of Peter alone as Quarles is. This chapter does nothing for his cause. In fact, it provides an example of Quarles dismissing the Gospel of Peter for the same reason that skeptics dismiss the Bible: there is insufficient reason to accept the extraordinary claims.

CHAPTER 50

The Gospel of Judas?

Ending our consideration of *Evidence for God*, we turn now to Craig A. Evans's essay on the Gospel of Judas. He says that in April 2006, the National Geographic Society held a press conference to announce the recovery, restoration, and translation of the Gospel of Judas. The history of the discovery, related by Evans, is intriguing:

> As best as investigators can determine, a leather-bound codex (or ancient book), whose pages consist of papyrus, was discovered in the late 1970s, perhaps in 1978, in Egypt, perhaps in a cave. For the next five years, the codex, written in the Coptic language, was passed around the Egyptian antiquities market. In 1983 Stephen Emmel, a Coptic scholar, ... examined the recently discovered codex in Geneva. Emmel was able to identify four tractates, including one that frequently mentioned Judas in conversation with Jesus. He concluded that the codex was genuine (i.e., not a forgery) and that it probably dated to the fourth century. Subsequent scientific tests confirmed Emmel's educated guess.

> The seller was unable to obtain his asking price. After that the codex journeyed to the United States, where it ended up in a safe-deposit box in Long Island, New York, and suffered serious deterioration. Another dealer placed it in a deep freezer,

mistakenly thinking that the extreme cold would protect the codex from damaging humidity. Unfortunately, the codex suffered badly, with the papyrus turning dark brown and becoming brittle.

Happily, the codex was eventually acquired by the Maecenas Foundation in Switzerland and, with the assistance of the National Geographic Society, was recovered and partially restored.

Evans tells us that:

> The Gospel of Judas begins with these words: "The secret account of the revelation that Jesus spoke in conversation with Judas Iscariot" (page 33, lines 1-3).

It singles out Judas as Jesus's greatest disciple.

> He alone is able to receive Jesus's most profound teaching and revelation. Jesus laughs at the other disciples' prayers and sacrifices. They do not fully grasp who Jesus really is and from whom and from where he has come. But Judas is able to stand before Jesus ... "I know who you are and from where you have come. You are from the immortal realm of Barbelo. And I am not worthy to utter the name of the one who has sent you" ... After this confession Jesus teaches Judas in private.

Jesus tells Judas that he will exceed the other disciples because he will sacrifice "the man who clothes me."

> That is, while the other disciples are wasting time in inferior worship and activity ... Judas will carry out the sacrifice that truly counts, the sacrifice that will result in salvation: he will sacrifice the physical body of Jesus.

It seems that this kind of idea was common in the second-century. Irenaeus writes in 180 CE about a group called the Cainites, "evidently because this group makes heroes out of biblical villains, from Cain, who murdered his brother Abel, to Judas, who handed Jesus to his enemies."

Evans then assures us that "it is highly unlikely that the Gospel of Judas preserves for us authentic, independent material." He presents a number of errors in the translations and interpretations of the Gospel of Judas and asserts that the story may also have been misunderstood:

When the Gospel of Judas is properly translated and interpreted we do not find in Judas Iscariot a hero, the wisest of the disciples, who assists Jesus and then enters glory. On the contrary, Judas is a tragic figure in a dramatic retelling and reinterpretation of the Passion of Jesus, a retelling that is marked by anti-Semitism and a mockery of the apostolic Church. The disciples have failed to understand who Jesus really is. Even the one who came closest to this truth—Judas Iscariot—in the end was the worst of a bad lot, sacrificing a human being to the rulers of this fallen earth ...However the Gospel of Judas is interpreted, all scholars agree that this second-century writing provides us with no genuine information about the historical Jesus and his tragic disciple who for whatever reasons decided to betray him. The Gospel of Judas is second-century fiction, not first-century history.

Response

This essay has the same fundamental issue as the previous one on the Gospel of Peter. It does not support the existence of God, and it does not support the historical credibility of the canonical Bible. If anything, it undermines it, as it shows how free people felt to embellish even sacred texts.

The story of Judas is another example of theological evolution over time in several ways. Firstly, it changes within the Bible apparently driven by the theological difficulties relating to Judas's culpability. This evolution continues into the Gospel of Judas. Secondly, there are inconsistencies introduced in the Bible apparently because different authors are trying to tie the story in with Old Testament writings and do so in different ways. Thirdly, there are modern additions to the story that attempt to reconcile the contradictions of the Bible. The evolution narrative explains the facts better than the idea that the Bible is historically accurate, which in turn undermines the credibility of the Bible. I will discuss each of these exemplars now.

We start with Paul, the earliest Christian writer, and note that Paul never mentions Judas, and writes as though it is God who is "delivering" Jesus up for His purposes. Even 1 Corinthians 11:23, where the translation "betrayed" is often used, is more accurately translated as "delivered up"[1].

---

[1] WEB, NLT, ESV, ERV, BSB, ASV, KJB, HCSB, ISV, and NIV all say "betrayed." But Young's Literal Translation renders is "delivered up."

Even if this is granted, we have one reference to betrayal and none to Judas by Paul. There are other verses that make it clear that for Paul it was God who was delivering

Next is Mark 14:21 and parallels in Matthew and Luke[2]. During the last supper, Jesus says:

> "For the Son of Man goes, even as it is written about him, but woe to that man by whom the Son of Man is betrayed! It would be better for that man if he had not been born."

Judas's betrayal is presumably part of God's plan, yet Judas remains culpable, with a strong condemnation by Jesus. This feels unjust.

John 13:27 has Jesus identify Judas by passing him a piece of bread (Jesus does not identify him in the other gospels):

> After the piece of bread, then Satan entered into him. Then Jesus said to him, "What you do, do quickly."

The moral quandary is not completely resolved, but now Jesus is not condemning Judas. Judas has Satan entering into him, and Jesus almost encourages him to do the betrayal.

From there it is a short step to the idea that Judas had some secret knowledge and was complying with Jesus's request, which is where the Gospel of Judas apparently gets to. It is understandable since we feel a sense of injustice if God made Judas do something (or perhaps allowed Satan to use him) and then blamed him for it. It seems likely that this moral difficulty drove the high rate of evolution that I have just described.

There is also the contradiction of how Judas died: Matthew 27:3–10 says he hanged himself while Luke (Acts 1:15–19) says that he fell headlong and his guts gushed out. Georgia Purdom writes an article for Answers in Genesis that attempts to resolve this contradiction[3]. She says:

> *Since the Bible is inerrant* [emphasis added] Judas cannot have died by hanging and died by falling and bursting open. Rather they are two different viewpoints of the same event ... Gruesome as it is, Judas's dead body hung in the hot sun of Jerusalem, and the bacteria inside his body would have been actively breaking down tissues and cells. A byproduct of bacterial metabolism is often gas ... In addition, tissue decomposition occurs compromising the integrity of the skin ... as he hit the ground (due

---

Jesus up. For example, Romans 4:25: "who *was delivered* up for our trespasses, and was raised for our justification" and Philippians 2:8 "And being found in human form, he humbled himself, becoming *obedient to death*, yes, the death of the cross.".

[2]Matthew 26:24 and Luke 22:22

[3]Georgia Purdom, 2009, *How Did Judas Die?* Available at answersingenesis.org/contradictions-in-the-Bible/how-did-judas-die.

to the branch he hung on or the rope itself breaking) the skin easily broke and he burst open with his internal organs spilling out.

This is an astonishing example of the evolution of a religion in progress before our very eyes. To reconcile the two stories all manner of speculation is introduced (the location of the hanging, the branch or rope breaking suddenly without cause, and so on). Not all Christians accept her explanation, which is consistent with this process eventually leading to the wide variety of denominations that we now see.

But consider the surrounding story: in Acts 1:15–19, Judas uses the money to buy a field, falls headlong and his body bursts open. Everyone in Jerusalem hears about this and so they call the field the Field of Blood.

In Matthew 27:3–10, Judas hangs himself after throwing the money into the temple. It does not say he hangs himself in a field. The chief priests pick up the money and decide to buy the potter's field as a burial place for foreigners, which is then called the Field of Blood.

Would Judas really have hanged himself in a field? Would the chief priests have bought that same field? Would Matthew really not have thought to mention that the field the chief priests bought was the location of the hanging? Did Judas or the chief priests buy the field? Was it Judas's body or the burial of foreigners that gave the field its name? Would Acts really not mention the hanging? Why would the branch or rope have broken after surviving for a while? What can explain these discrepancies? The answer is that they are explicitly trying to fulfill confusing Old Testament references and doing so in a variety of different ways (more about this shortly).

In other words, Matthew and Luke did exactly what the Answers in Genesis author did: they filled in gaps based on an underlying belief. Matthew even says as much (Matthew 27:9):

> Then that which was spoken through Jeremiah the prophet was fulfilled, saying,
>
>> "They took the thirty pieces of silver,
>> the price of him upon whom a price had been set,
>> whom some of the children of Israel priced,"

In fact, Jeremiah said no such thing, and so the NIV and WEB translators reference a mishmash of verses (Zechariah 11:12–13; Jeremiah 19:1–13; 32:6–9). This is not the first time that Matthew has poorly referenced proof texts[4]. Can any of this really be considered historical when the urge to fulfill scripture is so apparent and the resulting stories so irreconcilable? To me, this shows more religious evolution. The Answers in Genesis article is an example of this exact behavior in modern times by a sincere Christian; the Gospel of Judas seems to be another example in the second-century, and the Judas stories in the Bible seem to indicate that the first-century Christians were no less prone to this tendency.

So I, like Evans, do not think that the Gospel of Judas is historical. But I have also yet to be persuaded that the canonical Gospels are historical either. Yes, they have an historical setting. Yes, I think Jesus of Nazareth was an historical figure. Yes, I think that we can reasonably infer some of Jesus's history. But I do not think that we have enough evidence to accept this ancient writing as an indication of the miraculous or the divine. The evidence for the evolution of the Bible as well as for the evolution of Christianity, including an assortment of often incompatible doctrines, is clear for all to see. Evans can dismiss non-canonical sources all he likes, but that still does not make his essay evidence for God.

---

[4] The Old Testament never mentions Nazareth or Nazarene, yet Matthew 2:23 states: "[Joseph] came and lived in a city called Nazareth; that it might be fulfilled which was spoken through the prophets: 'He will be called a Nazarene.'"

Part V

Some Other Questions

CHAPTER 51

Why is Christianity so Big?

I used to have other reasons (meta-arguments, in the sense that they do not use the text of the Bible directly) for accepting the validity of the claims of the Bible. Ultimately they do not matter—for me, the whole thing falls apart with the lack of credibility of the Bible, taken on its own terms, rather than based on some meta-argument. In other words, the biblical text is itself not credible where it matters (discussed in Section III).

But people use these meta-arguments to establish the credibility of the Bible, regardless of how incredible the text is, so I wanted to look at a few of them, and one in particular, which is the continued existence of the Christian church. I do not intend to look at this rigorously, but rather to point out a way that might be helpful to understand this and to explore where this kind of thinking might get us. Daniel Dennett discusses the broader idea in his book *Breaking the Spell: Religion as a Natural Phenomenon.*

Some of the other meta-arguments are, for example, the Lord, lunatic, liar or legend argument, which is the logical fallacy of false alternatives: surely Jesus can be a complex mixture of the last three just like everyone else? Another is the question of martyrdom: these eyewitnesses were tortured to death rather than admit that they had not seen Jesus risen. But people choose to die for all sorts of things (including a variety of mutually incompatible religions), and, though impressive, it does not make them right. It *probably* means that they believed it, but that is not the same thing at all. I discussed this in Chapter 35.

So why is the Christian church so big? I used to work for a consulting company, which had survived for a long time and was well-regarded even though it was frequently a miserable place to work, did work that was not uniformly of high quality, and cost a fortune to hire. I came to view its success in evolutionary terms: there were characteristics that did not make it the best at what it did but made it successful in terms of its continued existence and profitability. Internally, it promulgated the myth that it was the greatest place to work. Obsessive secrecy and brutal hiring practices created a mystique around the company, which fed the system. We would call new hires "intellectual cannon fodder." It was not that it was the best at consulting—it was that there was a concatenation of circumstances that made everyone think that it was the best which allowed it to grow and thrive.

I think a similar thing on a much larger scale happened with Christianity (and much of this probably applies to other religions). Imagine that there are people who see something or do something or teach something that starts a religion. We know this happens all the time because of the amazing stories of the cargo cult type[1]. But major religions with mutually incompatible claims cannot all be true, which means that false religions have started and been hugely successful in the past. And, if you think it has only happened in the pre-enlightenment age, you need only look at Scientology and Mormonism[2]. Now each time, the early founders and adopters create a particular set of beliefs, and these, in turn, determine whether the religion will be successful in the world. It has nothing to do with truth—just the religion's growth or decline.

So what are some of the characteristics of Christianity that might combine to make it a successful religion?

Control and authority

Christianity tells us to have faith; to believe things without evidence; to suppress doubts (e.g. Mark 16:14b "he rebuked them for their unbelief and hardness of heart, because they didn't believe those who had seen him after he had risen."). All these things were, supposedly, inspired by God.

---

[1] The cargo cults occurred after certain societies made contact with more technologically advanced societies. The name comes from the Melanesian belief in the 19th and early 20th century that certain rituals, such as the building of a runway, will result in the appearance of Western goods ("cargo") via Western airplanes.

[2] There is a wonderful documentary about Scientology called *Going Clear* that is well worth a watch. I watched it with a devout Christian friend as I was losing my faith, and it was interesting to observe how many parallels I saw with Christianity, while he emphatically did not.

Some religions even tell us that God wrote some of their holy texts. But these texts are, nonetheless, spread around by people. Lots of people think their ideas are better than all the dolts surrounding them. It can be very frustrating when people do not listen, so it is easy to imagine that people want to imbue their statements with a little more authority.

Christianity has a strong ethos of sin which gets mixed up by Christians with morality and legality and all treated as the same. People who disagree are labeled as non-Christians. Even Christians who disagree are sometimes labeled as "not *real* Christians," which I have heard from well-meaning Christians.

In the end, Christianity tries to convince everyone that they are worthless. Incidentally similar to the sales technique of the consultancy for which I used to work. Everything is falling apart for you—you had better hire us quickly! But I am not so bad, you say. Well, did you know that even thinking bad thoughts is a sin? And that you deserve death, just for that? How do I know? God says so. You still believe you know better? "[D]on't lean on your own understanding" (Proverbs 3:5). "The fool has said in his heart, 'There is no God."' (Psalm 14:1).

Self-worth

After first convincing us that we are all rotten, Christianity tells us that we are all loved and accepted. You can have peace if you sign up with us. *Wait a minute, do you have peace?* Yes, of course, we all do. *But you seem just as bad as the rest of the world.* Of course—we are all sinners. But we have been called by God.

The creator of the universe cares for us and listens to all our prayers. *But does He answer?* Of course. Option a: He answers, but not always as you expect. We must trust in His divine will, even if he says no. "Says no" is code for ignores your prayer, but we do not mention that. Option b: If it did not work then you must not have had enough faith.

But either way, you are loved and looked after by the creator of the universe, even if you die or are maimed or your children die. It is all part of His mysterious will.

The appeal of this type of theology is that it cedes control to a greater power. We can feel that despite all the issues that we see in ourselves and the world we can know that God is in control of the bigger picture. The human mind seems to have found this idea attractive for a long time with our superstitions, seances, prayers, and religions and perhaps the Christian version of it strikes a chord.

There must be more to life

It is hard to face your own mortality; to believe that this short life is all you have. We want to believe that we will one day be reunited with our loved ones.

We also yearn for justice, and it seems to occur so rarely. Idi Amin dies at a ripe old age in a high-quality hospital, despite the atrocities he committed. An honest friend dies on honeymoon, hit by a drunken driver. How we want all the injustice that exists in this world to be set right.

Christianity comes along, offering you eternal bliss not just for you, but for your loved ones too. Justice will prevail. And the wrong you did will be washed away. It sounds too good to be true.

Wishing does not make it so. It just makes for an appealing set of beliefs.

Proselytize!

Go, and make disciples of all nations (Matthew 28:19). Do not worry if your beliefs seem foolish—that is done deliberately to show up humanity's weaknesses. God's ways seem foolish to humans. But if you study it carefully, you will get a feeling that seems like a glimpse of understanding, which you can help other people to gain.

Do not worry if you are martyred or persecuted. This is just the devil working through people to attack you. It is proof that you are right. People laughing at your beliefs just shows how little they understand. But they are lost, so you should pray for them and help them find their way. And, if it is God's will, he will help them come to Him. This exhortation to proselytize means that converts will at least try to spread the religion.

This is not necessarily appealing; many Christians quail at the thought of trying to proselytize. But if enough of them believe that it is part of the package, then they might just do it. The fact that someone is willing to do this may be impressive to others as they consider their own beliefs, and at the least, it gives Christian beliefs the opportunity to spread. Also, the history of Christianity is littered with cases where the proselytizing was not consensual.

Religious natural selection

Factors like these make Christianity survive and thrive in the world. It does not mean it is true. It just means that it fits well with some proportion of human psychology. The desire to receive approval, to fit in, to help others, to have justice, meaning, and secret knowledge are all met in Christianity. It is a potent cocktail that, through a kind of societal evolution, has spread Christian beliefs successfully around the planet. Of course, it helped that Constantine converted to Christianity: Christians went from a persecuted minority (perhaps 5%) before Constantine to a persecuting majority by the end of the fifth century[3].

It does not make it true or false. It just is. What makes it false is the lack of credibility of the texts. But the existence of the modern church might as well be used as a (rather ironic) demonstration of evolutionary principles.

We have seen several examples of the rapid evolution of theology, and, just as in biology, stresses are often the cause. In this case, a moral quandary or a contradiction provides the stress. For example, we saw this in the discussion of the birth narratives (Chapter 27); Jesus as God (Chapter 31); the increasing physicality of Jesus's resurrection appearances (Chapter 34); the criminals crucified with Jesus (Chapter 36); the Trinity (Chapter 37); the influence of Paul (Chapter 41); the imminence of the apocalypse (Chapter 48); and the culpability of Judas (Chapter 50). This is just a selection since the evolution is clear to see throughout this book.

And similar to what you would expect from evolution, Christianity is in no way homogeneous. The various forms are so different from each other they may as well be different species altogether. We find it incredible that the vast variety of biological life could come into being without God. And we find it incredible that the church, with all its variegated forms, could exist and thrive without God. But hard to believe means complex not false.

Daniel Dennett (referenced above) calls for a willingness to study religions and beliefs dispassionately. This essay hints that such an approach can help us understand why a set of beliefs may spread. This could apply to political, scientific, religious, or spiritual beliefs. We should not determine the truth of the beliefs based on this alone: evidence and rationality fill that role. But the notion that a dearly held belief could be more the result of your mind providing fertile soil for it than an objective measure of its accuracy should be disquieting.

Christianity has several characteristics that might suppress our ability to reject it, appeal to our sense of the numinous, and encourage us to spread its ideas around. These characteristics could cause wide-spread belief in a

---

[3]Bart Ehrman, *How Jesus Became God: The Exaltation of a Jewish Preacher from Galilee.*

false set of ideas. As an atheist, I need to consider whether something similar is going on with atheism. It does not matter what ideology you believe: democrat, republican, capitalist, communist, socialist, Christian, or atheist. That idea is not who you are; it is merely something you accept or follow. And we need to assess the truth of it based on reasonable evidence including an understanding of what caused us to believe it in the first place.

People have argued that Christianity supported the scientific revolution by separating God from nature, allowing us to investigate the latter without blaspheming the former. That may or may not be true, but I argue that we now need a similar revolution in the way we study religious beliefs and religion itself. We need to separate who you are from what you believe, allowing us to study belief without offending believers. The above discussion is a starting point, not a conclusion. It is a hypothesis, not a theory. It is something we should test and reject if it does not work. Christians should also advocate for this kind of study, as they should be unafraid of where a search for the truth will lead.

CHAPTER 52

Personal Experience of God

Speaking with Christians often yields the idea of a personal experience as the basis of faith. It is very hard to argue against this kind of thing, and it is often presented as an alternative "proof" for Christianity. After all, so many Christians claim this type of experience, and so where there is smoke there must be fire. But it is very easy to have smoke without fire, and many poor proofs do not add up to one good one. I would contend that these experiences just constitute another piece of evidence, and that, like other evidence we have looked at in this book, we should consider this evidence objectively before being persuaded by it.

Observations

Let us look at the personal experience side of things in more detail. Let us define two types of God experience: A **physical** experience is a tangible experience, such as a healing or concrete answer to prayer or a fulfilled prophecy. A **spiritual** experience is something intangible (though no less real to the person presumably), like a feeling of God's presence, or hearing his voice inside your head, or a feeling of acceptance or love or peace, or some other thing that we cannot independently verify. Paul's Damascus road experience would be spiritual (because the people with him could not confirm the details), while his resulting blindness and Jesus walking on water would be physical experiences.

My observations of the world lead me to believe that:

1. Many Christians claim to have had physical or spiritual experiences.

2. Many non-Christians claim to have had physical or spiritual experiences.

3. Many Christians claim to have had neither physical nor spiritual experiences.

4. Many non-Christians claim to have had neither physical nor spiritual experiences.

5. Some of the physical claims are reasonably well attested ("I prayed and demonstrably had an improvement in health").

6. By their nature, we cannot verify spiritual claims.

These observations need to be taken together before we draw any conclusions. As a Christian, I did this in the context of an *a priori* belief in Christ based on assurances in the reliability of the Gospels and other evidence. Now that I no longer believe that the Biblical witnesses were reliable, I look at these same observations and draw somewhat different conclusions. The essential point is that these experiences do not prove anything—we interpret them according to our context. So, if Christians have not made their case with extraordinary evidence, the above observations do nothing to help them. Of course, those who have had an experience themselves may be persuaded by focusing on it and brushing over the rest of the observations in the list; but this does not engage with the totality of the evidence.

Interpretation 1: Rationally explicable or insufficiently attested

My current interpretation is that these experiences fall into two categories: (1) something which has rational explanations (including, for example, fraud or brain functions); and (2) something which does not currently have rational explanations.

Spiritual experiences provide little problem for the atheist. We know that brain functions can explain many of them, including healing, as attested by the placebo effect for example. People in an emotional state with a strong desire to experience something can plausibly experience that thing. And frankly, there is also fraud, which, if nothing else, increases the emotional tension to try to experience something like it yourself. The line between fraud and genuinely trying to have an experience of God is probably somewhat blurred if my own emotionally fraught teenage experiences are at all representative of anyone else's.

Physical experiences would require extraordinary evidence, and, while I do not wish to be patronizing or belittle someone else's experiences, neither am I persuaded that the extraordinary evidence needed to support the claims exists. I will explore below what it would mean if some of these claims were to be true, but there is scant evidence for experiences that are outside the bounds of what is known to medical or other sciences. For example, a person might recover from alcoholism, but people do not regrow limbs; and claims of, for example, resurrections tend not to be well attested (or in fact to be outright fraud as in the famous recent case of *The Boy Who Came Back from Heaven*[1]).

Interpretation 2: What if some of the claims are real?

But let us suppose that you have already accepted Christianity for whatever reason, and you engage with the above observations. Importantly, not just your own experiences (if you have had them), but the totality of the observations above. Where does that leave you? Rationality immediately throws you into a veritable quagmire of fundamentally unresolvable theological difficulties.

Observation 2 (that many non-Christians claim to have had similar experiences) puts you into an instant and toxic antagonism with people of other faiths. Who, by symmetry, are equally antagonistic back towards you. You have to believe that your faith's experiences are valid, while others are all lying or deceived. But if the devil or the human brain is that good at causing others to believe they have had genuine experiences, how do you know that your experience is not from the same source? How are you supposed to differentiate? As we have seen, the evidence outside of the personal experience is not enough, and the teachings are not a great differentiator: for example, biblical teaching is spotty, requiring your human judgment to pick the bits that you are going to follow, which is no different from anyone else.

---

[1] Tyndale House published a book called *The Boy Who Came Back from Heaven*, which was a best seller. Alex Malarkey, the boy in question came out five years later to admit that it was all made up. NPR wrote an article about it in 2015, available at www.npr.org/sections/thetwo-way/2015/01/15/377589757/boy-says-he-didn-t-go-to-heaven-publisher-says-it-will-pull-book.

Not to mention the claims of alien abductions and hearing voices and so on, which at the least provides evidence that the human mind is capable of believing it is having experiences that it is not, in any real sense, having. In other words, other people's experiences cannot be sufficient to prove the case, and your own need to be handled with extreme skepticism.

Observation 3 (that many Christians claim not to have had such experiences) drops you instantly into theologies like the problem of pain (for physical claims), and predestination (for spiritual claims), which I will now discuss in turn.

The uneven distribution of physical experiences, such as healings, leads people away from Christianity, and is a challenge for the faithful: why does God answer some prayers but not all? Why do miracles alleviate some suffering, but leave an extraordinary amount in play?

Christians (including my former self) paper over this issue (how can God be all powerful and all good and allow evil in the world?) with all kinds of nice words like "divine restraint," or horrible words like "what does it matter what happens in this world since the eternal is all we should care about" or "we know we live in a fallen world." These words dissolve when faced with an actual person suffering. They are at best inadequate and at worst grotesque and unfeeling. How has religion allowed people to so detach themselves from the reality of this world by its constant obsession with the next when the former could (indeed must) be improved by any person with a conscience, and the latter has no proof at all? And religion still has the temerity to claim a monopoly on morality?

Faced with suffering and pain in the world, you might point to Christians who do good works attempting to alleviate it. But this is merely the act of giving in to basic humanity, as attested by the good done by non-Christians (and the evil done by the religious). The evidence would suggest that it is our humanity, not our religion, that compels us to serve and help each other. It also, though admirable, does nothing to resolve the fundamental theodicy problem.

The spottiness of spiritual experiences is no less problematic. Am I, who has not had a spiritual experience of God, and who has not found the evidence convincing (as you can see from this book) to experience eternal punishment? A predestination view would say that maybe God has decided that I am a vessel of wrath prepared for destruction[2]? It seems a bit harsh for applying a very modest level of skepticism—so much so that I find I am left even less convinced by the claims of personal experience, and, in fact, more convinced that the whole thing is an incoherent human concoction.

---

[2]Romans 9:22: "What if God, willing to show his wrath, and to make his power known, endured with much patience vessels of wrath made for destruction."

Reductio ad absurdum as a mathematician might put it.

I have listed three examples of theological difficulties (other religions, theodicy, and predestination) that arise immediately out of the above observations of personal experience (whether you are someone who has had them or heard about them). These theological difficulties did not drive me away from Christianity—in fact, I enjoyed turning them over in my head and in discussion, although primarily in the abstract rather than the concrete, and, of course, the ends were never satisfactorily tied-off. However, interpretation 1 resolves all three rather neatly. If you applied Occam's razor to this, you would conclude that personal experiences (taken together) do more to support atheism or agnosticism than any other view. Some dear friends of mine see this as evidence for spirituality and oneness and universalism and things of that ilk. While I am not personally persuaded by this, it makes more sense than any of the monotheistic interpretations that I have come across.

CHAPTER 53

The Heavens Declare . . .

Though we looked at some specific science claims in Section II, many people are inspired to faith by the wonder of nature, whether it be cosmology, biology, geology or any other discipline. In this essay I want to give an overview of the problems that I see with that, and, in fact, saw with it even when I used to be a Christian.

An analogy: Gödel's Incompleteness Theorem

This analogy is just to explain how I view the relationship between our observable universe and god. It is not intended as a proof, and it may be unprovable, which is ironic, as you will see.

In formal mathematics, there is a famous theorem known as Gödel's Incompleteness Theorem, and immortalized in the famous book *Gödel, Escher, Bach*[1]. In essence, the theorem states that for any consistent, formal mathematical structure (a system with axioms and rules, where you can use the rules on the axioms and on theorems to come up with new theorems) there exist theorems that you can write with the rules of the structure that are undecidable. Potentially you can determine whether or not the theorem is true, but only by reverting to arguments outside of the formal structure. Within the structure, you cannot deduce certain propositions.

---

[1] Douglas R. Hofstadter, 1999, *Gödel, Escher, Bach: An Eternal Golden Braid.*

The analogy to the universe is that god is, by definition, outside of the observable universe, and so he is like an undecidable statement, beyond the powers of science to determine, as science is constrained to act within the observable limits of the universe. I think it is an attractive analogy, though, of course, there is no such thing as a proof by analogy, so this is just to describe what I think, rather than to persuade you of its verity. However, there are some serious issues with the idea that science and observation of the universe in any form can lead you to belief in god, which I want to outline here.

Philosophical Problem: God of the Gaps

Tis a dangerous thing to engage the authority of scripture in disputes about the natural world, in opposition to reason, lest time which brings all things to light, should discover that to be evidently false which we had made scripture to assert.

This quote, by Thomas Burnett in the 18th century summarizes a fundamental issue that has long been understood even by Christians, which is the danger of teleological arguments[2] for the existence of God. Strangely though, while apologists now appreciate that a 'God of the Gaps' argument is flawed, proponents of these kinds of arguments for the existence of god merely assert that for some subtle reason, their argument does not fall into this category.

Gradually god has been squeezed into smaller and smaller domains of usage by this argument. For example, people say that the fine-tuning of the universal constants is so remarkable that it must be God. A tiny change would mean that we would not exist, so there you go! They go on to say that the probability of these constants being just so, is so vanishingly small that we must classify it as a miracle, and therefore someone must have done this miracle, ergo god. But this is wrong-headed. What if tomorrow a paper came out showing that these constants could only be this way because of some fundamental physics constraint (which would undermine the probability calculation that apologists performed using all manner of assumptions)? Then we say that god must have made that constraint? So we squeeze him out even further? The correct response is to look further for an explanation, not to shrug your shoulders and say it must be god.

In the old days, He scattered the stars across the sky and set the planets into motion; now He twiddles a few knobs to fine-tune the universal

---

[2]Teleological arguments are arguments from design or the intelligent design argument for the existence of God, or more properly a god.

constants? We find similar examples in evolution, abiogenesis, quantum mechanics or any other area of physics by going right to the edge of our understanding and pointing over the precipice and saying 'that must be God!'

Scientifically it has never been a helpful perspective because it stops further inquiry. Scientifically it has always been better to say 'we just do not know ... yet', followed by further exploration. This removal of God from science is what allows humanity to advance our knowledge. Scientists who are Christians have understood this for hundreds of years. But some modern apologists have forgotten their moral philosopher roots and have reverted to this kind of argument. We saw many examples in Section II.

Theological Problem: Deist to Theist

But suppose that you were able to demonstrate conclusively that some particular phenomena were inexplicable outside of a divine or spiritual entity? Given the above discussion, I doubt that such a thing is possible in the normal course of events, but let us go with it for now. You then establish a deity, but you still have all your work ahead of you to establish any of the major religions. It has done nothing to distinguish between Christianity, new age spirituality, Buddhism, Islam, Judaism, polytheism, etc. All of these and many others, including religions now dead, have an equal claim to the deity. As a Christian, it was evident to me that I believed in God and *then* His creation inspired me, not the other way around. Now that I have dropped the belief in God, I remain just as inspired by nature.

Theological Problem #2: But Is it Good?

Inspiration from the beauty of nature also requires cherry-picking. There are also aspects of life that are horrifying: 'red in tooth and claw.' We have to see both sides of nature's nature. It is not sufficient to say "well, of course, that is because we live in a fallen world. It is like this because people sinned." This is saying that the beautiful parts of nature prove that God exists and the ugly parts prove that man is evil. But, if you are willing to split up the evidence to support your view, discarding half the evidence for each of your two statements, then you need to be honest and say that the evidence is not supporting your beliefs at all. It might as well support the view that God made an evil universe and good human behavior has allowed it to be beautiful in some respects.

The alternative, of course, is that it speaks of capricious gods, like the old Greek and Roman pantheon. Those would make much more sense and are a much more sane view of gods if you consider the sheer randomness of everything around us.

Empirical Problem: The Stats Show Scientists are Less Religious

Another issue is that if scientifically studying the natural world leads to faith then you should expect the scientifically literate to be more faithful than the rest of the population. In fact, the opposite is true, and dramatically so. An article from Seeker[3] says:

> In 2009, the Pew Research Center for the People and the Press polled members of the American Association for the Advancement of Science on belief in a higher power. The study found that 51 percent of members polled expressed such a faith, compared to 95 percent of the American public. Additionally, the National Academy of Science charted belief in God as low as 5.5 percent among biologists and 7.5 percent among physicists and astronomers in a 1998 study.

In the end, science is agnostic, and most scientists end up not believing because it is unsupported. Many people are turned off from religion because they think they would have to give up their scientific beliefs, such has been the impact of the fundamentalists. I lost my faith at least in part because I realized that if Christians were willing to promote beliefs that I knew to be false, how sure was I that they were not doing the same for their central stories? That led me to further exploration into the historical credibility of the Bible, which in turn led me to atheism. I would be interested to know what proportion of professional historians believe. Because, in the end, it seems it is history, not science, that is the biggest challenge to faith.

---

[3]Robert Lamb, 2010, Seeker, *Are Scientists Atheists?* Available at www.seeker.com/are-scientists-atheists-1765139498.html.

Afterword

I began this book to discuss the evidence for God. Over time, a second, more important goal emerged, on how to have the discussion. This is a vital conversation and we need to talk about it.

I hope this book has challenged you as you think about your reasons for belief. But more importantly, I hope that you will begin to discuss your reasons for belief with everyone you know. The time of religion being a taboo subject is over. What is needed is to have the discussion in a respectful way.

When I began to publicize this book among my friends and family I was surprised to discover shows of support from unexpected sources. People who I had thought were Christians confessed to me that they were not. And people who are Christians confessed to me privately that they would like to read it, but that they were hesitant to announce the fact on social media.

What is it about this conversation that is shameful? Why is it that people take offense on both sides? Why is it that people go on the offensive on both sides?

The topic is intertwined emotionally with our very being. Many people have been hurt by religions and the religious. But in general good people do good things and we should strive to assume the best of intentions, even when we disagree or have been hurt.

However, we also must be aware of the dramatic impact that our religious beliefs have on society. That alone makes this a conversation worth having.

If this book has challenged you in any way, I ask that you discuss it with friends and family in order to continue the conversation. Be curious about their beliefs and, more importantly, the reasons for their beliefs. The question "Why do you believe that?" can and should be asked, and the search for truth should never stop.

Please also continue the conversation with me on social media or through my website: `glentonjelbert.com`. I would love to hear your thoughts, comments, questions, and ideas.

Printed in Great Britain
by Amazon

38711828R00205